Discursive Democracy

Discursive Democracy

Politics, Policy, and Political Science

JOHN S. DRYZEK
Department of Political Science
University of Oregon

CAMBRIDGE
UNIVERSITY PRESS

PUBLISHED BY THE PRESS SYNDICATE OF THE UNIVERSITY OF CAMBRIDGE
The Pitt Building, Trumpington Street, Cambridge, United Kingdom

CAMBRIDGE UNIVERSITY PRESS
The Edinburgh Building, Cambridge CB2 2RU, UK   www.cup.cam.ac.uk
40 West 20th Street, New York, NY 10011-4211, USA   www.cup.org
10 Stamford Road, Oakleigh, Melbourne 3166, Australia
Ruiz de Alarcón 13, 28014 Madrid, Spain

First published 1990
First paperback edition 1994
Reprinted 1999

Printed in the United States of America

Typeset in Garamond

Library of Congress Cataloging in Publication data

Dryzek, John S., 1953
Discursive democracy : politics, policy, and political science / John S. Dryzek
p.   cm.
Includes bibliographical references.

1. Democracy. 2. Consensus (Social Sciences). 3 Policy sciences.
4. Rationalism.   I. Title.
JC423.D73   1990
321.8 - dc20   90 - 1502
                                            CIP

British Library Cataloguing in Publication data

Dryzek, John, 1953–

Discurcive democracy : politics, policy, and political science

1. Democracy. Politics..
I. Title.
321.8

ISBN 0 521 47827 8 paperback

To

RHYS EDWARD DRYZEK

*who came into the world
at the same time*

Contents

Preface

Discursive democracy is woven here from threads supplied by a classical (Aristotelian) model of politics, participatory democracy, communicative action, practical reason, and critical theory. The product, or so I shall argue, is a coherent, integrative, and attractive program for politics, public policy, and political science. Ultimately, discursive democracy looks forward to a world of free and congenial political interaction where politics, properly understood, is returned to its Aristotelian primacy in the order of things. More immediately, discursive democracy charts escapes from some contemporary impasses in political arrangements, public policy, and social science. Politics, policy, and science alike are currently beholden to instrumental and objectivist notions about rationality in human affairs. My case for discursively rational alternatives is constructed on foundations provided by the ruins of instrumental rationality and objectivism.

These thoughts took form over a number of years. They were shaped by comments and criticisms on individual chapters by Terence Ball, Deborah Baumgold, Steven Brown, John Champlin, James Farr, Robert Goodin, Susan Hunter, David Jacobs, Brian Ripley, Rex Stainton Rogers, and Douglas Torgerson. Two anonymous readers for Cambridge University Press did an exceptionally thorough job. Chapters 5 and 7 are based on papers originally coauthored with Susan Hunter and Brian Ripley, who would not necessarily endorse the broader claims for discursive democracy made in this volume. Chapter 9 uses some results from a study in which my coinvestigators were Margaret Clark and Garry McKenzie. Steven Brown gave permission to reproduce in Chapter 9 some results from his work. Discussion with my communicatively competent climbing companions Terence Ball, James Farr, and Stephen Leonard involved learning much about political theory, mountains, and Laphroiag single-malt Scotch.

Though a study like this requires little or nothing in the way of financial support, a summer research grant from the University of Oregon provided some initial momentum. This book breathes free Oregon air and so is happier than if it had been undertaken in more instrumentally rationalized and objectivist surroundings. Much of the writing was done in my home village of Maids Moreton, England. There I found the real inspiration for discursive democracy, not in ancient Athens, but in the public bar of The Wheatsheaf.

Several of the chapters that follow build upon previously published articles. Chapter 2 draws upon "Discursive Designs: Critical Theory and Political Institutions," *American Journal of Political Science*, 31 (1987): 656–79; Chapter 3 upon "Complexity and Rationality in Public Life," *Political Studies*, 35 (1987): 424–42; Chapter 5 upon "Environmental Mediation for International Problems," *International Studies Quarterly*, 31 (1987): 87–102; Chapter 6 upon "Policy Sciences of Democracy," *Polity*, 22 (1989): 97–118; Chapter 7 upon "The Ambitions of Policy Design," *Policy Studies Review*, 7 (1988): 705–19; Chapter 8 upon "The Mismeasure of Political Man," *Journal of Politics*, 50 (1988): 705–25; and Chapter 10 upon "The Progress of Political Science," *Journal of Politics*, 48 (1986): 301–20.

PART I

Introduction

CHAPTER 1

Democratizing Rationality

There is, as usual, much that is wrong with the world. Economic crisis, environmental crisis, energy crisis, debt crisis, legitimation crisis, international crisis, crisis of the welfare state succeed one another. Overloaded governments grapple with ungovernable societies. Few think governments can succeed, given widespread pessimism about the possibilities for effective public policy or planning. On the other hand, there is limited faith in the market, and increasing numbers of individuals reject material rewards, be it in favor of postindustrial lifestyles or the revelation of fundamentalist religion. Ex-Marxist societies now look only to what is already in trouble elsewhere.

My intent here is to explore a diagnosis for at least some of the world's present political ills and to think about a cure. The diagnosis is that many of these ills have much to do with the decline of once-confident and still pervasive forms of rationality. The cure involves large doses of what I shall call discursive democracy for the individual actions, political institutions, policy practices, and social sciences that lay claim to rationality.

Diagnosis

Individual political behavior, the policies of governments, the structure of political systems, and the assumptions and strategies of political scientists who study these phenomena are all more or less rational. Over the centuries since the Enlightenment, rationality has come to demand two things. The first is effective instrumental action; instrumental rationality may be defined in terms of the capacity to devise, select, and effect good means to clarified ends.[1] The second is the idea that rational choices concerning theories and beliefs about matters of fact, and even about values and morals, should be made through reference to a set of objective standards that are equally applicable – and accessible – to all individuals. This second aspect of post-Enlightenment rationality is generally referred to as objectivism.[2]

Instrumental rationality and objectivism go hand in hand. The former governs rational behavior, the latter rational belief and morality. Thus they provide a complete guide for the would-be rational individual. In social life, objectivism provides glue for the coordination of the actions of large numbers of instrumental rationalists in a fashion that is itself instrumentally rational (in terms of any goals of the social system at hand). Together, instrumental rationality and objectivism conjure up a clean and orderly world where modern science, technology, and economics flourish. However, I shall argue that modernity also allows some very different possibilities in polity, economy, and society.

Instrumental rationality is perhaps more ubiquitous than objectivism. Indeed, economists – and increasing numbers of political scientists, even a few sociologists – assume that instrumental rationality captures the essence of all human behavior. Most analysts of international relations believe it captures the foreign policy behavior of whole states. Advisors to and critics of government action, including professional policy analysts, want public policies to involve instrumentally rational pursuit of some set of clear goals.

Some further manifestations of this kind of rationality in political analysis – and political life – are less obvious and will be explicated in the chapters that follow. So instrumental rationality under conditions of free criticism undergirds liberal polyarchy, the dominant kind of political system in the West (see Chapter 2). Instrumental rationality is also embedded in many of the practices and methods of political science (see Chapter 8).

The counts against this kind of rationality are as follows.

1. Instrumental rationality destroys the more congenial, spontaneous, egalitarian, and intrinsically meaningful aspects of human association. This criticism is a familiar one. At the turn of the century Max Weber claimed instrumental rationality (in conjunction with objectivist systems of rules) provided justification and organizing principles for bureaucracy. Weber also argued that instrumental rationality expressed in bureaucratization portends an

"iron cage" around human existence. More recently, Jürgen Habermas has extended Weber's prognosis beyond bureaucracy to speak of the "colonization" of the "lifeworld" of culture and social interaction by the administration, ministration, influence, and control of technical expertise in the service of private profit or political power. Administrators, marketing consultants, police, social workers, counselors, physicians, lawyers, and clinical psychologists are in the vanguard of this invasion of processes that were once constructed and conducted by ordinary people. Moreover, an instrumentally rationalized world is one in which individuals themselves are like economic men – calculating machines with an impoverished subjectivity and no sense of self and community.

2. Instrumental rationality is antidemocratic. This point too is Weberian insofar as bureaucratization entails the concentration of political power. The tendency is diluted to the extent instrumental rationality is exercised under conditions of free criticism, in what Popper (1966) would call "piecemeal social engineering" in the "open society." But the risk to democracy still persists in the open society, especially in its real-world approximations, such as liberal polyarchies. For even if they are elected, someone (or some group) must do the engineering; that is, they must exercise power over others. Open societies therefore experience a tension between a desire for rationality and egalitarian principles. A further threat to democracy arises because individuals reduced to calculating machines are susceptible to totalitarian appeals promising to restore meaning to their lives.

3. Instrumental rationality represses individuals. On the one hand, instrumental rationality gives us the power and technology to create the material conditions for human freedom. On the other hand, in maintaining this focus, the playfulness and creativity that would allow human subjects to realize this freedom are suppressed. This paradox is what Horkheimer and Adorno (1972) call the dialectic of Enlightenment, from which they believe there is no escape (save perhaps through artistic expression). Somewhat different but related statements about repression are made by contemporary feminists, who argue, for example, that reproductive technology and population control ideology cede control of the female body to technical experts. Thus the promise of control *of* a woman's own fertility degenerates into control *by* others (Diamond, 1988).

4. Instrumental rationality – and the political institutions in which it is manifested – is ineffective when confronted with com-

plex social problems. Instrumental rationality goes hand in hand with an *analytic* sensibility, the idea that complex phenomena are best understood through intelligent disaggregation into their component parts. These parts should then be apprehended – and any problematic aspects of them resolved instrumentally – in piecemeal fashion.[3] Indeed, such decomposition forms the organizing principle for bureaucratic division of labor. My criticism here is therefore anti-Weberian; Weber predicted bureaucratization precisely because of the efficacy of its rationality in dealing with ever more complex problems. My anti-Weberian argument about complexity will be developed in Chapter 3.

5. Instrumental rationality makes effective and appropriate policy analysis impossible. This criticism is, of course, less global than the first four, applying as it does mostly to the interdisciplinary field of public policy analysis. For the most part, this field is still under sway of the idea that public policies should properly be instrumental interventions in society, economy, and polity. If the first four counts are accepted, then mainstream policy analysts are accomplices to tyrannical but otherwise ineffective public action. A critique of policy analysis along these lines will be developed in Chapter 6.

6. Instrumental rationality informs inappropriate and unfruitful social science instruments and methods. A critique of the most widely used method in political science – the opinion survey – will form the substance of Chapter 8. Whereas at first sight this concern might seem parochial and disciplinary, I shall also argue that widespread use and acceptance of such instruments functions in a particularly subtle way to reinforce some unsavory aspects of the dominant political order.

Aside from its complicity in these six items of an indictment against instrumental rationality, objectivism, for its part, may be charged with three further counts.

1. Objectivism is inspired by a false account of the science it idolizes. Postempiricist philosophy of science has demonstrated that a universally applicable "logic of scientific inquiry" does not exist. Any such set of rules is destroyed in its encounter with the history of science, especially in connection with exemplary episodes in this history (see, e.g., Kuhn, 1970b, p. 200; Burian, 1977; MacIntyre, 1977, p. 468). The outcomes of encounters between rival theories and research programs defy objectivist standards.

2. Objectivism is repressive. It imposes its own standards and

practices, whether by argument in its own terms or by force, upon traditions and ways of life that do not share its viewpoint. The victims include indigenous cultures, nonscientific medical practices, and dissenting epistemologies such as feminism (for a good overstatement, see Feyerabend, 1987). One of objectivism's most enlightened partisans congratulates ancient Athens on its use of "some form of imperialism" to overcome "tribalist exclusiveness and self-sufficiency" (Popper, 1966, p. 181).

3. Objectivism inhibits the progress of political science and politics. In Chapter 10 I shall argue that to the extent that the political world is informed by purely objectivist ideas about cognitive rationality it is inhospitable to defensible political science and to authentic political reflection more generally.

Cures

If these counts against instrumental and objectivist rationality are accepted, at least three escapes from their clutches are conceivable. Two involve reconsidering what it means to be rational, whereas a third contends reason is irredeemable.

The least radical of the three retains and reaffirms the essential precepts of instrumental and objectivist rationality but is open to their modification and supplement. Perhaps the most well-known effort along these lines is found in the work of Popper (1966, 1972a). Popper argues that the most effective problem-solving form of social organization is not centralized planning or Weberian bureaucracy but an open society in which instrumental rationalists can freely criticize one another's designs. The open society is itself styled after a model of the scientific community in which objectivists freely criticize one another's theories. Popper's claims will be dealt with in Chapter 2. Von Hayek (e.g., 1979) tenders a parallel line on behalf of markets, which rely on price signals rather than verbal interchanges to coordinate the efforts of large numbers of instrumental rationalists in a nonhierarchical fashion. Several other extensions of instrumental rationality will be introduced and criticized in Chapter 3.

The most radical escape repudiates human reason, minimally in some specified domain, but sometimes more universally. A wide range of intellectual positions advocate repudiation in one form or another. Some advocates of the free market depart from von Hayek in arguing that invisible hands thoroughly dispense with the need for extensive cogitation and calculation (see, e.g., Friedman and Friedman, 1979, pp. 6–9). Admirers of decentralized political processes argue that interaction therein can be a complete substitute for analysis in determining the content of political decisions and public policies (e.g., Lindblom and Cohen, 1979). Some ecologically sensitive opponents of industrial society believe the nefarious effects of instrumental rationality in human domination of the natural world (not to mention other humans) can be surmounted only by a turn to spiritual and intuitive relations among persons and with nature (e.g., Spretnak, 1986). Christian and Islamic fundamentalists recommend a very different kind of spirituality, one that seeks salvation in the authority of the revelations of a transcendent deity.

It is not just instrumental rationality and objectivist rationality that are under siege here, but also rationality in the sense of an ability to provide *any* good cognitive warrants for actions or positions. So skeptical continental philosophers such as Foucault (e.g., 1980) see in reasoned discourse only entrapment and repression of varying subtlety. Theories about politics and systems of thought (or what he calls "discourses") more generally are by their very nature prisons that discipline their adherents. One can escape these bonds only through a romantic devotion to the aesthetic dimension of experience. Foucault subjects past and present social formations, the complicity of social scientists in them, and their rationalities to merciless criticism. But ultimately he traffics in pure negation and intimates no better alternative. Postmodernists (e.g., Lyotard, 1984), deconstructionists (e.g., Derrida, 1976), and epistemological anarchists (e.g., Feyerabend, 1975, 1978, 1987) are equally relativistic, though occasionally, in contrast to Foucault, playful rather than unremittingly negative. Such "anti-theorists" or "all-purpose subversives" now abound (Skinner, 1985, pp. 12–13). Most of them are indeed "suspicious continental characters with farfetched ideas and unpronounceable names" (Ball, 1987a, p. 2). But the case of Rorty (1979) demonstrates that such skepticism reaches into the Anglo–American academy. Rorty argues that all claims to knowledge, including those of philosophy itself, which long tried to adjudicate such claims, are bounded by time, space, culture, and experience.

Beyond reaffirming extended instrumental and objectivist rationality and throwing reason out lies a third alternative, which is to attend more carefully to what reason can mean. I shall argue here against the near hegemony of instrumental and objectivist rationality in the modern world. Instrumental rationality will always be with us, but it merits restriction to a domain more limited than that which it currently occupies. Objectivism, though, can be dispensed with entirely. The spaces thus vacated can then be occupied by a different kind of rationality, discursive and democratic rather than instrumental and authoritarian in character, which can answer the charges of the "all-purpose subversives." This discursive and democratic rationality may regulate the remnants of instrumental rationality and replace objectivism.

Alternative Rationalities

Whereas both their adherents and critics are preoccupied with them, instrumental rationality and objectivism have no monopoly on reason. Over four decades ago Max Horkheimer (1947) contrasted ancient conceptions of what he calls "objective" reason (not to be confused with objectivism) to the Enlightenment's legacy of "subjective" (i.e., instrumental) rationality. Horkheimer's objective reason is defined by its appreciation of "a comprehensive system, or hierarchy, of all beings, including man and his aims. The degree of reasonableness of a man's life could be determined according to its harmony with this totality" (1947, p. 4). Here there is no manipulation of objects by (human) subjects, but instead only the harmonization of subjects.

Horkheimer pays tribute to Aristotle as one exponent of his objective reason. But to speak in terms of harmonization hardly does justice to Aristotle's notions, especially about politics and practical reason (*praxis* and *phronesis*). Aristotelian practical reason involves persuasion, reflection upon values, prudential judgment, and free disclosure of one's ideas. The precise political implications of this kind of rationality are a matter of ongoing contention, occasioned in part by the difficulty of appropriating the epistemological categories of the ancient Greeks to contemporary modes of thought. And indeed, some self-styled Aristotelians, especially in Germany, today follow a conservative and parochial approach to ethics and politics at odds with my own appropriation of Aristotle in the service of free discourse.[4] But irrespective of the niceties of interpretation, Aristotle clearly grounded practical reason in collective life. An individual isolated outside the *polis* could not be rational, for rationality was a product of collective interaction. In this sense, it is practical reason, and not power, that defines the very idea of politics. As Fay (1975, p. 54) puts it, "'politics' refers to men's deliberate efforts to order, direct, and control their collective affairs and activities, to establish ends for their society, and to implement and evaluate these ends."

This "classical" conception of politics (and its special rationality) was long eclipsed by definitions of politics in terms of power and the instrumental pursuit of interest on the part of individuals or states (see Ball, 1983a, pp. 39–40). It is left to Hannah Arendt (1958) to retrieve the classical ideal, albeit in somewhat nostalgic fashion. Arendt argues that echoes of the classical ideal of unconstrained and egalitarian political debate about principles can indeed be heard in the modern world, if only in the fleeting circumstances surrounding revolutions (Arendt, 1962). Thus her spontaneously republican "councils" occur in the French Revolution, the Paris Commune, the Soviets of the Russian Revolution (before their capture by the Bolsheviks), and the Hungarian Revolt of 1956. In all cases, though, these councils are soon crushed by force of arms or subverted by instrumental rationalists such as Lenin.

Alasdair MacIntyre (1984a) shares Arendt's affinity for Aristotle and her rejection of modern precepts, but in the realm of moral philosophy rather than politics. He argues that moral philosophy lost its bearings when it rejected Aristotle's account of the virtues in favor of enlightened liberalism. Subsequently, liberal morality degenerated into moral relativism and solipsism, an arbitrariness of goals entirely consistent with instrumental conceptions of what it means to be rational. This degeneration occurs with the failure of liberal objectivists to yield any transcendent standards for morals that would convince other liberals, let alone anyone else. MacIntyre suggests a revival of Aristotelian and communal approaches to ethics, emphasizing the prudential application of principles to particular cases, in order to retrieve the possibility of reasoned discourse about values. Later, he allows that the Aristotelian tradition is just one among many, each with its own ideas about justice and rationality (MacIntyre, 1988). Nevertheless, MacIntyre believes that reasoned discourse can extend across the boundaries of traditions. But this extension is likely only when a tradition encounters a crisis (in terms of its own standards) severe enough to move its adherents to look for answers in some other tradition and to allow partisans of that other tradition to formulate answers intelligible in both traditions.

The works of Arendt and MacIntyre constitute part of a larger movement sympathetic to practical reason. This movement "beyond objectivism and relativism" is celebrated by Bernstein (1983). He argues that the objectivist search for the solid ground of overarching criteria and universal decision rules for (instrumentally) rational choices is being repudiated in areas ranging from philosophy of science to textual interpretation to political theory. But the alternative need not be retreat into a hopeless relativism of closed systems of thought or culture across which no rational choices are possible. For rational persuasion is indeed possible across the boundaries of scientific paradigms, political theories, cultures, or normative positions, even in the absence of transcendent criteria. Criteria, on Bernstein's account, are always multiple, mutable, open to criticism and defense, and susceptible to selective adducement and differential weighting in different cases. In other words, they are resources for rational arguments in debates between proponents of different views. Such debates are possible so long as systems of thought intersect at some points (see also MacIntyre, 1984a, p. 276). If there were no intersection, there would be no competition, and so nothing even worth disagreeing about. For example, competing scientific paradigms are (almost by definition) about the same object(s) and are produced in a community with shared values about what it means to do science. Even as they differ, Darwinians and punctuated equilibrium theorists agree that it is evolution they are trying to explain and that values of consistency, accuracy, and fruitfulness matter; they do not live in different and totally incommensurable worlds. Darwinians and punctuated equilibrium theorists alike might find it more difficult to communicate with believers in the literal truth of Genesis, but even fundamentalist Christians feel the need to style their creationism "scientific." In so doing, they open themselves to arguments that appeal to the values of science.

One of the figures celebrated by Bernstein is Jürgen Habermas. As a fellow member of the Frankfurt School of critical theory, Habermas shares Horkheimer's preoccupation with the Enlightenment legacy. But whereas Horkheimer, like Arendt and MacIntyre, condemns post-Enlightenment conceptions of reason, Habermas is more equivocal. He argues that modernity brings increased potential for a more attractive kind of reason as well as the kinds that Horkheimer, Arendt, and MacIntyre bemoan.

Habermas (e.g., 1984, 1987a) follows Horkheimer, Adorno, and

Weber in denouncing the restrictions and constraints that instrumental rationality, once so liberating, has institutionalized in bureaucratization, administration, and social control. But modernity also promises a presently unredeemed potential for *communicative* rationalization in the form of uncoerced and undistorted interaction among competent individuals.

Both instrumental and communicative rationalizations are rooted in processes whereby the lifeworld (to use Habermas's term) becomes increasingly subject to modern forms of consciousness. The lifeworld itself is the "symbolic network in which subjects interact" (White, 1988, p. 102), where culture, social relations, and individual personalities are maintained and constructed. Modern consciousness liberates the lifeworld from unthinking conformity to traditional values, customs, and other kinds of normative constraint, thus releasing individuals to engage in instrumentally rational action. However – and this is what Weber, Horkheimer, and Adorno miss – these same developments also enable discursive and critical reconstruction of the lifeworld. Subjects can coordinate their actions through talk rather than unthinking compliance with norms, and it is through talk that an attack can be launched against instrumental rationalization. To date, instrumental rationality has got the better of this conflict, in large measure due to the raw power of state and capital. Instrumental rationality is bolstered further through the "cultural impoverishment" of the lifeworld by "expert cultures" monopolizing science, technology, art, law, and other kinds of activity upon which resistance might otherwise draw (White, 1988, pp. 116–17). Yet resistance based on reflection, talk, and communicative action remains a possibility.

It is, then, no coincidence that the potential for communicative rationalization increases with that of its seeming nemesis, instrumental rationalization. An additional link between these two forms of rationalization arises in that instrumentally rational action in a setting comprised in part by other human beings is effective only to the extent the individual can comprehend and deploy language, if only to recognize and make offers, threats, and bluffs. Such uses of language in turn imply a commitment to some constitutive rules of linguistic interaction (Midgaard, 1980). Moreover, coordinated instrumentally rational action on the part of more than one person (be it a group of scientific investigators, a task force, or a committee) presupposes effective communication within that group. So

Apel (1972, p. 8) argues that the practice of science (and, one might add, any instrumental rationality it embodies[5]) presupposes a "metascientific rationality of intersubjective discourse" within communities of practitioners. The same might be said for communities of technologists, whose purview is more clearly instrumental than that of scientists. Now, given the complicity of technologists in the control of both human and nonhuman nature, one might claim that any such group is party to the instrumental domination of individuals and objects external to it. But in this case, one task for communicative rationalization becomes the destruction of such privilege and its implicit hierarchy.

There are some major differences across the figures I have just introduced, and I shall have cause to return to these differences. Nevertheless, the commonalities among the ideas and possibilities discussed in this section should be apparent. Classical politics, practical reason, critical theory, Horkheimer's objective reason, and communicative rationality form a coherent set. Opposed to this first set are modern politics, deductive–nomological theory,[6] Horkheimer's subjective reason, objectivism, and instrumental rationality. Both sets exist not just in the world of political theory, but also in terms of real-world politics.

This second set is associated with both bureaucratic–authoritarian and liberal democratic political forms. Let me now suggest that the political form most hospitable to the first set is a more participatory democracy – "strong democracy," in Barber's (1984) terms. Although there is no simple dichotomy between liberal and participatory democracy, one can think of them as the two major democratic possibilities. As one moves toward the participatory pole of the spectrum they help define, politics becomes increasingly discursive, educational, oriented to truly public interests, and needful of active citizenship. In contrast, the liberal pole is dominated by voting, strategy, private interests, bargaining, exchange, spectacle, and limited involvement. My argument about these two kinds of democracy will be developed more fully in Chapter 6.[7]

The second set currently dominates the real world, but the first set – to which the name discursive democracy may now be attached – is not lost. Today this first set shows signs of renewal in a variety of political movements, be they Green, feminist, peace oriented, or communitarian, and, I shall argue, in a variety of institutional experiments. Given that this study is organized around challenges to conventional conceptions of rationality, let me now pick out from the first set the concept of communicative rationality for more intensive scrutiny.

Communicative Rationality

Communicative rationality is rooted in the interaction of social life. Communicative *action* is oriented toward intersubjective understanding, the coordination of actions through discussion, and the socialization of members of the community (see especially Habermas, 1984). Communicative *rationality* is the extent to which this action is characterized by the reflective understanding of competent actors. This situation should be free from deception, self-deception, strategic behavior, and domination through the exercise of power. Communicative rationality is a property of intersubjective discourse, not individual maximization, and it can pertain to the generation of normative judgments and action principles rather than just to the selection of means to ends. However, communication is concerned in part with the coordination of actions, so communicative rationality cannot totally replace instrumental rationality; rather it can only restrict the latter to a subordinate domain.

This idea that rationality consists of cogitation in interaction does have a respectable heritage. As I have already noted, Aristotle is a key figure in this history. Kant and Rousseau also figure prominently inasmuch as they sought justification of values and principles in "the formal conditions of consensus formation" (Habermas, 1979, p. 184), though Kant for one was ultimately more concerned with the isolated subject than with social interaction. For reasons that will shortly become apparent, I shall stress the Aristotelian and not the Kantian or Rousseauean aspects of communicative rationality.

The more well-known contemporary heirs to Aristotelian themes of *phronesis* and *praxis* include Arendt (1958), Gadamer (1975), MacIntyre (1984a), and Habermas (1984). Despite major differences, especially concerning the extent to which talk and action must or should be constrained by tradition, the common aim of these philosophers is to resurrect authentic and reasonable public discourse. Such discourse has been eroded over the centuries by instrumental rationality manifested in hierarchy, administration, and technocracy, by liberal attempts to locate objectivist solid ground, and more recently, by postmodern relativism. Let me now explicate communicative rationality further as an ideal; murkier real-world approximations to it will appear in later chapters.

Communicative rationality clearly obtains to the degree social interaction is free from domination (the exercise of power), strategizing by the actors involved, and (self-) deception. Further, all actors should be equally and fully capable of making and questioning arguments (communicatively competent). There should be no restrictions on the participation of these competent actors. Under such conditions, the only remaining authority is that of a good argument, which can be advanced on behalf of the veracity of empirical description, explanation, and understanding and, equally important, the validity of normative judgments.

This normative dimension means that values are not treated as arbitrary and idiosyncratic (though neither are they regarded as amenable to objectivist proof). Any actor offering a normative judgment can be called upon to back it with reasons. The logic of normative reasoning has been explored by Taylor (1961) and applied to public policy evaluation by Fischer (1980). In these terms, one can argue on behalf of a value judgment on the basis of its consistency with a broader system of values or its concurrence with a culture of joint subscription. Alternatively, a normative judgment can be justified on the grounds that its adoption by all individuals would produce felicitous consequences. So Habermas (1971) speaks of the "generalizable" status of certain kinds of values, and Anglo–American analytical philosophers such as Hare (1963) speak of the "universalizability" of principles. Thus any disinterested individual would subscribe to such value judgments (cf. Rawls, 1971). The possibility of normative persuasion, which unfortunately Kant, Hare, and Rawls would treat as normative *legislation*, contradicts the frequent simplifying assumption made by social scientists that values ("preferences") are fixed. In the real world, of course, value judgments, including those about process, change with experience.

Any consensus about matters empirical or normative emerging from a communicatively rationalized political interaction can be described as rational through reference to the conditions of its production. Will consensus indeed prevail in this hypothetical ideal state? With unrestricted deliberation it might. On the other hand, it might not if, as Elster (1983, p. 38) believes, there is a "plurality of ultimate values." Human beings may prove so irreducibly different that consensus about normative judgments is precluded even under ideal conditions simply because individuals therein adhere to different conceptions of what it means to be human, or what Moon (1983) calls a "model of man" or "paradigm of personhood." More concretely, MacIntyre (1988) argues that ideas about what is rational and just can only develop within a tradition, which in turn must have been shaped by its encounters with *particular* sets of social circumstances. Similarly, Hanson (1985, p. 409) believes we can never repudiate the particular traditions in which we find ourselves, or their elements of arbitrariness, "since it is only on the basis of tradition that we understand at all."

One widely held negative interpretation of Habermas's position on communicative rationalization holds that in denying any potential for irreducible disagreement, he is seeking an objectivist solid ground for both truth and morality and perhaps even detailing a utopia, where all individuals would reach the same conclusion (see, e.g., Gould, 1988, pp. 18, 126–7). If so, he is guilty of the same homogenizing sin as post-Enlightenment liberalism, not to mention Western moral philosophy from Kant to Popper and Rawls, which cast rationality and tradition as opposites. A specific critique along these lines is tendered by Benhabib (1982, 1986), who argues that, if nothing else, Habermas "ignores the contingent, historical, and affective circumstances which made individuals adopt a universal-ethical standpoint in the first place" (1986, p. 298). Benhabib's unwillingness to renounce the validity of particular, contextual interests resonates with a feminist argument to the effect that abstract states of the kind postulated by Habermas (and for that matter by Rawls) are essentially masculine constructs, populated as they are by universal and ahistorical *men* (Leonard, 1990). Such theories therefore reflect an essentially masculine urge to transcend contextual particulars. A feminist model of *woman* cannot be so estranged from particular contexts and relations, for woman is always of and in this world.

Thus cautioned, communicative rationality can withdraw from the brink of objectivist homogeneity in one of three ways. The first, and least helpful, would admit an element of local arbitrariness into the determination of consensus, which could then only be sought within particular traditions or ways of life. But the shared understandings and common socialization that facilitated *phronesis* in the Athenian *polis* are rarities in contemporary society to the extent each individual interacts with many and varied others.

A second solution would recognize that consensus on *what* is desirable based on a reciprocal understanding of the accepted legitimate (if different) opinions and conceptual frameworks of other actor(s) is possible in the absence of a shared commitment to the ultimate reasons *why* it is desirable. MacIntyre (1984b, pp. 500–1) notes that disagreement on the fundamental principles of morality (pure ethics) often proves compatible with consensus on the moral side of practical issues (applied ethics). In other words, prudential, context-specific moral reasoning can overcome differences in abstract commitments.[8] Even failing this kind of consensus, simple compromise between different views is defensible to the extent it is reached under communicatively rational conditions (Habermas, 1982, pp. 257–8). The views in question would have to be either opposing conceptions of generalizable interests or reflectively held and discursively scrutinized interpretations by individuals of their particular needs. The critics of communicative rationality who charge it with homogenization and contextual insensitivity are mistaken, for communicatively competent individuals hear and respect different voices.

Communicatively rationalized consensus or compromise should not, of course, be confused with the systematically distorted compromises reflecting the skewed distribution of power found in real-world liberal and bureaucratic politics. The conditions of consensus and compromise are crucial and prevent communicative rationality's degeneration into a hopeless pluralism here (White, 1988, p. 74). Communicative rationality enables actors to state their *real* concerns about the issues at hand in the expectation they will be taken seriously, if not shared.

A third solution is in fact advanced by Habermas himself (1979, p. 90) and endorsed by Bernstein (1983, pp. 191–4). On this account, communicative rationality provides only procedural criteria about how disputes and arguments might be resolved and about how principles might be constructed. The procedures in question are discursive and so differ from those advanced by Kant and Rawls, which require only that the isolated individual engage in a thought experiment. In further contradistinction to Kant and Rawls, there is no attempt at substantial determination of universal principles for individual conduct and social arrangements. Communicative rationality tolerates a plurality of values, practices, beliefs, and paradigms of personhood (masculine or feminine). Moreover, it neither presupposes nor seeks to generate any universal theory of human needs (White, 1988, p. 70).

The approach followed in the remainder of this study is consistent with these second and third solutions. I shall, though, argue that pure proceduralism is incoherent, for a commitment to the procedures of communicative rationality implies approval of certain broad kinds of political institutions even as it allows greater plurality in other realms of life. There is a parallel here with Arendt's analysis of politics. Arendt stresses that objectivist claims to truth (about facts or morals) are irrelevant to authentic politics, which can only flourish with the interplay of *different* opinions.[9] But just as Arendt's commitment to variety leads her to endorse the councils that allow variety to flourish, so a commitment to communicative rationality leads me to endorse the institutions of discursive democracy. The debate about the substance of these institutional arrangements must, however, remain open-ended.

The pervasiveness and power of particular traditions and ways of life is undeniable and cause for celebration rather than regret. But this recognition does not mean one must follow Burkean conservatives (even if they do disguise themselves as neo-Aristotelians) in accepting the authority of the traditions one inherits and the dead hand of their past. For "the critical resource that enables us to re-appropriate the past . . . is an active historical consciousness that legitimizes the choices we make *vis-a-vis* competing traditions. The appeal to tradition can never rest on tradition itself; . . . rather, it always has to be made on the basis of a critical historical perspective that selects from the past those moments worth preserving" (d'Entreves, 1987–8, p. 242).

This endorsement of both communicative rationality and the integrity of traditions departs from Habermas's mistaken belief that "'tradition' means just that we carry something forward as unproblematic which others have begun before us" (Habermas, 1989). As Hanson (1985) stresses, following MacIntyre (1984a, p. 222), any tradition is constituted by prolonged and open-ended argument about the key concepts of the tradition itself, in Hanson's own case liberal democracy (1985, p. 418). This intramural argument can then be called to account by the standards of communicative rationality in order to expose distortions, false consensus, and the like. However, Hanson still believes we are all ultimately prisoners of tradition; in his (American) case, "we are liberal democrats by virtue of our historical situation" (1985, p. 429). Concerning this particular tradition, I shall argue that we should not and need not be liberal democrats. My general point is of course that communicatively rational discourse can involve the reconstruction, rejection, synthesis, or even creation of traditions, not just their extension. So here I part company from Hanson, Gadamer (1975), and even MacIntyre, who does not recognize the possibility of a rationality that transcends particular traditions.

In sum, differences across contexts, traditions, opinions, and paradigms of personhood are profound and perhaps ineliminable. But debates among partisans are not only possible but also more or less communicatively rational. And rational consensus is no empty hope.

The Uses of Discursive and Communicative Rationality

Most of the authors mentioned approvingly so far in this chapter deploy variations of communicative or discursive rationality in a fashion that removes them from concrete political concerns. Thus Horkheimer (1947) outlines his objective reason not as a real-world possibility but as a lament for what we cannot have under a triumphant, instrumentally rationalized, and nefarious modernity (see also Horkheimer and Adorno, 1972). For Arendt (1958) and Ball (1983a) the classical model of politics does no more than demonstrate that the present exhibits just one kind of politics, defined by power, interest, and large numbers. So the classical model just helps us understand this present better, offering no realistic alternative to it. Habermas, Bernstein, and MacIntyre operate at the metaphilosophical level. By now it is a standard criticism of Habermas's work (though no less true for the repeated telling) that he fails to develop anything that meets the specifications he himself has laid out for a critical theory. That is, he has formulated no theory addressed to a specific audience and designed to liberate them from their sufferings (see, e.g., Benhabib, 1981, pp. 54–5; Leonard, 1990).

My own concerns are more practical. Consider, in this light, the case of Arendt. To begin, she believes that politics, authentic or otherwise, will always be for a self-selected elite (e.g., Arendt, 1969, p. 233). So politics can be discursive but hardly democratic. She then draws a dichotomy between the truly "political" and the inescapably "social." True politics consists of free, relaxed discourse about matters of principle: liberty, participation, institutional reconstruction, and so forth. The "social," in contrast, is the domain of collective problems, of inequality, crime, poverty, exploitation, unemployment, environmental decay, and the like. To

Arendt, this mundane domain is best left to expert (instrumentally rational) administrators. Arendt implicitly affirms the idea that just as in ancient Athens true politics is only for rich, fat, idle, male slaveowners.[10]

Arendt's dichotomy, though not her elitism, is echoed by Habermas (e.g., 1987a), who believes that the proper home of communicative rationality is the lifeworld of social interaction, where individuals construct and interpret the identities of themselves and others, their morality, aesthetic sensibilities, and common culture. Communicative rationalization frees the lifeworld from the dead hand of custom, myth and illusion on the one hand and the domination of specialists and manipulators on the other.[11] Except for the fact that it is not predominantly political, Habermas's communicatively rationalized lifeworld resembles Arendt's authentic politics. Likewise, Arendt's "social" category is echoed in Habermas's idea of the "system." This system is where strategizing, technical manipulation, cost efficiency, and instrumental rationality serve state and economy and the more general functional necessities of social system maintenance.

Arendt's politics disdains social problem solving quite explicitly. Habermas is less forthright on this score, but if indeed social problem solving is an aspect of social system maintenance that can only proceed through feedback and the exercise of instrumental rationality, it has no proper place in the lifeworld. However, a critique of Habermas along these lines is not on solid ground, for he argues at a high level of abstraction, which makes it hard to tell what he thinks about social problems and their resolution.

My intent here is to pave the way for discursive democracy by violating the dichotomies explicit in Arendt and, I would still claim, implicit in Habermas. I shall argue that discursive rationality should be expanded into things "social" and "systemic." Among these I include social problems (especially complex ones), political and policy-making institutions, policy analysis, and empirical political science. Thus I seek not to defend the lifeworld against further "colonization" by the system but to conduct a counteroffensive by taking discursive rationality to the heart of the "enemy's" domain. It follows that I do not believe that the spheres of instrumental and communicative rationality are separate and incompatible. I shall argue that instrumental and communicative attitudes can coexist; the choice is seldom a matter of one or the other but rather of the proportions in which the two shall be combined.[12]

By conducting a counteroffensive, I hope to engage the concerns of an audience beyond that sought by metaphilosophers and cultural critics of contemporary society. My intended broader audience would encompass not just modernity's malcontents but also the members of what is still the dominant tradition in the Western world, organized around objectivism, liberalism, instrumental rationality, "modern" politics, and deductive–nomological theory. This tradition has encountered crisis *in its own terms.* If MacIntyre (1988, pp. 364–5) is right, such a crisis is exactly the occasion when a tradition can open up to its rivals and when the rivals, for their part, can generate solutions to the tradition's problems *as those problems are defined by the tradition's own adherents.* In this light, I shall argue that a rival tradition under the umbrella of discursive democracy offers both a critique of present practices in a number of areas and an escape from current impasses in these areas.[13] The intent is to show that discursive democracy offers attractive alternatives in politics, policy making, policy analysis, and reflexively, political science. I shall also touch on other areas to which discursive democracy might contribute. In short, what I offer is a constructive dimension that has so far been missing from the critical theory of society.

Throughout, I will try to demonstrate that these alternatives constitute a coherent set, that they really are the stuff of a rival tradition. Thus discursively democratic institutions demand a particular kind of public policy, which in its turn cannot flourish without such institutions. Political science as currently practiced is reinforced by, and helps legitimate, dominant political and economic institutions. So a communicatively rationalized political science would criticize these dominant institutions to the extent of *their* obstruction of free discourse. Moreover, that kind of political science can prosper only to the extent these institutions are themselves discursively democratic.

Though it is but one alternative, discursive democracy is not just *an* alternative to the dominant tradition. Rather, discursive democracy attempts to capture what is *the* alternative implicit in, and made possible by, "modern structures of consciousness" (to use Habermas's term). I shall say little about the premodern or postmodern possibilities currently found on the margins of Western social life and philosophy, such as magic, Dadaism, poststructuralism, fundamentalist religion, Burkean conservatism, fascism, and nihilism.

A Preview

The argument begins in Part II with a focus on political institutions. The institutions of liberal polyarchy currently dominate Western polities. The *rationality* of these systems is established most effectively by Popper's (1966) famous proclamation on behalf of the open society.[14] Chapter 2 takes on the open society in the name of discursive democracy. The idea of "discursive designs" is proposed as the institutional manifestation of discursive democracy, offering an alternative to the more familiar liberal institutions of the open society. This program for political organization also constitutes a reply to those who charge critical theory with excessive abstraction and aridity.

Whether or not this program should actually be pursued is another matter entirely. The capabilities of discursively democratic institutions are explored further in Chapter 3, where I argue that they can cope with complex problems better than both liberal open societies and Weberian bureaucracies. Thus discursive democracy is preferable not just in terms of intrinsic meaning and congeniality in the threatened lifeworld, but also in the problem-solving terms of Popperians and Weberians.

Discursive democracy may have its attractions, but realistically, can it be a material force for emancipation in a hostile world? Some contradictions and crises that open up a space for discursive democratization are introduced in Chapter 4. But discursive designs will always be under siege in a society dominated by state and market imperatives. The ambiguity these dangers and threats impart to the potential of discursive designs is also dealt with in Chapter 4. At their worst, such institutional designs could prove little more than subtle agents of social control for state and market actors. In the light of their ambiguous potential, some advice is offered to those contemplating discursive design in a hostile world, concerning in particular the need for relentless critique.

Many of the world's more complex and intractable social problems today reside at the international level. Thus the international system provides an acid test for institutional proposals claiming problem-solving power, which is the subject of Chapter 5. Cur-

rently, the international polity possesses little in the way of problem-solving capabilities, a condition often attributed to its highly
decentralized character. But that difficulty turns into a virtue when
it comes to discursive designs, for there exists no state analogue or
hierarchical structure to preempt or subvert them. Somewhat coun-
terintuitively, then, the international system could be a promising
place to experiment with discursive institutions.

Political institutions remain in sight in Part III, but the emphasis
shifts to public policy and the policy analysts and designers who
help create it. Chapter 6 explores the relationship between democracy and policy analysis, conceptualized in broad terms as that
knowledge-based activity concerned with social problem solving.
Most policy analysis efforts to date are cast in the image of exclusively instrumental rationality and as such constitute a "policy
science of tyranny" that facilitates the control of centralized power.
Efforts to construct a policy science consistent with liberal or pluralist democracy provide little in the way of problem-solving rationality and at best merely reinforce the structure and operation of
pluralism. Only a communicatively rational policy science of participatory democracy, oriented to the public sphere rather than the
state, is well placed to reconcile the twin demands of effective social
problem solving and democratic principles. It should be stressed
that the quality rather than just the quantity of participation is at
issue here. The role of the policy analyst in such processes is not
that of a technocrat but rather that of a participant in and facilitator
of open discourse about policy (albeit with some special capabilities). That analyst should also focus continually on the conditions
of policy discourse. Parenthetically, it may be noted that this kind
of policy analyst is well placed to monitor the direction taken by
discursive designs in light of the dangers identified in Chapter 4.

Aside from its reconciliation of rationality and democracy, the
kind of policy science sketched in Chapter 6 can release this field
from some of the inhibitions that critics of (instrumentally rational) policy analysis and planning have imposed upon it. Chapter
7 argues that as long as they are committed to conventional notions
of policy rationality, analysts and planners really would do well to
bridle their ambitions in a complex and uncertain world. But communicatively rational conditions render more ambitious policy design (i.e., large-scale policy commitment), an attractive proposi-
tion in the face of large-scale problems or opportunities. Discursive
democracy could therefore release creative energy in the polity.

The mood of Part IV is more reflexive as I turn to the practice and progress of political science, again conceived in broad terms, as an intellectual community that reflects on politics. Chapter 8 deploys the classical model of politics in the critical style of Arendt, who takes modern politics to task, and Ball, who takes on the whole of empirical political science. My own target is limited to the most widely used instrument in the empirical study of politics, the opinion survey, and the kind of rationality it embodies. I shall argue that this instrument can yield precious little information about the prospects for a democratic political order, or for that matter communicatively rational politics. Moreover, widespread opinion surveying functions in very subtle fashion to reinforce a political order of instrumental domination and control and to obstruct more democratic possibilities. Thus the analysis of Chapter 8 remains relevant to real-world politics, even as I focus on the discipline of political science.

If the opinion survey is an inappropriate and undemocratic instrument for the empirical study of politics, what should take its place? In Chapter 9 I argue that Q methodology, an approach unfamiliar to most political scientists, is especially appropriate. Q methodology does justice to the political capabilities of individuals, and its assumptions and implications are conducive to the egalitarian discourse sought by discursive democracy (though Q can also tap distortions of discourse). This approach conceptualizes political situations in terms of "concourses" of verbal interchanges rather than strategic exercises of power.

In Chapter 10 I turn to the progress and rationality of political science in its entirety and the discipline's potential contribution to emancipation processes. Rejecting objectivist accounts and drawing on postempiricist philosophy of science, I argue that the progress of political science consists of an ever-increasing capacity to cope with contingency in the empirical and conceptual problems society presents to the discipline. The fact that these problems and disputes are socially constituted and historically specific raises the question of the conditions under which they are constituted. These conditions may, and do, feature distortion by established power and wealth. To the extent this distortion holds, the discipline's problem-solving success is mere complicity in an irrational society, hardly something to be proud of. On the other hand, to the extent that the conditions of problem formation are characterized by free discourse, problem solving can indeed be the stuff of a justifiable discipline. Conditions of free communication between polity and discipline are likely only to the extent the polity is itself communicatively rational. In other words, a truly rational and progressive political science is possible only in a rational society. Thus we come full circle to institutions. For if it is true to its rational foundations, political science *must* criticize society and polity to the extent their institutions violate canons of uncoerced communication and free, competent political interaction. Discursive democracy provides a program for both the polity and those who study it.

PART II

Political Institutions

CHAPTER 2

Discursive Designs

Political institutions and practices can be judged, justified, and criticized in many more or less specific ways. Are they efficient? Do they provide for the basic needs of society's less fortunate members? Do they imperil the mental health of their inhabitants and their clients? Do they promote freedom or necessitate repression? Are they aesthetically pleasing? Do they provide agreeable spectacles? Do they promote justice, environmental quality, inflation, or national security? Do they allow for meaningful political participation?

The scrutiny and justification of political institutions undertaken in this chapter proceeds in light of their claims to rationality. For though it may require some digging to find them, all political institutions and practices have roots in theories of knowledge and rationality of the sort introduced in Chapter 1. One does not have to be a critical theorist to accept this point; Immanuel Kant, Bertrand Russell, and Karl Popper would concur (Williams, 1989, p. 50). Now, theories of knowledge rarely (if ever) *determine* institutional structure. More usually, they legitimate and justify or (conversely) criticize and undermine particular practices. Nevertheless, theories of knowledge and rationality can inform political development to the extent they permeate the understanding of political actors. The program for discursive democracy in political development sketched in this chapter finds its theory of knowledge in critical theory, and so its rationality is communicative. This program is central to my constructive project for critical theory.

This pursuit of principles for political organization can expect little sympathy from many critical theorists. For critical theories are most confidently directed *against* particular repressive or exploitative social relations based on class, gender, race, spatial location, dominant kinds of rationality, and so forth (although a critical theory will also normally specify the broad kind of action necessary to combat oppression). A theory of this sort is therefore tested through action on the part of the audience to whom it is addressed, as they come to realize the character and source of their oppression, throw off its yoke, and decide for themselves what kind of life they shall lead henceforth. Validation of the theory is complete when these individuals agree it gave a correct account of their sufferings and effectively charted the course of their relief.[1]

A critical theory of this sort does not rule out statements about the proper character of actual practices or states of affairs. But a fear of foisting institutions and practices on already oppressed groups by outsiders who cannot know the true interests of these groups makes critical theorists reluctant to go into specifics. Any steps in this direction endanger their attempts to establish innocence of frequently leveled charges that they are repressive purveyors of utopian blueprints (see White, 1980).

Although aware of such hazards (see Chapter 1), I shall claim that critical theory and communicative rationality can indeed inform the creation of political practices and institutions. How, then, may this movement toward real proposals be justified?

A Constructive Moment for Critical Theory

Most critical theory is exactly that – critical (at least when it is more than metatheoretical). Thus the intention is less to disclose what is right than to expose what is wrong, though in practice it is hard to engage in exposure without some minimal disclosure. I shall suggest that the balance of critical theory be tipped toward more disclosure. To see why, consider three kinds of critique the theorist might pursue.

The first may be termed pure critique, in which the theorist compares reality with some fixed standard. For critical theorists, this standard can be the ideal speech situation (which I shall discuss in detail later). Other analysts might appeal to different utopias, such as the Rawlsian principles of justice (Rawls, 1971) or the neoclassical economist's perfect market. Indeed, the most common justification for constructing utopias is to better criticize the present (so I attach no pejorative connotations to the word "utopia" here).

A second kind of critique may be termed indirect. Indirect critique uses the precepts of communicative rationality (or some other ideal) to construct a counterfactual but contextually specific discourse, which can then be deployed in the criticism of reality. Hanson (1985) endorses the idea of indirect critique in his history of democratic theory and practice in the United States and quotes Habermas (twice) to the effect that critique should proceed by answering this question:

How would the members of a social system, at a given stage in the development of productive forces, have collectively and bindingly interpreted their needs (and which norms would they have accepted as justified) if they could and would have decided on organization of social intercourse through discursive will-formation, with adequate knowledge of the limiting conditions and functional imperatives of their society? (Habermas, 1975, p. 113; quoted in Hanson, 1985, pp. 42, 415).

The critic might then (say) reconstruct the discourse of the 1960s New Left as it would have been had womens' voices been heard and use this reconstruction to criticize the actual discourse of that New Left. This particular move would be contextually appropriate because womens' voices were available, although ignored or disdained. The theorist makes no claim to have identified the discourse as it should have been, still less should be, for even the counterfactual the critic constructs remains open to critical evaluation. So although this second type of critique involves more disclosure and less exposure than the first, both types are relentless.

I shall have cause to deploy both these first two kinds of critique in the pages that follow. But for the most part my approach contains more disclosure than either of them. I stress this constructive moment in critical theory – and hence a third type of critique – because, with apologies to Marx, the theorists have criticized the world, but the point is to change it. Pure and indirect critique can of course be forces for change. But critique that intimates no feasible or attainable alternative fails in its practical task. For defenders of the status quo, warts and all, can argue that really "there is no alternative" (to use one of Margaret Thatcher's favorite expressions). And if there is no alternative, then ultimately there is no critique. My attitude to critical purists here echoes that of former Australian Prime Minister Gough Whitlam's comment on the purists in his own Labor Party: "The impotent are indeed pure."[2]

Political theory today often proceeds in terms of abstruse language and incomprehensible idioms, remote from the experience of most political actors. This, to Gunnell (1986), is the alienation of political theory. In moving from metatheory to pure critique to indirect critique to constructive critique, critical theory becomes progressively less alienated and more able to relate to the concerns of ordinary political agents.

Constructive critical theory offers conceivable and practical alternatives to the status quo. Clearly, though, the implication of perfection for some realizable political practices and arrangements should be avoided. Any proposals that are offered must also be subjected to both pure and indirect critique. Constructive critical theory should not forget its critical roots; it is not an alternative to pure and indirect critique but a necessary addition to them.

Having justified my constructive project, let me now identify its most prominent constructive rival, which makes a useful foil.

The Rationality of Political Arrangements

In the scrutiny of political arrangements, no less than elsewhere, rationality is often interpreted in purely instrumental terms. In other words, political institutions are judged and justified according to how well they can generate and implement policies to resolve well-defined problems through pursuit of clear goals.

A long tradition encompassing such otherwise varied figures as Plato, Comte, Saint-Simon, Weber, Lenin, Mussolini, Herbert Simon, and Robert Heilbroner argues that the most instrumentally rational arrangements are those in which power is centralized and authority is organized on a hierarchical basis.[3] For the purposes of this chapter I shall take it as given that this tradition has met its death at the hands of Sir Karl Popper. Popper has argued convincingly that instrumental rationality in politics can flourish only to the extent that policies are proposed, and their actual effects judged, under conditions of free criticism. Imperfect knowledge in an uncertain world requires cautious action, and a maximum of critical feedback both before and after the fact. Hierarchy and centralized power are by their very nature impervious to such criticism.

The idea of critical rationalism as developed by Popper and his followers justifies piecemeal social reform, social experimentation, and liberal democratic polyarchy (i.e., multiple centers of power) through reference to a fallibilistic and falsificationist, but still objectivist, view of knowledge and rationality.[4] Everything we do, as individuals, as investigators, as policy makers, or as groups, can only be tentative. Thus the Popperian "open society" and its offspring are the forms of sociopolitical organization most conducive to instrumental rationality. Critical rationalism (not to be confused with critical *theory*) today constitutes the most fully articulated and prominent program linking abstract issues of epistemology and rationality to concrete ideas about political organization.[5] So critical rationalism is not just an articulate and influential account of Western science and social science; it also justifies some of our more cherished and prominent institutions.

In the remainder of this chapter I shall attempt to show that critical theory can do better than critical rationalism. My choice of target is therefore different from the much easier one normally attacked by critical theorists and others sympathetic to communicative rationality. The latter are usually obsessed with instrumental rationality as associated with positivism and embodied in authoritarian and technocratic structures; in other words, their preferred target is the one already destroyed by Popper. Positivism is the doctrine that causal laws of society can be deduced from basic assumptions, verified by empirical test, and then added to a stockpile of inviolable truth. Instrumental rationalists can then use these laws as the basis for their manipulations of social systems. So positivism (and its concomitant instrumental rationality) have been held responsible for bureaucratic hierarchy (Iggers, 1972), instrumental and manipulative policy science (Fay, 1975, pp. 38–43; see also Chapter 6 of this study), and (in a version traceable to Engel's interpretation of Marxism) coercive political practices in the Soviet Union (Ball, 1984). My Popperian target is a worthier opponent than positivism.[6]

I will challenge critical rationalism, and its preferred institutions, from the direction of communicative rationality and critical theory. By way of indicating the elements required of my alternative constructive program for political organization, I will begin by briefly laying out the moves successfully accomplished by critical rationalism in similar pursuit. The ensuing development of a parallel program for critical theory will, if successful, help defuse familiar charges that this approach is abstract, obscure, arid, and politically irrelevant. I will conclude with a comparison of the capabilities of institutions and practices inspired by the two approaches, though a full comparison in the light of complex social problems will have to wait until Chapter 3.

Epistemology to Politics: Lessons from Critical Rationalism

Let me now outline the critical rationalist approach to political organization. In the comparative sections at the end of this chapter and in the next one I will argue that critical rationalism falls short of the critical theory alternative, even if the Popperian program "works" the way its followers believe.

The Popperian specification of principles for political organization begins with an exemplary scientific community governed by free conjecture and criticism in its problem solving, constrained only by its (objectivist) subscription to a shared set of rules for the conduct of science. This community constitutes an image of the kind of social life most conducive to (instrumental) rationality. Now, *real-world* scientific communities always feature obstacles to free interchange such as hierarchy, conformity, and punishment of transgression. The Popperian scientific community is unattainable and functions only as a counterfactual ideal to which actual and proposed arrangements can be compared and by which they can be evaluated. This ideal is a critical standard for all human social practice, including politics.

The specifically *political* translation of this ideal is the open society (see especially Popper, 1966). The primary task of politics is seen as the resolution or amelioration of social problems, and the most rational way to perform this task is through free conjecture about and criticism of public policies. The ideal scientific community and the open society are equally ethereal. No true, fully open society has ever existed and probably ever will.

These utopian beginnings can, however, yield some clear implications for political structure. Approved critical rationalist institutions and practices exist at two levels. First, model institutions and practices can be designed and effected by committed critical rationalists. Second, real-world approximations that have developed autonomously can be endorsed.

Dealing first with exemplars rather than approximations, model political *practice* takes the form of policy experimentation. Just as the open society imitates the scientific community, so should public policies imitate scientific experiments (see Campbell, 1969). Popperian "piecemeal social engineering" specifies that each public policy should be implemented under controlled conditions so that clear inferences about its effects can be made (see Popper, 1972a).

Several well-publicized policy experiments have been undertaken along these lines in recent years, and their methodology is now the staple of policy evaluation textbooks (the most famous is the New Jersey Negative Income Tax Experiment). Given the fallibility of social scientific knowledge, Popperians (but not all policy evaluators) specify that policies should be open to criticism both before and after their adoption and implementation. Given an unavoidable multiplicity of social values, criticism should be admissible from any quarter, expert or lay.

The model *institutions* that such practices help to constitute may be captured by the idea of an "experimenting society," essentially an array of institutions for the facilitation of piecemeal social engineering. Given the instrumental manipulation of social conditions central to Popperian ideas about problem solving, some governing elite of manipulators must exist. However, this elite should be subject to a maximum of control by the governed and wield authority only at the behest of the latter. Arrangements should be made for maximal generation and dissemination of information about policies. (The provisions of the U.S. 1970 National Environmental Policy Act and 1972 Technology Assessment Act are exemplary in this respect.) If the issues involved are highly technical, then a public forum should be provided before which experts would debate one another (see James, 1980, pp. 172–3). Specific reform proposals along critical rationalist lines include the "overlapping loops of information and control" in government outlined by James (1980), whose level of detail reaches the constitution of residents' associations and their relationship to city councils.

Despite sporadic attempts to realize these model practices and institutions, precious little in contemporary political life measures up to Popperian ideals. But all imperfect practices and institutions are not condemned alike. Distinctions are made between existing institutions in complete violation of the critical rationalist model and those that offer a very rough approximation. These distinctions yield a general preference for decentralized representative democracy and hostility to bureaucratic, legalistic, or highly centralized decision making. Thus Popper himself can make a passionate case for the essential rationality of existing liberal democracy, especially when comparing it with more authoritarian alternatives (see Popper, 1966).

The critical rationalist reach from scientific ideal to liberal democracy is united by a culturally invariant conception of rationality as effective problem solving, which has both objectivist and instrumental facets. Objectivism resides in procedures for ascertaining the veracity of beliefs and theories. These procedures go hand in hand with an instrumental attitude toward devising and selecting means to ends, for both facets involve specifying tests to indicate the adequacy of theories or means, and then criticizing these theories or means in the light of experience, especially through reference to the results of controlled manipulations. Theories and means are homologous in the critical rationalist world. Indeed, it is here that the essential connection between objectivism and instrumental rationality is most strongly established. The conception of rationality uniting them is claimed by critical rationalists to be applicable to science, social science, art, and public policy alike. The transcendent quality of this rationality means that institutions and practices themselves should be created through instrumental manipulation under criticism.

This sketch of the critical rationalist program for political organization now stands complete at six elements: (1) a counterfactual ideal, (2) a political translation of that ideal, (3) model political practices, and (4) model political institutions for pursuit of the ideal, (5) imperfect real-world approximations to these models, all united by (6) a conception of rationality. If critical theory is to mount a credible challenge to this orthodoxy, then a counterpart for each of these components is required. These counterparts will now be developed and discussed.

The Counterfactual Ideal: Ideal Speech

Critical theory's counterfactual ideal is the ideal speech situation, in which discourse proceeds among actors with equivalent degrees of communicative competence. This situation is unconstrained in the sense of being free from domination, self-deception, and strategic interaction. Given that discussion is unlimited, it is conceivable that the whole sum of human experience can be adduced. Hence any consensus attained in this situation, be it about empirical questions of truth or normative matters of justice, has a rational quality. The ideal speech situation is of course nothing more than the full realization of the precepts of communicative rationality.

Now, the ideal speech situation does not exist, and clearly cannot exist in this world of variety in opinions and traditions. Its canons are always and unavoidably violated in the real world. But as Habermas postulates, the ideal speech situation is anticipated in every act of communication between individuals (see, e.g., Habermas, 1970) such that it is not just an invention of the philosopher or political theorist. Any individual communication, collective decision, or social practice that *could only* be justified by diverging from the precepts of ideal speech is indefensible. The ideal speech situation and its hypothetical consensus can be used both within traditions (Hanson, 1985) and across traditions to criticize real-world practices. Like any utopia, including the Popperian scientific community, its primary practical value is critical. It is not designed to legislate any particular values, institutions, or practices.

Some critical theory purists might want to cut short any pursuit of principles for political organization at this juncture. Both White (1980) and Habermas (1982) take pains to stress that the ideal speech situation is not supposed to be a blueprint (any more than Rawls's, 1971, original position is intended to be a place to which rational actors can retreat). Critical purity might at most allow comparative evaluation. So we may confidently judge the American polyarchy to come closer to the ideal than did the Third Reich. But we can also try to push critical theory further.

The Political Translation: An Authentic Public Sphere

Communicative rationalization and the ideal speech situation can apply to all domains of social life. Their specifically *political* aspect emerges in the idea of a public sphere, a concept used somewhat loosely in critical theory and political theory more generally. Despite its elasticity, this concept is central to any attempt to pursue a communicatively rationalized lifeworld (see McCarthy, 1984, p. xxxvii). Keane (1984, pp. 2–3) defines the public sphere in the following terms:

A public sphere is brought into existence whenever two or more individuals . . . assemble to interrogate both their own interactions and the wider relations of social and political power within which they are always and already embedded. Through this autonomous association, members of public spheres consider what they are doing, settle how they will live together, and determine . . . how they might collectively act.

In these terms, the public sphere can function as an ideal to which appeal is made or as an actual situation. In the latter sense, Habermas endorses the public sphere that sprang forth with eighteenth-century bourgeois society. The emerging bourgeoisie sought to limit more traditional and hierarchical authority through the development and exercise of informed public opinion (see Habermas, 1962; also Held, 1980, pp. 260–3). Unfortunately, the subsequent development of capitalism overwhelmed the community of interest characterizing the early bourgeois public sphere. The state came to work for rather than against the bourgeoisie, and discourse gave way to the exercise of political power. Arendt (1958) argues that the public sphere has sometimes flourished but is today degenerate, as disinterested discourse has been corrupted by pursuit of private interest. Habermas, in contrast, is more sanguine about the possibilities for revival of the public sphere, especially in conjunction with the rise of new social movements (Habermas, 1987b, pp. 364–6), to which I shall return later.

For the purposes of this chapter I will set aside accounts of the public sphere that ground its health in specific historical circumstances and stress instead the use of the concept as an ideal to which appeal is made. Rodger (1985, p. 205), following Habermas, speaks of an "authentically open public sphere," open in the sense that the precepts of communicative rationality are followed. A polity grounded in these principles would in fact consist of an *array* of authentically open public spheres. In later chapters I shall treat the public sphere in more concrete terms, as a target and a site for political action.

Model Practices: Discourse and Holistic Experimentation

The idea of a public sphere can inspire model political practice with at least two facets. The first is simply *discourse*, or free and open communication in political life, oriented toward reciprocal understanding, trust, and hence an undistorted consensus. This kind of activity characterizes the Aristotelian notion of pedagogical and discursive politics, celebrated more recently by Hannah Arendt, as discussed in Chapter 1. Arendt, of course, takes pains to stress that politics, properly understood, does not concern the resolution of social problems.

Arendt's fear, shared by many critical theorists, is that goal-directed pursuit thrusts imperatives on political interaction. Debate about the effectiveness of the means of collective action, rather than just about its ends, involves consorting with the "diabolical powers" of instrumental rationality (see Keane, 1984, pp. 184–6), which lead only to technocracy, bureaucracy, and at best the Popperian experimenting society. Arendt herself fears totalitarian terror of the sort that transpired in the French Revolution if we attempt to solve social problems through political means (Arendt, 1962, p. 108). Taking such hazards to heart, the practical political program of critical theory might end with institutionalization of principles of discourse, perhaps in the weak form suggested by White (1980, pp. 1015–6), for whom principles of ideal speech should take a form analogous to First Amendment freedoms in U.S. constitutional law. That is, anyone wishing to override tolerance, free expression, and participation would require an exceptionally substantial burden of proof.

On the other hand, critical theory can also allow for political practice in the form of experimentation concerning social conditions (see, e.g., Habermas, 1973, pp. 36–7). It is crucial that such experimentation avoid any distinction between "subjects" and experimenters; hence the instrumental manipulation characterizing piecemeal social engineering is ruled out. The appropriate practice may be termed *holistic experimentation*, as sketched (outside a critical theory context) by Mitroff and Blankenship (1973). Participants in holistic experiments are all subjects in the true sense of the word. The purpose of the experiment is an improvement in the aspects of the group's condition considered relevant, upon reflection, by its members (rather than before the fact by some external experimenter). In this pursuit, continual trial and error are allowable, and the individuals involved can reconstruct their relationships with one another and with the outside world as *they* see fit.[7] Holistic experimentation violates just about all the canons of systematic piecemeal social experimentation. Unlike the piecemeal approach, no elaborate controls are necessary, for generalization of the results to any larger population or any future time period is irrelevant.

Holistic experimentation leaves open the possibility that political practice inspired by critical theory can get its hands dirty in the details of collective action in a way forbidden by Arendt's loftier conception of communicative politics. In similar spirit, some recent contributions to the field of policy analysis (which is defined by its concern with social problem solving) have attempted to apply critical theory constructs to the conditions of deliberation about policy proposals (see Chapters 6 and 7).

Model Institutions: Discursive Designs

It is perhaps at the juncture of model institutions that a critical theory program for political organization is currently weakest, to the point of petering out entirely. Now critical theory is not necessarily unsympathetic to the specification of institutions. A need for the rationalized lifeworld to assert its primacy through being "objectified" in social and political institutions is sometimes recognized (Wellmer, 1985, p. 58). However, critical theorists tend to be chary of overly precise specification, for as noted in Chapter 1, discursively democratic institutions must be sensitive to variety in political and cultural traditions and social conditions.

In this spirit, McCarthy (1978, p. 332) commends context-sensitive, but still hypothetical, institutions that would "justify the presumption that basic political decisions would meet with the agreement of all those affected by them if they were able to participate without restriction in discursive will-formation." In pursuit of such institutions, Bernstein (1983, p. 228) argues that we should "seize upon those experiences and struggles in which there are still the glimmerings of solidarity and the promise of dialogical communities." He pleads that it is "imperative to try again and again to foster and nurture those forms of communal life in which dialogue, *phronesis*, practical discourse, and judgment are concretely embodied in our everyday practices" (Bernstein, 1983, p. 229).

Such scattered comments are the closest intimations of a project for the construction of discursively democratic institutions to be found in the literature. Unlike the critical rationalists, critical theorists have so far failed to generate much in the way of model institutions, still less attempted to apply them to political reality.

Critical theory is at a competitive disadvantage here for two reasons. First, critical rationalism would like its model institutions embodied in the apparatus of liberal governments. Critical theorists, by contrast, are profoundly suspicious of the contemporary state. Their ideal is a separate public sphere (see Rodger, 1985, p. 213; Keane, 1984, p. 257). Hence the proper location for any discursive designs is the public space between individuals and the state. Excessively formalized institutions risk co-optation and de facto absorption by the state. Second, as already noted, critical theory renounces instrumental manipulation of social conditions, even in pursuit of manifestly desirable ends.[8] Critical rationalists lack any such inhibitions about legislating for political practice.

Overly precise specification of model institutions involves skating on thin ice. Far better, perhaps, to leave any such specification to the individuals involved. The appropriate configuration will depend on the constraints and opportunities of the existing social situation, the cultural tradition(s) to which the participants subscribe, and the capabilities and desires of these actors.

Is this fear of designing institutions warranted? Often the verb "design" connotes manipulation of conditions and as such is part of the vocabulary of instrumental rationality. If one draws a parallel between the design of political institutions and architectural or engineering design, then critical theorists should indeed fear it.[9] But the design of social and political practices can be *itself* a discursive process in which all the relevant subjects can participate. Any conjectures and proposals for model institutions can be offered for validation by these individuals.

The stage is now set for a move from abstract formulation of authentic public spheres to real-world institutional design. It is perhaps easiest to begin with a specification of what model institutions should *not* contain. First, no individuals may possess authority on the basis of anything other than a good argument. All that counts, in Habermas's phrase, is "the forceless force of the better argument." Hence hierarchy, even in the mild form of representative government as endorsed by liberals and Popperians, is ruled out. Second, no barriers to the participation of interested parties should exist. Third, there should be no autonomous formal constitutions or rules.

More positively, meaningful participation requires communicatively competent individuals. Competence in turn may need a boost with regard to resources, time, and information. In this context, some critical theorists see substantial potential in the current "information revolution" (Luke and White, 1985), which might render obsolete the idea that true democracy requires face-to-face contact of the sort possible only in small autonomous communities.[10] Herein lies a connection to the prospects for participatory democracy, which I shall develop more fully in Chapter 6.

Model discursive institutions may require the embodiment of communicative ethics in rules of debate. So, for example, Fisher and Ury (1981) describe cases of "principled negotiation" relying upon four rules: separation of individual egos from the problem-solving tasks at hand; emphasis on the interests of parties rather than on bargaining positions; efforts to generate proposals of net benefit to all the actors involved; and a striving for criteria separate from the (particular) interests of each party. Unlike existing legalistic political structures, any such rules must themselves be redeemable in discourse among the parties subject to them. These rules must always have contingent status. A *fully* authentic public sphere could of course dispense with formal rules entirely.

One bone of contention concerning discursive designs is the kind of decision rule that would obtain. Unreflectively, one might simply try to apply the hypothetical rational consensus of the ideal speech situation, which would suggest unanimity as an operative principle. Consensus on what is to be done could be reached through the exercise of Aristotelian *phronesis*, the prudential application of ethical principles in particular cases.

A first plausible objection here (anticipated in the discussion of communicative rationality in Chapter 1) is that even in the ideal speech situation consensus could not be expected. If participants hold to different fundamental values and interpretations, then one should expect them to disagree on practical questions too [unless MacIntyre (1984b, pp. 500–1) is right in claiming that practical deliberation can overcome abstract differences]. A second objection would hold that even granting hypothetical consensus under conditions of ideal speech, the exigencies of any real-world discursive designs would preclude consensus. For *phronesis* assumes and requires a background of shared norms and socialization experiences on the part of participating individuals. People from different cultural backgrounds are unlikely to come to agreement, especially under real-time constraints (see, e.g., Elster, 1983, p. 38).

If a substantial shared background on community norms does exist, then *phronesis* can proceed and unrestricted unanimity is a defensible decision rule. If such a background is absent, then as noted in Chapter 1, participants can still reach consensus based on reasoned *dis*agreement, by striving to understand the cultural tradition and/or conceptual framework of the other participants. This disagreement would ideally concern only different conceptions of the public interest rather than competing private interests. It is in this spirit that Barber (1984, p. 135) argues that the key to conflict resolution in participatory democracy is the transformation of private interests into publicly defensible values in unrestricted debate. On the other hand, interpretations of needs peculiar to one or more individuals are not ruled out, and compromises between different interpretations may be necessary (see Chapter 1). Individuals can then seek consensus on *what* is to be done while differing about *why*. Understanding of and respect for the motivations of those holding to a different "why" is crucial. This kind of procedure would preserve the decision rule of consensus, which does not require bland uniformity across participants or perfect agreement on norms.

Let me now formalize the idea of a discursive design, which is central to the whole notion of a constructive moment in critical theory.

A discursive design is a social institution around which the expectations of a number of actors converge. It therefore has a place in their conscious awareness as a site for recurrent communicative interaction among them. Individuals should participate as citizens, not as representatives of the state or any other corporate and hierarchical body. No concerned individuals should be excluded, and if necessary, some educative mechanism should promote the competent participation of persons with a material interest in the issues at hand who might otherwise be left out. The focus of deliberations should include, but not be limited to, the individual or collective needs and interests of the individuals involved. Thus the institution is oriented to the generation and coordination of actions situated within a particular problem context. But complicity in state administration should be avoided. As long as a state is present, discursive designs should be located in, and help constitute, a public space within which citizens associate and confront the state. Within the discursive design, there should be no hierarchy or formal rules, though debate may be governed by informal canons of free discourse. A decision rule of consensus should obtain. Finally, all the features I have enumerated should be redeemable within the discursive design itself. Participants should be free to reflectively and discursively override any or all of them.

To the best of my knowledge, nobody inspired by critical theory has ever tried to articulate and effect political institutions of the sort sketched here. Some critical theorists believe discursive forms are rare and vanishing. Where, then, might incipient forms be located?

Incipient Discursive Designs

Let me suggest that intimations of discursive designs can be found in some contemporary attempts to resolve conflictual social problems. These practices go by different names in different contexts, and none pays conscious tribute to communicative rationality. Examples include mediation of civil, labor, international, and environmental disputes (see Wall, 1981); alternative dispute resolution procedures more generally (sometimes known as "informal justice"); regulatory negotiation (Harter, 1982); policy dialogue (Gusman, 1981); principled negotiation (Fisher and Ury, 1981); and "problem-solving" workshops in international conflict resolution (Burton, 1979).

Although differing in nuance, these practices share the following features. First, they proceed in the context of a pressing unresolved problem of interest to all the parties. Second, that context is characterized initially by a degree of conflict, indicating interaction between divergent ends favored by these actors. Third, some neutral third party (a mediator, facilitator, or convener) generally initiates, lubricates, and oversees discussions among the interested parties. Fourth, discussion among the actors is prolonged, face to face, and governed by formal or informal canons of reasoned discourse. Such canons might rule out threat, concealment of information, delaying tactics, embarrassment of another party, statement of a bargaining position, and so forth. Participation therefore means that the parties involved reconstruct the nature of their relationships, at a minimum in the case at hand, perhaps too in their broader interactions. In some cases, especially international conflict resolution, this reconstruction ipso facto contributes to problem resolution. Fifth, any product of the process is a reasoned, action-oriented consensus. No judgment is reached by the third party. The fact that agreement is purely voluntary has generally led to high degrees of subsequent compliance. Sixth, such exercises are fluid and transient, lasting no longer than a particular problematic situation. As such, they tend to involve ordinary political agents rather than professional participants.

Short of being convinced by the arguments of this book, people will enter such practices if they see good reason to do so. One good reason might be a stalemate in other areas of decision, such as courts. Another might be a genuine desire for improved communications with protagonists. A third reason could be naked self-interest: There is more to gain from participation than abstention.

One suspects this third calculus may dominate in a world of ubiquitous strategic pursuit of self-interest. Such pursuit is of course anathema to communicative rationality. Hence any incipient rationalized interaction immediately confronts the need to transcend the motivations that attracted the participants. This requirement perhaps explains why a third party is necessary: to ease participants over hurdles leading to an unfamiliar kind of interaction. One sign of successful dialogue is the increasingly inactive role of this third party.

Although no panacea, these procedures have often managed to generate substantial consensus among initially hostile parties, which may account for the current explosion of interest in such discursive processes in a variety of problem areas. Several anthologies of cases have appeared recently. For example, in the area of environmental mediation alone, Talbot (1983) discusses six site-specific cases, the most complex of which involved the construction and operation of power plants on the Hudson River in New York. Bingham (1986) undertakes a broader, if less detailed, survey. Bacow and Wheeler (1984) combine breadth and depth in their casebook, focusing on relatively large-scale and complex conflicts. Let me now pick out mediation and regulatory negotiation for more intensive scrutiny. Other examples of incipient discursive designs will be discussed at appropriate points in later chapters (especially Chapters 5 and 6).

Mediation

Mediation is, by definition, a process in which the parties to a dispute attempt to reach a mutually agreeable solution under the aegis of a third party by reasoning through their differences. To this end, a mediator will begin by identifying and selecting the parties to mediation (if they are not self-selecting). Preliminary interviews with these parties can indicate the extent to which a mutually satisfactory outcome is conceivable. If the initial communications offer some encouragement, the mediator can proceed to provide a conduit for initial communications among the actors, disseminate pertinent information to all sides, and set the initial rules for debate.

Beyond these minimal tasks, the mediator can also take actions to reduce rigidities in the bargaining positions of adversaries, attempt to reconceptualize issues through reference to novel problem definitions or normative judgments, offer inducements to the parties involved, and oversee subsequent compliance with any agreements reached.[11] Many of the mediator's tasks require oversight of the process of mediation. But the mediator must also attend to the substantive content of proposals on the agenda and how they relate to the interests of the parties involved.

It is important to distinguish mediation from procedures such as arbitration and legal adjudication, in which the third party reaches a verdict. The product of mediation is not a verdict, but consensus among the actors involved, sensitive to the central concerns of these parties.

Mediation in practice can sometimes involve little more than a veneer of participation in decisions masking the co-optation of the relatively powerless by the securely powerful. Amy (1983a) documents several cases in which environmental mediation has been used as a strategic tool by developers. Environmentalists get to say their piece, and the project under discussion will be modified to produce "responsible development," but when all is said and done, the mine, shopping mall, dam, or power station will be constructed. Co-optation and other hazards will be addressed at length in Chapter 4, where it will be seen that mediation and similar exercises have a thoroughly ambiguous potential with regard to communicative rationalization.

However, mediation can also stimulate discourse and reflection about goals, interests, and values and reciprocal education over the issues at hand. Such processes, too, have been observed and described in several cases of environmental mediation (see, e.g., Watson and Danielson, 1982). Participation in mediation puts the individual in the company of others who do not share his or her normative principles, which can stimulate reflection on these values (Amy, 1983b, p. 355). Mediation contains intimations of discursive politics in the form of both a search for reasoned consensus and understanding of the legitimate, if different, interests of other parties.

One larger point here is that incipient discursive designs such as mediation can and should be subject to the kind of critique made possible by the ideal of a discursive design as articulated earlier. It would not be hard to reconstruct particular cases of mediation as they might have been had this ideal been followed and to use these reconstructions for an indirect critique of reality.

Regulatory Negotiation

Regulatory negotiation has recently gained some popularity in U.S. policy-making circles, largely in reaction to perceptions of failure in existing means for the promulgation and enforcement of government regulations. The traditional regulatory process is somewhat complicated. The relevant agency has substantial discretion, though the courts have often specified very precise procedural requirements the agency must follow, and legislative direction can tie its hands still further. There is widespread unhappiness with the results of this process. Those regulated complain of the burden of excessive and unnecessary regulations. Those the regulations purportedly protect point to weak enforcement, wholesale noncompliance, and cozy relationships between regulators and regulated. Neutral observers bemoan the often perverse incentives of regulations insensitive to real conditions and a lack of coordination across different regulations.

Regulatory negotiation is a discursive procedure designed to improve matters. It bears some similarity to mediation, for it involves face-to-face negotiation among the parties interested in a regulation (such as public interest groups, the regulated industry, and the regulatory agency itself), directed toward reasoned consensus on the appropriate content of regulations (see Harter, 1982, for more detail). In recent years regulatory negotiation has been attempted with varying degrees of success in areas such as environmental, work safety, and aviation safety regulation.

The most intensive experiment in regulatory negotiation to date is the National Coal Policy Project, operational in the late 1970s (see McFarland, 1984, for a chronicle). The project brought together representatives of the coal industry and environmental groups to discuss the appropriate future of coal policy in the United States. A remarkable degree of consensus was reached concerning this future. Some of the accords represented recognition of the interests of the other side. For example, the coal industry agreed to public finance for environmentalist representation at public hearings, and environmentalists supported the idea of a simplified one-stop permitting process for new coal-burning plants. Moreover, there was a dramatic change in the terms of discourse as the project proceeded. With a little prodding, the participants began talking in a language new to both sides, that of welfare economics. The overarching value implicit in this language is allocative efficiency, which again was of little prior concern to either side. Now a switch from the language of strategic interaction to the language of welfare economics is perhaps little more than the replacement of one kind of distorted discourse by another that is equally distorted. Yet it suggests the possibility of a reciprocal scrutiny of normative judgments, penetrating beyond particular concerns such as the profits of the coal industry or the preservation of a hillside in Utah.

The eventual failure of the National Coal Policy Project recommendations to find acceptance in public policy may be traced to its exclusion of several interested parties: some environmentalists, the United Mine Workers, and consumer groups. In addition, the project's members ignored some political and constitutional realities, such as the division of policy-making authority in a federal system (see McFarland, 1984). But as a discursive exercise in something like a public space the project remains suggestive.[12]

When all is said and done, we will not find Athens in regulatory negotiation or the Paris Commune in mediation. The incipient discursive designs discussed here have their defects from the perspective of the model discursive design defined earlier, just as real-world social experiments are defective from a critical rationalist angle. So mediators sometimes manipulate proceedings and suppress discourse, and regulatory negotiators happily exclude actors lacking political "clout." Any such process confined to discussions among political leaders always runs the risk of alienating their followers. Participants are often representatives of the state, corporations, or interest groups rather than citizens per se. And the dividing line between incipient discursive designs and the state is not always as clear as it should be.

Unfortunately, none of these cases has been able to benefit from a critical theory contribution. Critical theorists for the most part remain ensconced in the heights of theoretical abstraction. For their part, instigators of and participants in these incipient discursive designs probably remain unaware of the existence of critical theory. But as Trotsky once said, "you may not be interested in the dialectic, but the dialectic is interested in you." These incipient discursive designs indicate the potential for discursive democracy in today's political world. And they are often located where one would expect, in the space between individuals and the state.

Real-World Approximations: New Social Movements

The incipient discursive designs introduced in the previous section fall far short of model institutions, but at the same time they are something more than undesigned real-world approximations. Aside from such cases, institutions and practices in sympathy with the precepts of discursive democracy can exist in several locations. Fidelity to the principle of unremitting critique means that any such institutions and practices must be criticized as well as endorsed.

One school of thought on this question is thoroughly nostalgic, looking only to history for exemplars such as the Athenian *polis*, the early bourgeois public sphere, or the extraordinary spontaneity surrounding epic revolutions.

More sanguine are those who see discursive potential in an array of contemporary political movements concerned with peace, ecology, opposition to nuclear power, feminism, civil rights, community autonomy, and so forth. These movements can be interpreted as engaging in a communicative assertion of the claims of a threatened lifeworld against encroachments by the state and capitalism. They should not, however, be confused with the conservative reactions against modernity expressed through the religious right in North America or neofascist parties in Europe. They do, though, share a great deal in common with the radical Christian activism of Liberation Theology, the Quakers, and the United Church of Christ. New social movements fight for the unredeemed promises of modernity, for, as Offe (1985, p. 853) puts it, "a selective radicalization of 'modern' values." So feminism, for example, only moves in radical directions after society intimates legitimization of the idea of gender equality. These movements are also permanently concerned with the definition and re-creation of their own identity (Cohen, 1985).

Their radical and modern character means that new social movements can contribute to the establishment or revival of free discourse in a public space (Habermas, 1981, 1987a, pp. 393–6). These movements are generally committed to the promotion of communicative rationality (if not by that name) in the political life they engage. In addition, the internal politics of these movements is generally organized on a freely discursive basis (Keane, 1984, p. 25; Rodger, 1985, pp. 209–13; Weiner, 1981). Indeed, given their affinity for the classical model of politics introduced in Chapter 1, the description new *political* movements would be more appropriate, though it is probably too late for such renaming to stick.

This classical style in their internal workings means that no leadership can bind a movement's members to compromises with the state or other conventional political actors. Thus continued confrontation with such actors is to be expected, with demands made in stark, all-or-nothing terms (Offe, 1985, pp. 830–1). Uncompromising demands of this sort might involve the shutdown of nuclear power, the total removal of nuclear missiles from a territory, or an end to destructive agricultural practices. So new social movements are unlikely to be found participating in the incipient discursive designs discussed in the previous section, which constitute a very different sphere of action. Indeed, one of their defining features is their lack of interest in sharing state power (Cohen, 1985).

One of the more impressive examples of an uncompromising discursive movement is that of the Solidarity in Poland (see Touraine et al., 1983), which in the early 1980s constituted both a challenge and an alternative to the state. Its uncompromising stance in those early years helps to explain its suppression. Solidarity's more recent entry into the Polish state suggests it has succumbed to the lures of more conventional politics, both internally and externally, though not without some resistance from its membership. With this move, Solidarity has ceased to be of interest to critical theory.

In the West, a wide variety of social movements and citizen actions evidences participatory and egalitarian momentum. One of the more prominent movements is the Greens. The U.S. Greens pursue collective decisions through discussion and consensus involving local groups, working parties, the circulation of issue papers (which anyone can write), and conferences. Like the incipient discursive designs outlined earlier, these Green discussions often make use of third-party facilitators, though the intent is to work out programs rather than to resolve conflicts (of course, conflicts do arise in these programmatic debates).[13] Green hostility to conventional politics is reflected in the reluctance of the U.S. Greens to declare themselves a political party. The European Greens are less inhibited on this score, but they are no less aware of the perils of seduction and so explicitly demarcate a sphere of political action outside their participation in parliamentary and electoral politics.

A Conception of Rationality: Communicative Rationality

The final element of a critical theory program for political organization, required to make it fully competitive with critical rationalism is of course the unifying conception of communicative rationality.

Table 2–1. *Two programs for political organization*

Element	Role	Critical rationalism	Critical theory
Counterfactual ideal	Critical standard for all social practice	Idealized scientific community	Ideal speech situation
Political translation	Critical standard for *political* practice	Open society	Authentic public sphere
Model political practice	Refers to actual practices	Piecemeal social engineering	Discourse and holistic experimentation
Model political institutions	Constituted by practices and arrangements	Experimenting society	Discursive designs
Real-world approximations	Endorsed but not necessarily inspired by program	Liberal polyarchy	New social movements
Conception of rationality	Unites and underpins the other elements	Instrumental and objectivist rationality under criticism	Communicative rationality

Nothing need be added here to the discussion of communicative rationality in Chapter 1.

Critical theory's program for political organization is now fully comparable with critical rationalism. The two programs are summarized in Table 2-1. But the fact that a path can be charted by critical theory is no reason for following that path and rejecting critical rationalism. Through comparing the capabilities of the two traditions, I will now attempt to show that the claims of critical theory are indeed substantial, not only in its own terms but also in the terms of critical rationalism.

A First Comparison: System and Lifeworld

The natural home of communicative rationality is the lifeworld of culture and social interaction. In contrast, instrumental rationality is manifested in the idea of a social *system*, in which all structures, actions, and practices have only an instrumental function, most especially in terms of their contribution to system maintenance. Habermas (1987a) echoes Weber's fear that we are witnessing an invasion of the lifeworld by the unrelenting instrumental rationality or *zweckrationalitat* of the system. Such a process deprives the world of meaning and removes control from human subjects. Moreover, any action conceived in solely instrumental terms always proves more than a means to some end. As Tribe (1973) demonstrates at length, it also helps determine who or what we shall become. So a decision to (say) devote financial resources to "relevant" subjects in higher education may be an economy measure and contribute to the profitability of industry, but it also makes us a less humane society, with different kinds of preferences. Under such conditions, our seeming choice of futures is illusory.

Some critical theorists, notably Horkheimer and Adorno (1972), have accepted the dismal Weberian prognosis of triumphant instrumental rationality concomitant with modernity. Thus the lifeworld can expect only invasion or colonization by money and power, be it through advertising; media manipulation; experts in nutrition, sex, and aesthetics; or the helping agents of the welfare state. On the other hand, as noted in Chapter 1, Habermas (1984, 1987a) sees nothing inexorable in the progress of instrumental rationality and system imperatives. The trouble is that although the potential of instrumental rationality has been realized, an equal potential for communicative rationalization has atrophied. But actions to protect the autonomy of the lifeworld are indeed possible. And these actions need be not defensive and conservative but rather assertive and communicative, as the preceding discussion of new social movements should suggest.

Today, the lifeworld battles not just bureaucracy and capital but also the social interventions of liberal polyarchy. Even if these interventions involve well-intentioned piecemeal social engineering, that engineering is done *to* people on behalf of system requirements. And, it must be said, the lifeworld battles the critical rationalism of Sir Karl Popper in its entirety. For in his celebration of modernity and (justified) fear of totalitarianism and other romantic and irrational threats to liberal society, Popper presents a prescriptive model of man that is uniform, atomistic, and in rational pursuit of an arbitrary set of purely subjective preferences (Williams, 1989, pp. 172–81). The world constituted by such individuals would be antiseptic, cold, comfortless, rootless, and aimless, with no place for tradition, diversity, or community. There would be no place for commitment to anything except the colorless methodism of critical rationalism itself. Such individuals and such a world provide no defense against the very authoritarian and romantic appeals Popper fears most (Williams, 1989, pp. 160–5).

This first comparison of the qualities of our two programs for political organization is hardly fair, for it proceeds in the terms established by critical theory itself. Let me turn now to the terms established by critical rationalism.

A Second Comparison: Problem-solving Capabilities

To Popperians and in everyday usage, rationality consists largely of effectiveness in instrumentally solving problems. If problems can only be solved through purely instrumental action, then clearly problem solving has no place in the critical theory program. Indeed, some of the major proponents of communicative rationality in public life, especially Arendt, believe there should be no more to politics than talk. She emphatically opposes social problem solving. If, like Arendt, one wishes to maintain the communicative purity of political life, then its rationality is of an order quite different to that of instrumental reason, which is tied to problem solving. Indeed, to call these two things rationality might be to stretch a single concept too far. The two programs would remain incommensurable, the one committed to problem solving, the other to communicative rationalization.

However, contrary to views advanced by critical rationalists and critical theorists alike, there is more to social problem solving than instrumental action. Important social problems are pervaded by conflicting values (Dryzek, 1983a), which instrumental action cannot resolve. The claim to be made in the rest of this chapter and in the one that follows is that communicative rationality can contribute to the resolution of social problems, especially complex ones. Although a departure from Arendt and other heirs of Aristotle, this tack renders the two kinds of rationality commensurable. Moreover, I shall argue that increasing complexity in the modern world facilitates the rise of discursive designs.

Unlike Popperian "critical" rationality, communicative rationality allows for reasoned consensus on normative judgments that, if attained, could motivate actions.[14] Thus problem-solving impasses caused by conflicting values might be circumvented. In the real world, of course, an overarching consensus may be unattainable, except in cases where shared socialization enables the exercise of *phronesis*. However, understanding across different frames of reference can allow practically equivalent results, as I argued earlier.

Equally important to the fact of undistorted consensus is the content of norms arrived at, which can, in the terms developed by Habermas (1971), constitute *generalizable* rather than *particular* interests, though as I have noted, the discovery of such norms is not essential. A generalizable interest exists beneath the surface misconceptions of actors. In offering an argument on behalf of a candidate for generalizable status, an individual is in effect claiming that rational, uncoerced, and knowledgeable individuals would subscribe to it in the situation at hand. Discursive designs facilitate the discovery of generalizable interests through the kinds of argument to which they are conducive. One way for an argument to prove persuasive in such a forum is through transcendence of interests particular to any subset of the parties involved. Arguments based on generalizable interests have much greater power. Interests or values are "tested" by the group as a whole, which can pass judgment on their generalizable status. It should be stressed that any such judgments allow continued differences over the ranking, or even definition, of generalizable interests.

All actors are likely to have both generalizable and particular interests in the context of any given issue. Critical theorists are rightly averse to giving instances of generalizable interests, for to offer one outside the context of discourse endows it with a peremptory status totally out of keeping with the principles of communicative rationality. As Wellmer (1985, p. 58) observes, "it is not the task of the theoretician to determine what the content of a future social consensus will be." We should bear in mind that communicative rationality is best thought of as a *procedural* standard, dictating no *substantial* resolution about values to be pursued. But some examples that could conceivably arise in discourse include the following. In the context of nuclear deterrence, all humanity has a generalizable interest in avoiding war. Minorities such as government officials of the superpowers or members of the military–industrial complex have particular, and discursively indefensible, interests in strategic advantage, defense expenditures, prestige, and so forth. In the context of ecological resources (say a fishery) each individual has a particular interest in maximizing his or her immediate "take" (fish catch) and a generalizable interest in the overall quality of the resource (sustainable yield of the fishery).

The continuing integrity of the ecological systems on which human life depends could perhaps be a generalizable interest par excellence.

As populations grow, natural resources are depleted, and individuals interact with increasing numbers of others in complex ways, the values microeconomists call public goods and their obverse, common-property resources become ever more important relative to their private counterparts. The orthodox (and very Hobbesian) microeconomic theory prescribes centralized coercion to ensure adequate supply of public goods and protection of commons resources (see, e.g., Olson, 1965; Hardin, 1968).[15] Discursive action facilitates the provision of public goods in a decentralized and noncoercive manner, for public goods and the condition of commons resources are kinds of generalizable interests. The very reason public good supply is problematical is the domination of generalizable by particular interests. An additional attraction of public good supply through discourse is that this procedure enhances subsequent compliance with any agreements reached simply because the parties involved will have freely consented to the content of accords (see Mernitz, 1980, Chap. 4; Amy, 1983b, p. 350). Moreover, discourse can also define the very content of public goods through scrutiny of precisely which generalizable interests are at issue in a particular situation.

Any ability of discursive designs to supply public goods might be reason enough for endorsing their institutionalization. But their potential contributions to social problem solving go still further.

Both technocracy and open society inspire policy practice that can only involve instrumental manipulation and engineering of people (and nature). Discursive designs, in contrast, can facilitate a less manipulative and more symbiotic kind of problem-solving intelligence in political life. For the very act of joint seeking after improved conditions through participation in discursive institutions can itself help constitute both improvement in these conditions and reduced social tensions. For example, residents of a deprived urban area previously subject to the manipulation of policymakers can improve and exercise their problem-solving competence by participating in discursive institutions that will help determine the conditions of their lives henceforth.

Beyond their immediate contribution to problem solving, discursive designs, however incipient, have three more noteworthy qualities. First, they expose the deficiencies of established institutions operating in the same area. Mediation can make litigation look foolish and expose public hearings for the charades they generally are. Second, not being bound up in constitutions and formal rules (or other controls), they allow for their own supercession. Their procedures can develop in the directions their participants feel most appropriate. Third, their very presence and successful functioning help erode the idea that it is legitimate to exercise authority on the basis of anything other than a good argument.

Conclusion

Critical theory and communicative rationality are fully capable of inspiring a realistic program for political organization. To the degree collective choice is so inspired, the scope for influence or control through material riches or the means to coerce others is reduced. Beyond this promise of a more authentic politics of free discourse, the project may offer one of the few avenues for dealing effectively with growing conflict associated with social problems.

However, the future's problems are probably going to be even more complex than today's. And if Max Weber is right, increasing complexity demands more in the way of instrumental rationality, not less. Weber himself would expect this instrumental rationality to be manifested in centralized power and bureaucracy; critical rationalists would reply that decentralized, experimenting society institutions are more appropriate and more likely to survive evolutionary selection. Can discursive designs cope with complexity in social problems? In Chapter 3 I shall argue not only that they can but also that they can do so better than either Weberian bureaucracy or the Popperian experimenting society.

CHAPTER 3

Complexity

Complex social problems demand effective political responses. My intent in this chapter is to challenge received notions about the character of these responses. Specifically, I will argue that actions based on exclusively instrumental rationality have highly limited capabilities in a complex environment. By implication, the forms of social organization in which instrumental rationality is enshrined, be they Weberian bureaucracies or liberal open societies, are similarly limited. The case against instrumental rationality will be made through reference to three of its most effective modern extensions: analytical problem disaggregation, systems modeling, and structured integration of diverse perspectives on complex issues. The first of these three extensions, the analytical strategy, is central to both bureaucracy and the open society. The second, systems modeling, is a more clearly bureaucratic approach and as such would find little favor with Popperians. The third, integration, finds some place in large formal organizations but is essentially Popperian and critically rationalist in its open problem-solving spirit. After exposing the limits of these three extensions, I shall argue that discursive democracy can contribute more to the resolution of complex social problems than any of the three. This efficacy does not, though, mean that all vestiges of instrumental rationality need be purged. To the extent my argument is convincing, the appearance of some of the real-world intimations of discursive designs in the vicinity of complex problems becomes understandable.

The Weberian Anxiety

Following Max Weber, it has been regarded as axiomatic that increasing orders of social complexity require ever more refined means for the exercise of instrumental rationality in decision making if effective control of a problematic environment is to be achieved and maintained. The Weberian thesis can be applied to any kind of decision process, be it that of a human brain, a corporation, or a government. Currently, the instrumental cognitive capacities of the individual brain are the target of banal aids to "positive thinking" and more sophisticated "modern technologies of reason" (March, 1978, p. 588). In the form of systems analysis, linear programming, decision analysis, and the like, the latter technologies can also be applied and exercised by and in small groups confronted with complexity. With high orders of complexity any such technical assistance becomes insufficient, and harmonization of the efforts of large numbers of individuals is required. Such coordination in turn requires the growth of forms of social organization in which instrumentally rational overseers coordinate the instrumentally rational efforts of other individuals.

Herein, of course, lies Weber's own fear of advancing *zweckrationalitat* in hierarchy and bureaucracy constructing an "iron cage" around human existence (see, e.g., Weber, 1968). This fear can be alleviated somewhat by Popper's analysis of the political conditions most hospitable to instrumental rationality. For at least Popper allows the zookeepers of the iron cage to be plural, equal, and critical of one another (see Chapter 2). He even lets the animals criticize the zookeepers. Nevertheless, Popper does not break the bars of the cage, for presumably hierarchy and bureaucracy will always be necessary to implement piecemeal social interventions, however much their design is a matter of liberal political debate. Even one of his sympathizers charges that, when pressed, Popper comes down on the side of technocracy (Williams, 1989, p. 183).

The Weberian scenario has rarely met much enthusiasm. At best, centralized instrumental rationality has been regarded as an unfortunate necessity (see, e.g., Hauser, 1967; Huntington, 1974). At worst, its progress has been portrayed as a nightmare against which humanity can only cry out in impotent rage (Horkheimer and Adorno, 1972). One finds only sporadic suggestions that an uphill struggle can be waged against instrumental rationalization on behalf of human spontaneity and congeniality (e.g., Bookchin, 1982).

I will argue, contra Weber and his heirs, that complexity does not dictate instrumental rationalization. But first, just what *is* complexity?

Complexity

The most widely cited definition of complexity speaks of "nonsimple" relationships among elements sufficient to render the properties of a system capable of apprehension only as something more than the sum of the system's parts (Simon, 1981, p. 195). A shorter definition is as follows: Complexity exists to the extent of the number and variety of elements and interactions in the environment of a decision process (Dryzek, 1983b, p. 346). An illustration of complexity in action may be more instructive than further semantic explication.

Consider the problem of air pollution. Air pollution is one aspect of a larger phenomenon called pollution and itself covers a number of different kinds of emission and damage. Thus the air pollution problem is not a well-bounded case, ripe for resolution. However, to explore the pollution problem (or problem nexus) further, we need to start naming categories while cognizant of their artificiality and interpenetration. One such category might be "acidic emissions," publicized as acid rain, which we can consider in a little more detail.

To begin with, the causes and consequences of acid rain are shrouded in no little mystery. Acidic emissions can be traced to a variety of sources, natural and man-made. The latter include coal-burning power stations, metal smelters, and automobiles. Acid rain is a product of chemical transformation of emissions in the atmosphere that vary with meteorological conditions. This rain can damage buildings, trees, soil, and aquatic life. But the damage is not easily measured, and each instance invariably has other plausible causes.

Now, complexity as discussed so far in this case pertains only to natural, ecological systems. An ecological adage has "everything connected to everything else" (Commoner, 1972). But the acid rain issue involves complex *human* systems too. Human social systems possess a further level of complexity due to their teleological components: human minds capable of devising the actions they take, thereby introducing systematic variety into the interactions they make with other humans and nonhuman objects.

Human actors concerned with acid rain include the institutions and agencies of various national, regional, and local governments; individual public officials; environmental groups and their members; car drivers; corporations such as automobile manufacturers, coal producers, and makers of emission control equipment; fishermen and foresters; labor unions; and environmental scientists. These actors are motivated by concerns ranging from forest growth to economic growth. Some motives are transparent, some ulterior. For example, Canada's concern over its net import of acid rain may be crocodile tears, for any U.S. curbs on acidic smokestack emissions will increase the competitive edge of Canadian hydroelectric exports in U.S. markets. Though not necessarily unfathomable, the behavior of actors can be unpredictable, possibly subverting policy intentions, if only by so simple an act as switching off a "scrubber" on a smokestack or falsifying data about tree damage. Worse still, these actors do more than help constitute the environment of policy making; they also permeate the boundaries of that process. Herein lies the seeds of arguments against democratic politics of the sort advanced by Thurow (1980), Huntington (1974), and Friedman and Friedman (1984), who would coerce at least the public policy process into simplicity by excluding troublemakers.

Complexity in today's world is on the advance. Growth in populations, urbanization, industrialization, travel, trade, specialization, and communication possibilities increases the number of people with which any given individual will have significant interaction. Population and economic growth increase human pressure on, and hence interaction with, natural systems. Expanding education gives individuals greater latitude to devise their actions and interactions. The mobilization of once-passive groups such as women, ethnic minorities, sexual deviants, and the poor increases complexity across the boundaries of the policy process (see Nias, 1975). But perhaps the most powerful engine of complexity is technology, especially as manifested in the information revolution, which opens up vast new possibilities for human interaction and action.

Extending Instrumental Rationality to Cope with Complexity

Instrumental rationalists possess several means for forging a response to growing complexity. Three such extensions of instrumental rationality will be explored in this section: analytical problem disaggregation, systems modeling, and integration of different perspectives on a complex issue.

Analysis

Consider first the disaggregation strategy. The kind of problem solving prized most highly in Western society, as in Western science and technology, is analytical in spirit. Analysis means, quite literally, breaking down a complex phenomenon into components for the sake of fuller understanding. In social problem solving, analysis translates into disaggregating any problem into a "tree" of sets and subsets, devising a solution for each subset, and piecing together an overall solution by simple aggregation of these partial solutions (see, e.g., Simon, 1981). The solution thus generated is in effect a mirror image of the decomposition. To illustrate, a hypothetical decomposition of the acid rain problem is presented in Figure 3-1. Analysis of this kind can be called upon to organize a hierarchical division of labor in bureaucracies. But this sort of analysis is also the essence of the *piecemeal* social engineering prized by critical rationalists, for only with problem disaggregation can Popperian trial and error in policy making proceed.

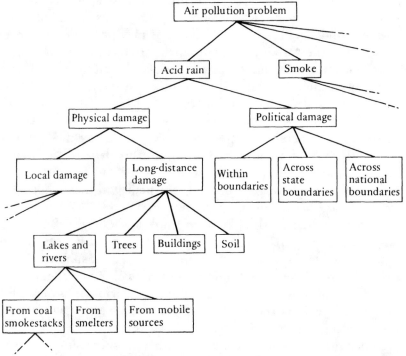

Figure 3–1. Possible decomposition of acid rain problem.

This strategy can work for *moderately* complex problems, which Simon (1981, pp. 209–13) dubs "near-decomposable." Under such conditions, a static ceteris paribus in the environment of policy enables clear inferences about the effects of instrumental interventions. But growing complexity can frustrate the decomposition strategy, for interactions across the boundaries of sets and subsets become too rich, irrespective of the quality and veracity of the theory informing decomposition and the intelligence with which the tree is drawn (see Alexander, 1965; La Porte, 1975). Any intervention may merely displace (sub-)problems across set boundaries. Only by chance will that intervention contribute to convergence on a less problematic state. Moreover, any dynamism will inhibit inference about its real effects (both primary and secondary). Successive attempts to deal with any apparent negative secondary and tertiary effects of an intervention may themselves only make matters worse.

A further limit to the analytical strategy arises with its need for clear, simple, and uncontroversial goals, for dissensus on such goals will mean like dissensus in problem definition, problem disaggregation, and the direction of problem solving in the various subsets. And after the fact, conflicting perceptions of what is desirable and undesirable in social conditions may preclude agreement on whether the various interventions have succeeded or failed.

To illustrate these limitations, consider the fate of two recent interventions in air pollution policy. First, one way of dealing with the box marked "smoke" in Figure 3-1 is to mandate the installation of electrostatic precipitators in coal-burning plants. Unfortunately, the ash thereby precipitated is alkaline. Hence the acidity of emissions rises, and the subproblem in the box labeled "acid rain" becomes more acute (and a problem concerning the disposal of solid waste ash is created). Second, air quality in the vicinity of a smokestack (the "local damage" box in Figure 3-1) can be improved by legislating an increase in smokestack height. But pollution is not thereby reduced, just transported long distances. Moreover, emissions spend more time in the atmosphere, which facilitates the chemical transformations necessary to produce acid rain. Thus the world's largest single source of acid rain is now a tall smokestack at a nickel smelter in Sudbury, Ontario, where once stood several smaller stacks.

Under highly complex conditions, then, a succession of seemingly intelligent piecemeal choices will yield no necessary convergence on a less problematical overall state. Worse still, no single indicator, or finite set of indicators, can tell us whether or not matters are improving. Any improvement on a single indicator (such as total suspended particulates in urban areas) may mask problem displacement to another medium or location. Further examples of such processes in operation in the realm of ecological problems alone may be found in the application of synthetic pesticides and fertilizers, energy-intensive agriculture, and mammoth development projects like the Aswan Dam (See Ehrenfeld, 1978, for a catalogue). Ecological systems combined with teleological and conflictual social structures exhibit complexity, nonreducibility, conflict, and dynamism to still greater degrees. Analytical problem solving can, then, be overwhelmed by complexity.

Systems Modeling

The idea of systems modeling is to capture the interactions constituting complexity. The modeler can increase the "analytic size" of the system at hand (i.e., the number of elements and interactions attributed to it by the analyst) in order to cope with the real size of this system (see Brewer, 1975a, pp. 176–7). Systems modeling is, though, more than just a tool. In the hands of Niklas Luhmann, it becomes a way of organizing thought, and organizing society, in a battle with complexity (see the essays by Luhmann in Habermas and Luhmann, 1971).

Some recent attempts of the U.S. Environmental Protection Agency (EPA) to grapple with complexity along such lines are instructive. By the early 1980s the EPA had been administering piecemeal, single-medium pollution control programs for more than a decade, undeniably reducing specific pollutants in particular locations. But success was often bought at the price of rising levels of other pollutants in different places. By 1985, Administrator Lee Thomas was raising the specter that "somewhere in the country, toxic metals are being removed from the air, transferred to a waste water stream, removed again via water pollution controls, converted to a sludge, shipped to an incinerator and returned to the air" (Thomas, 1985, p. 6). Sensitive to these nightmares of recurring cross-medium transfer of pollutants, discourse within the EPA came to revolve around ideas such as "integrated environmental management," a "whole-systems approach," "cross-media analysis," "integrated risk management," and concomitant reduction of the rigid division of labor between the agency's units.

These sentiments spawned models of cross-media pollution transfers. Each model incorporates the risk to human health from each relevant pollutant. Thus analysts can trace the health effects of any given antipollution regulation across media and ultimately identify the most cost-effective location and means for the achievement of a specified reduction in risks to human health (see Mosher, 1983; Alm, 1984; Thomas, 1985). The requirements of (instrumentally) rational decision would suggest construction of an integrated national (or global) model. However, the early EPA models refer only to particular localities such as Philadelphia, specific industries such as iron and steel (in a given location, such as northeastern Ohio), and broad categories of pollutants in a given region, such as hazardous wastes in New England.

The EPA's whole-systems efforts are hampered by the legal requirements that the agency must operate under a series of single-medium statutes (such as the Clean Air Act). Serious application of the whole-systems method would at least require Congress to redraft every environmental law to take into account all the others. Wholesale commitment to the approach would demand abdication of any semblance of democratic control to a computer model in the hands of an administrative agency, Max Weber's scenario with a vengeance (a scenario happily embraced by Luhmann). But these practical problems have no bearing on the essential problem-solving efficacy of the whole-systems approach, which falls short when confronted with profound complexity.

To begin with, this kind of modeling exercise requires some single metric to inform both model construction and subsequent action. The EPA models stress risks to human health. Now, health and threats to it can be measured in a number of ways, none of which is uncontroversial. Nor is there unproblematic interpersonal comparability on this metric. The respiratory illness of a steelworker does not necessarily have the same meaning as the skin disease of a farmer inadvertently exposed to toxic sludge left over from air pollution control in steel mills. Worse still, other values beyond human health may be at issue: aesthetics, life-styles, the intrinsic value of ecosystems, intergenerational equity, and so forth.

A contributing factor to the complexity of environmental problems is the variety of value positions brought to them by human stakeholders. Large-scale modeling efforts have trouble handling this facet of complexity, especially when, as in the EPA case, value systems apply differentially across different media. For example, aesthetics probably applies more to air pollution than to water pollution. Like any model of a complex system of concern to humans, the EPA approach involves an unwarranted simplification of normative judgment.

A further consequence of this simplification reflects the fact that different value systems or conceptual frameworks can inform different interpretations of a complex system. Any system model, no matter how large and complicated, embodies but a single perspective on reality (see Brewer, 1985). The EPA models are essentially engineering ones. Ecological models of pollution would embody different variables and pathways and political models different ones still.

The systems modeler is inevitably caught between the Scylla of attempting to capture *all* elements and interactions and the Charybdis of excessive simplification. Any attempt to fully capture reality means the modeler ends up with rich contextual description at the expense of problem-solving assistance. For example, the EPA modelers could no longer use a single summary coefficient to represent a cross-medium transfer. They would have to investigate how and why each instance of the transfer happened. In practice, of course, all models are simplifications and summaries of some sort (otherwise they would not be models at all). So the EPA ignores economic and political system variables and draws arbitrary boundaries around particular industries and locations. The risk of model simplification under complex conditions is simplemindedness, a charge leveled at the global modeling efforts sponsored by the Club of Rome (Meadows et al., 1972). Large-scale modelers tend to simplify their own lives by relying on too many questionable assumptions, not the least of which is that the relationships they establish are valid across time and space [see Brewer (1983) for a discussion of this and related issues].

Perhaps the most fundamental shortcoming of large-scale systems modeling is its inability to apprehend the goal-directed, teleological aspects of complexity in human social systems. The behavior of human actors (such as polluters and their opponents) has to be assumed constant, uniform, and predictable if the model itself is to behave. But examples of intentional human action subverting the best-laid plans of policy engineers are legion (as the literature on policy implementation amply attests).

Integration

If any model can represent but one perspective on a complex situation, then a legitimate variety of perspectives is inevitable. To cope with this variety, adherents of different perspectives can try to integrate them in pursuit of a more complete view. Any such pooling need not produce a (horribly complex) supermodel, but instead sensitize the individuals involved to the scope and variety of possible effects of interventions in the system at hand. One could seek interventions that are robust across different perspectives (Dryzek, 1983b, pp. 360–1). This strategy may be termed "integrative" of diverse specialities. It is obviously consistent with the critical rationalist predilection for a variety of inputs into problem-solving processes discussed in Chapter 2.

The relevant participants might represent different academic disciplines, each of which in isolation offers an oversimplified account of a complex reality. For example, one might invite engineers, ecologists, meteorologists, moral philosophers, lawyers, economists, psychologists, and political scientists to discuss the acid rain issue. Participation might also be extended to occupants of policy-making positions.

Several variants on this strategy are conceivable. The integrative encounter could proceed in adversarial fashion; so Mason (1969) suggests a "dialectical" encounter of thesis and antithesis in strategic planning. Similarly, George (1980) commends "multiple advocacy" among foreign policy advisors. Alternatively, a collegial atmosphere may be more conducive to creative synthesis and less prone to subversion by the demands of the ego. Proposals along collegial lines include Lasswell's "decision seminar" (Lasswell, 1960) and Brewer's "policy exercise" (Brewer, 1985). Such ideas find reflection in some contemporary private and public sector organizations, which respond to complexity by nurturing loose collegial groups, often partially isolated from the bureaucratic core.

The integrative approach can expose the blind spots of any single perspective, a blindness only exacerbated by incorporation into large-scale systems models. Thus Straus (1979) proposes negotiation over the details of models with such exposure in mind. The strategy promises more complete apprehension of the complex system involved. But one suspects that such integration will fall short as long as it is tied to a decision structure in which a privileged group manipulates, or advises the manipulators of, a system "out there." This shortcoming will persist even if this group consists of good Popperian piecemeal social engineers: intelligent, broad-minded, and unencapsulated by disciplinary and organizational socialization.

To begin with, if the group's members adhere to conventional notions of instrumental rationality in problem solving, then their individual contributions will still involve analytical problem decomposition. The consequent disaggregations may be broadly informed, but *any* decomposition fails for highly complex problems.

More fundamentally, *social* complexity means that the teleological elements in the system out there are still capable of springing surprises on this group of would-be policy engineers (or advisors to engineers). Finally, social complexity means that one unwarranted decomposition is between a collective decision process and its environment (because social actors are also political actors and so straddle the boundary of the policy process). Integrative strategies with restricted participation make such a distinction. To illustrate, all the examples of decision seminars discussed by Brewer (1975b) are confined to "experts"; only in the famous Chilean Vicos project are "local leaders" admitted.

If the integrative strategy remains tied to an imagery of a privileged problem-solving group manipulating a problematic external environment, then just like the critical rationalist designs discussed in the previous chapter, it is hamstrung by its inability to think of rationality in anything but predominantly instrumental terms. As the best that extended instrumental rationality can offer, the approach highlights the inherent shortcomings of conventional conceptions of problem solving under extreme complexity.

When confronted with complexity, the failure of the three extensions of instrumental rationality is not just a contingent fact of particular applications but is rather inherent in their operational logic. Critical rationalists might respond that provided these techniques are applied in an open-society atmosphere, then criticism and correction of their failings is an ever-present possibility. Clearly, though, analytical disaggregation and systems modeling are not self-correcting, even in such an atmosphere. Confronted with failure due to interaction effects across subsets, the analyst's response qua analyst can only be to seek still more subsets, now labeled secondary and tertiary effects. And if systems modeling fails because its perspective is oversimplified, the modeler's response qua modeler can only be to add more components to the model, perhaps approximating reality more closely but at the same time reducing the model's power as a problem-solving aid. For both disaggregation and systems modeling, a critical rationalist spirit can only compound error. Only practitioners of the integrative approach can escape this trap, and then only if one of the perspectives they embrace can highlight the limits of integration and expand its boundaries. The remainder of this chapter elaborates one such alternative.

Reconsidering Reason

Many of the more intelligent discussions of complexity in social decision (e.g., La Porte, 1975) have a hand-wringing quality, bemoaning the dire consequences of complexity but offering little hope of escape from its grip. This lacuna owes much to these observers' ties to dominant Western conceptions of rationality. Although recognizing the shortcomings of particular applications of this kind of rationality, they cannot bear to renounce the enterprise entirely, for therein would lie the road to irrationality and chaos.

Others, though, are less hesitant, suggesting that complexity be confronted by replacing instrumental rationality (at least at the system level) with other forms of reason. So incrementalists commend the political rationality attainable in the give and take of pluralist politics (Lindblom, 1959; Wildavsky, 1966). Free traders such as von Hayek (1979, pp. 65–97) believe market rationality can best synthesize dispersed fragments of information in a complex and uncertain world. Ecological critics of industrial society suggest a less calculating and more symbiotic intelligence attuned to the rhythms of the natural world (Bookchin, 1982). This spirit is consistent with classical conservatism of the sort espoused by Edmund Burke, for whom the complexity of society is best left well alone by would-be rationalists and coercive simplifiers.

More literally reactionary reactions to the failure of instrumental rationality in apprehending complexity involve a renunciation of reason altogether. A few conservative enthusiasts of the "restoration" of a market order and some ecological opponents of economic growth (e.g., Ehrenfeld, 1978) yearn for an earlier, simpler age, in which it was not necessary to think so hard. A related yearning is felt by those who would coerce the world into becoming a simpler place, be they socialist proponents of a siege economy for industrial reconstruction or the architects of Nazi Germany.

Automatic processes and invisible hands in politics and in markets have defects too familiar and numerous to recount here. Moreover, there are limits to their ability to cope with complexity. The shortcomings of incremental muddling through will be discussed in the next section. Markets can be overwhelmed by complexity because the more complex a situation, the greater the probability that failure of a single element (such as a key supplier) will be disastrous. This vulnerability explains why private sector organizations grow vertically, in order to absorb and administer uncertainty and interdependence (see Butler, 1983, p. 156). Markets can only cope with the uncertainty and interdependence attendant upon complexity by contracting for contingent claims. As complexity grows, the ability of market actors to anticipate contingencies is overwhelmed, and the capacity of the price system to transmit information is exceeded. Hierarchical organization may be more efficient than the market here because it can be programmed to cope with contingencies as they arise, so there is no need to anticipate every possibility in a system of contracts for contingent claims (Williamson, 1975, pp. 21–6).[1]

Beyond clinging to instrumental–analytic reason and renouncing it in favor of automatic invisible hands lies communicative reason, which, like political and market rationality, grounds rationality in the interaction of human subjects. But communicative rationality places little faith in invisible hands, seeking instead more cogitation in interaction.

Communicative Rationality and Complex Problems

Any complex problem has multiple facets, each of particular concern to a specific group of people. That concern may be immediate, as when a forester bemoans the acid rain falling on her trees. More universally, concern is vicarious. Thus damaged trees may also attract the attention of environmentalists. Each aspect of a complex problem therefore has ties to a human population. In the analytical terminology, these individuals are located at the various points in the disaggregation of sets and subsets.

Having admitted people into our *problematique*, we can let them all loose on problem solving. The interactions defining complexity and bedeviling instrumental–analytic problem solving can be mirrored by joint, cooperative actions undertaken by individuals located in or concerned with the various facets (subsets). Thus nonreducibility in problems can be mirrored by nonreducibility in problem solving. Obviously, any individual with multiple concerns (straddling subsets) can make a special contribution to this endeavor. Such joint projects are anathema to piecemeal social engineers, for projects of this sort cloud the possibility of clear causal inference from policy intervention. The locus of problem solving therefore shifts away from the instrumental manipulation of systems by would-be policy engineers and toward cooperative efforts on the part of a wide range of participants (who may, as individuals, still take instrumental actions). The cognitive burden at the center of the decision process is correspondingly reduced.

What could stimulate such efforts? Incrementalists have long intimated the presence of some invisible hand guiding political transactions in contemporary polyarchies, without explication beyond vague reference to "partisan mutual adjustment" (e.g., Lindblom, 1965). The trouble here is that adversarial stalemate, paralysis, conspiratorial externalization of the costs of a particular compromise, and drift are as likely as problem amelioration, even when the individuals involved pay lip service to the nature and severity of a common problem. In practice, such processes *decompose* problems on the basis of participants' concerns. Such decomposition can lead to chaos of the sort that plagued U.S. energy policy in the 1970s. Thus extensive participation and discussion are not necessarily helpful and may even exacerbate complexity and paralysis in policy making (cf. Nias, 1975) rather than help cope with them.

To state a thesis, coordinated problem solving will occur to the extent that there is communicative rationalization in the decision process. Communicative rationality is oriented toward intersubjective understanding and the generation of action-oriented consensus. Any agreement on the ends of policy that emerges can act as a device for coordination among individuals party to the agreement. Free, public, and reflective subscription to common ends coupled with commitment to coordinated action in their pursuit inhibits subsequent subversion by narrow self-interest.

Here, a cynic might argue that any such arrangement is highly vulnerable to the subsequent defection of free riders seeking personal advantage at the expense of collective interests. Thus Williamson (1975, p. 45) argues that participatory "peer groups" are not live options for political–economic organization and that our only alternatives are markets and hierarchies. However, this conclusion follows not from empirical observation but from Williamson's assumption that individuals are always opportunistic: If it is expedient, they will lie, break promises, and conceal information. The empirical evidence is more encouraging. Counterpressures ruled out by Williamson's assumption include the convergence of expectations around agreements, social pressures, and "tit-for-tat" sanctions imposed by individuals upon transgressors (see Young, 1979). Experimental work on the prisoner's dilemma finds that a period of group discussion always reduces the number of subsequent free riders (Dawes, McTavish, and Shaklee, 1977). And managers in large organizations recognize that compliance and implementation are facilitated by meaningful participation in decision making by those responsible for executing decisions (Vroom and Yetton, 1973, pp. 83–7, 108–14).

Even without complete agreement on common goals, communicative rationalization enables consensus based on mutual recognition of legitimate, if different, interests (see Chapter 1). Such understanding and consensus can cut across the different facets of a complex problem. Only with communicative rationalization can interaction across these subsets become felicitous rather than confounding and involve joint, cooperative problem solving rather than strategic politicking in continued pursuit of self-interest. One further benefit promised by communicative rationalization is enhancement of the problem-solving competence of individuals, which accords with the pedagogical value of political life stressed by Aristotle.

Communicative rationality confronts the teleological aspects of social complexity head-on by providing for the harmonization of the volitions of disparate actors through rationalized political interaction. In analytical social problem solving, these volitions subvert the intentions of policy and surprise its engineers and as such are the substance of implementation and compliance failures. In the strategic interaction of polyarchy these same volitions lead to self-perpetuating chaos when the policy process confronts complexity.

Under communicative rationality, one unwarranted analytical distinction that falls by the wayside is that between a decision process and the social system on which it is operating. By (conditionally) welcoming citizen participation, communicative rationality embraces interaction across that boundary rather than dreading it. But participatory democracy of itself has an ambiguous potential. Without communicative rationality it will only add to the burdens of complexity. On the other hand, communicative rationality without open participation will remain hobbled by the vestiges of control by a privileged group, and hence a dominant instrumental rationality, in exactly the same manner as the integrative strategy discussed earlier.

Given these pitfalls, what is to prevent continued pursuit of private interest, compromise, paralysis, and chaos when participation is extended? Optimistic judges of human nature might argue that free discussion will itself allow communicative principles to come to the fore. This faith in human spontaneity receives some backing from the experimental prisoner's dilemma finding, noted previously, that the mere fact of discussion increases cooperative behavior. Realistically, though, the intervention of some third party (of the kind discussed in Chapter 2) may be required to convince participants of the virtues of communicative rationality.

Even if communicative rationality can be secured, one final difficulty remains. Williamson (1975, pp. 45–6) argues against widespread participation in decisions on the assumption that the (instrumental) rationality of individuals is always bounded. Given this imperfect information-processing capacity, the "all-channel network" characterizing universal participation in all decisions will impose strict limits upon group size. After all, the number of links in such a network increases with (roughly) the square of the number of members. But Williamson errs in assuming that all members must participate in all facets of all decisions. Communicatively rationalized discourse requires only that there be no barriers to competent participation. Individuals can attend selectively to the aspects of decision or the interactions between elements that concern them. Further economy may be achieved to the extent of subscription to common ends or action principles, which may free individuals from negotiation over the details of action. Alternatively, the number of participants could be held to manageable levels along the lines suggested by Dahl (1985a, pp. 86–9).

Dahl argues that the complex and interdependent moral and technical issues associated with the control of nuclear weapons could be handled by the creation of a "minipopulus" of citizens chosen by lot for one-year terms. This body would help constitute informed public opinion on the nuclear issue. Its competence would be promoted by full-time participation and access to advisory committees of technical specialists (constituted by professional associations rather than government). Burnheim (1985) goes further than Dahl to suggest that existing representative and bureaucratic institutions be replaced by what he calls demarchy. Demarchy involves government by agencies whose members are selected by lot from among those who both (a) volunteer and (b) have a "legitimate material interest" in the agency's issue area. This kind of statistical representation should ensure that all relevant perspectives on a complex issue are covered.

Confronting Complexity in Practice

If discursive designs are potentially devices for solving social problems along the lines suggested in the previous section, then one place to look for signs of their realization would be in the vicinity of complex, nonreducible, and controversial social problems. Contrary to the expectations of both mainstream critical theorists and Weberians, it is here that instrumental rationality is breaking down. The location of incipient discursive designs such as mediation and regulatory negotiation is now understandable. How well, then, are these incipient institutions coping with complexity?

The symmetry of this chapter would now suggest discussing an air pollution case. Although a number of discursive exercises have addressed air pollution, their scope has been somewhat restricted. For example, mediation of a case involving increased emissions from coal conversion of a power plant at Brayton Point in Massachusetts addressed only local levels of suspended particulates and sulfur dioxide. Negotiations about emissions from a paper mill in Berlin, New Hampshire, engaged only the Brown Paper Company and the federal EPA. Policy dialogues about air pollution at the national level have generally addressed but a single regulation. And one of the most ambitious attempts at regulatory negotiation, the U.S. National Coal Policy Project, brought together only national environmentalist and industry groups. Several interested parties were excluded.

Can such procedures operate effectively under high orders of complexity? The theoretical argument of this chapter suggests an affirmative answer, but only experience will tell whether this extension is feasible. The limited evidence to date is encouraging. For example, Bacow and Wheeler (1984, pp. 195–247) chronicle the successful mediation of a dispute occasioned by proposed construction of a dam and water supply system near Denver, Colorado. The following summary should give a flavor of the complexity of this "Foothills" case.

The environmental values at issue in the first instance concerned the flooding of a scenic valley and obstruction of a free-flowing river. This prospect aroused the ire and opposition of several environmental groups and the federal Fish and Wildlife Service. On different grounds, residents of the western slope of the Rocky Mountains feared the scheme would ultimately steal "their" water. A broader environmental question concerned the future scope and content of growth in the Denver metropolitan region, checked by limited water supply. The federal EPA moved to block the project, arguing that additional water would mean more growth and hence traffic in a region already in violation of federal air quality standards. Other federal agencies actively involved for diverse reasons included the Bureau of Land Management, the Forest Service, and the Army Corps of Engineers. Locally based governmental actors included the Denver Water Board, several state agencies, and the local governments of the region. A plethora of interest groups raised questions about environmental impact, the openness of the planning process, water quality, recreation, and so forth. Lawsuits flew back and forth. In sum: "The Foothills case is an example of . . . a *polycentric* problem. There were numerous issues, each of which was intricately laced to the others" (Bacow and Wheeler, 1984, p. 242). Nevertheless, a mediated accord was reached. This agreement provided for construction of the dam, but with substantial mitigating measures. The accord also committed the governmental actors to a more open and participatory mechanism of decision for future development-related issues. This kind of process was embodied in the more broad-ranging Metropolitan Water Roundtable, which succeeded the Foothills effort (Bingham, 1986, pp. 36–41).

Complexity and the Preconditions for Communicative Rationalization

The Foothills case illustrates the potential for communicative rationalization in a complex situation. Further indication that complexity is no barrier comes from the case survey of Bingham (1986), who finds no decline in the success rate of mediation as the number of participants increases. It remains the case, though, that the calculus of self-interest can prevent rationalized interaction entirely. If A (e.g., an acid polluter in the Rhine Valley) is hurting B (a forester in the Black Forest) but nothing B does hurts A, why should A agree to talk to B? Actor B might try to promote discourse by looking for some way to hurt A (perhaps by a legal action) or offering A some inducement. Such strategies are hardly in the spirit of discursive democracy.

However, as the world becomes more complex, the larger is the probable number of interactions between A and B and hence the greater is the likelihood that B can also hurt A (e.g., B may be polluting the headwaters of a river flowing past A). Thus increasing social complexity raises the chances of a calculus rooted in self-interest leading actors into communicative interaction. The resulting discussions may deal with two or more seemingly different issues (e.g., both air and water pollution). In a complex system it may be easier to solve several interlocking problems simultaneously rather than one at a time (cf. Mitroff and Blankenship, 1973).

A related point here is that complexity can help convert relatively intractable zero-sum problems (in which A's gain has to be B's loss) into more soluble positive-sum relationships (in which mutual gain is possible). If A and B interact on issues X and Y, then A's gain on X may be more than enough to compensate for A's loss on Y. With such considerations in mind, an astute third party may raise additional issues in order to increase the number of potential trades across problems and thus entice A and B into discussion. However, such a strategy will do little to facilitate discourse on issues of fundamental moral conviction, such as abortion or capital punishment, whose zero-sum character is immutable.

Conclusion

The Foothills case, like most real-world instances of mediation and related procedures, is no paragon of communicative rationality. Its flaws include sequential attention to issues on the negotiation agenda, occasional covert manipulation by the mediator, and charges of noncompliance with the agreement. None of the parties, least of all the mediator, had communicative rationality in mind. However, some mediators have called for the expansion of informed public participation in mediation (see Straus, 1979; Bacow and Wheeler, 1984, pp. 246–7).

Without such expansion, exercises such as mediation remain vulnerable to charges that they are just further manifestations of the conspiratorial interest group liberalism disparaged by Lowi (1979), reflecting at best bargained compromise between special interests rather than generalizable concerns or publicly defensible interests. At worst, these exercises might constitute subtle extensions of the domination of established power.

As they stand, then, incipient discursive designs have an ambiguous potential. In addition, even the identification of successful instances would not prove that they represent *significant* forces for emancipation in modern society. Thus their relationship to larger systemic processes needs to be investigated. In this light, the next chapter will locate the forces presently conducive to discursive democratization and explicate the connection of discursive designs to these forces. This chapter will also consider how well discursive democratization is likely to fare in the face of the countervailing forces generated by a hostile political and economic environment.

CHAPTER 4

Discursive Dynamics

To the extent discursive democracy poses a radical challenge to dominant institutions, it would flourish in a world beyond capitalism, interest group politics, and bureaucracy. Discursive democracy looks forward to such a world as a practical hypothesis, but how do we move toward it? Specifically, what are the forces and circumstances that could produce more in the way of discursive democracy in politics, how likely are they to transpire, and how might they be exploited? Conversely, what forces operate to frustrate discursive democratization? If these negative forces prove less than invincible, what kind of path and pace should be sought?

Forces Favoring Discursive Democratization

In Chapters 2 and 3 discursive designs were defined, their capabilities and consequences explored, and real-world approximations to them located. But concrete examples of the sort I have provided do not prove the importance of discursive designs. If these institutions merit recognition as manifestations of significant forces for emancipation in the modern world, then it must be demonstrated that there are important general developments abroad conducive to their actualization and impact. In this section I shall identify some such developments.

Spaces exist for the generation of discursive designs to the extent dominant political and economic institutions are crumbling under the weight of their contradictions. One of the more effective analysts of such contemporary contradictions in state, economy, and society is Claus Offe, whose main concern is the fate of the Keynesian welfare state.

According to Offe (1984), the Keynesian welfare state exists and expands in order to curb the self-destructive anarchy of capitalism. Without this institutional fabric, the instability, income insecurity, poverty, and alienation generated by capitalism would foster discontent sufficient to undermine the prevailing political–economic order. The current contradiction of the welfare state arises because the state depends on a flourishing capitalist market system for both its revenues and its popularity in the eyes of the populace, which now holds government officials accountable for the condition of the economy. Offe does not mention that revenues are also needed if the state is to compete successfully in a hostile international environment.

This dependence on economic conditions means that governments dare not pursue policies that might threaten business confidence and so precipitate disinvestment and economic downturn (Block, 1977; Lindblom, 1982b). The trouble is that the welfare state produces policy outcomes that may indeed cause disinvestment and recession. These outcomes take the form of taxation to finance the state's operation and work disincentives arising from income guarantees. Thus, Offe claims, the Keynesian welfare state is now pulled in two different directions. It must both consolidate itself in order to curb the anarchy of capitalism and contract so as to avoid recession. In the language of Habermas (1975), it is torn between its legitimation and accumulation functions.

Before turning to the likely implications of such developments for discursive democracy, let me add an additional dimension of crisis Offe does not stress. Capitalism is addicted to economic growth; it must either grow or suffer disinvestment and depression. States dependent on the health of their economies share this addiction. But the capacities of the earth's ecosystems to tolerate the burdens of growth, especially resource exhaustion and pollution, are finite. Thus state and market offer no escape from a deepening ecological crisis.[1]

Now, the simple facts of contradiction and crisis will not necessarily produce discursive democracy. Indeed, they may not produce anything at all. Offe, for one, believes that the Keynesian welfare state is quite capable of muddling through in the face of the contradictions he has identified. And Held (1987, pp. 240–2) points out that any protests that do occur are likely to remain fragmented and directionless. Worse, protest may not even be evident so long as the costs of crisis can be displaced onto those least able or likely to organize: single parents, the very old, the very young, others for whom withdrawal is more likely than rebellion, and future generations.

Any more dramatic political reactions to contradiction and crisis may move in directions very different from discursive democracy. One major conceivable alternative would involve dismantling the Keynesian welfare state in favor of a pure capitalist free market. But although conceivable, such a development is highly unlikely. Not only would this alternative reinstate the anarchy that produced the welfare state in the first place, but also it would exacerbate ecological crises. A very different conceivable alternative would involve a more authoritarian and centralized political economy. But for the reasons detailed at length in Chapter 3, such a system could anticipate only paralysis in the face of increasingly complex problems, especially ecological problems.

This elimination of pure market and authoritarian possibilities still does not mean that the future belongs to discursive democracy. There are no historical laws in operation here. Discursive democracy can only be chosen, not caused; it belongs to the realm of freedom, not necessity. The contradictions and crises I have surveyed do no more than undermine some of its alternatives and help make discursive democracy an attractive choice. Aside from its intrinsic appeal as a meaningful way of life that counteracts the instrumental rationalization of society, discursive democracy offers an escape from at least some dimensions of crisis. It offers a way of resolving seemingly intractable conflicts and stalemates, a means for coping with seemingly irresoluble complex social problems, and a procedure for defining and providing public goods. So there are many good reasons to choose discursive democracy. And the choice is facilitated by the ever-increasing possibilities for discursive and critical reconstruction of the lifeworld released by the continuing development of modern forms of consciousness (see Chapter 1).

Forces Frustrating Discursive Democratization

If discursive democracy is a matter of choice, then one major dimension of choice concerns the pace of democratization. Both convulsive and gentle change have their difficulties.

Convulsive change would presumably find sympathy to the degree critical theorists and other advocates of communicative rationality are heirs to a revolutionary heritage. At least two further arguments might be tendered on behalf of choosing revolution. First, revolution is exhilarating. As William Wordsworth put it in reacting to the French Revolution, "Bliss was it in that dawn to be alive." Second, the power vacuum that often accompanies the revolutionary moment is a space that can be filled by discursive politics. It is in these terms that Arendt (1962) celebrates the "councils" that spontaneously occupied this space in the French, Russian, and Hungarian (1956) revolutions and in the French resistance during World War II. These councils epitomize the free and egalitarian discourse and solidarity that to Arendt is the essence of authentic politics (see Chapter 1). But all soon succumbed, be it to Jacobin terror, Bolshevik discipline, Soviet tanks, or the more gentle touch of Charles de Gaulle.

The outcome of any thoroughgoing social revolution is almost always a strengthened state with a longer bureaucratic reach able to more effectively secure economic growth, industrialization, and military strength (see Skocpol, 1979; Goldstone, 1986, pp. 207–322). In other words, the powers of instrumental rationality are invigorated by revolution. Social justice, still less freely discursive political life, rarely flourishes in the wake of successful revolutions.[2]

Even if we ignore the lessons of history, there is another reason sufficient to warrant rejection of revolution. Any revolutionary assault on behalf of discursive democracy would have to be launched from the lifeworld of social interaction, introduced and discussed in Chapter 1. Now, as I just noted, the lifeworld is becoming increasingly subject to modern kinds of consciousness and as such might seem to promise an increasingly secure basis for such an assault. Yet many aspects of the lifeworld remain incapacitated to the extent of penetration by the forces of the state, capital, and instrumental rationality. Individuals who are passive clients of welfare state bureaucracies or captive consumers of corporate products and life-styles are unlikely to become communicatively competent citizens overnight. The general point here is that it is hard to imagine a thoroughgoing revolution that is discursively democratic in its process as well as its aim, for not everyone would happily and competently go along. Individuals whose primary identity is that of client, consumer, or conformist to tradition are likely to resist. And if revolutionaries compromise on process by coercing such individuals, then they are no better than all the Leninists who have shown that an instrumentally rationalized revolution produces only an instrumentally rationalized society.

The extent of the colonization of the lifeworld (to use Habermas's expression) is, then, the final nail in the revolutionary coffin. This rejection of the convulsive alternative does not, though, lead to quiescence. For colonization can meet with resistance, as burgeoning new social movements demonstrate (see Chapter 2). A welfare state in crisis may lose its grip on its clients, and the scripts that corporate capitalism feeds to consumers might come to seem increasingly absurd, especially in light of ecological crises. But the point is that any resistance that does occur in complex contemporary societies is likely to arise at different times in different places in different ways on the part of different groups and never by masses or majorities. Such is hardly the raw material for revolution.

Having ruled out convulsive change, it should be recognized that a reformist approach to discursive democratization faces hazards of its own. For the foreseeable future, reform will have to proceed in a hostile environment defined by an economic system of corporate capitalism with extensive state intervention and a political system that mixes liberal polyarchy with pervasive bureaucracy. The culture that bolsters these systems and is reinforced by them remains what MacPherson (1970) calls possessive individualism.

Perhaps the most obvious danger this environment presents to incipient discursive designs is that of co-optation, mentioned in Chapter 2. State and corporate actors may seek some association with, or even participation in, discursive forums. The door is open to manipulation by these actors. They can cloak private interests in a rhetoric of public concern, perhaps even in the genuine belief that what is in their own interest must also be in the public interest [Elster (1983, pp. 41–2) discusses supply-side economics in this light]. They can make superficial concessions to opponents and thereby secure passive acquiescence on the part of potential troublemakers. They can offer symbolic participation in policy implementation in order to hide a low quality of service delivery to the poor and so generate support for an unjust regime (Ugalde, 1985). As Elster (1983, pp. 38–9) points out, not all participants in discourse need be equally motivated by the common good. The result may be compromise between some actors' private interests and other actors' notions of the public interest. Overall, the consequence might be that feared by Benhabib (1981, pp. 57–8), the degeneration of radical demands for the decentralization and "socialization" of state power (of the kind sought in discursive designs) into a conservative program for the privatization of that power.

More insidious possibilities are identified by Amy (1986) in the context of a critique of environmental mediation.[3] His central point is that the very act of entering into mediation can corrupt seriously held principles. According to Amy, mediation proponents generally treat the claims of different parties (such as developers and environmentalists) in terms of equally valid interests, between which compromise should be sought. The moral hazard here is that seriously held, properly nonnegotiable principles – such as belief in the integrity of a wilderness area or hostility to the idea of urban growth in an arid environment – are downgraded to the status of interests, on a par with more prosaic concerns like profit. Thus moral relativism is promoted, disputes are depoliticized through their removal from any context of deeper structural conflict (e.g., concerning the kind of society that should develop), and actors whose principles are compromised are effectively coopted by powerful corporate interests.

To the extent these charges are valid, mediation is just a subtle form of political control in the interests of the powers that be, who, realizing they can no longer ignore troublemakers, offer them an illusory share in control over policy. Mediation would merely secure the continued dominance of the development imperatives of the state and the capitalist market economy.

Powerful forces do, then, stand ready to frustrate incipient discursive designs. If serious principles can be so corrupted, where might these principles be fought for instead? Is there anything to be said for these alternative venues?

Alternatives to Discursive Designs

The facile answer normally given by opponents of alternative (informal) dispute resolution and mediation is that legislatures, courts, and perhaps even administrative agencies are the proper locations for decision when principles are seriously held and conflict with the imperatives of dominant actors (see, e.g., Schoenbrod, 1983; Fiss, 1984).

The dominance of powerful special interests in legislatures and regulatory agencies is too well documented (see, e.g., Lowi, 1979; Thurow, 1980; Friedman and Friedman, 1984) for these two alternatives to be taken seriously. At best, one can expect them to yield only expedient compromise between different special interests, the very sin of which procedures such as mediation stand accused. For their part, some of the critics of special interests and iron triangles see salvation in extending the scope of the free market (e.g., Friedman and Friedman, 1984). For example, in the context of environmental policy, Scott (1986) suggests the establishment of a "market" in acid pollution entitlements. By rationing the number of entitlements, total emissions could be forced down. The problem here is that in accepting such quasi-market mechanisms the principles of environmentalists (and others) are converted not just into interests but also into commodity values, complete with a price tag (Kelman, 1981).

Upon closer examination, courts fare little better than legislatures, regulatory agencies, and quasi-market systems. Courts are devices for adjudicating disputes and elaborating rules; they are not mechanisms for solving problems, let alone complex ones of the kind discussed in Chapter 3. Those wishing to see their principles embodied in legal decisions must pin their faith on a nebulous "public interest" to which courts sometimes try to respond. This interest can cover everything from social justice and social harmony to national security and economic efficiency. Further, the language of law is the language of rights (and rules). "Generalizable" principles, which might include community integration and ecological integrity (not to mention the canons of communicative rationality) are not readily expressed in that language. The severe constraints of law's language game are deadly to freely discursive democracy. Legal systems are closely tied to the (classically) liberal order of possessive individualism, reductionism, and analytical disaggregation, which may be contrasted with an order hospitable to discursive democracy, featuring community, holism, and interdependence.

The institutional alternatives to discursive designs are not, then, very attractive [see Dryzek (1987, pp. 67–148) for further discussion of the shortcomings of these alternative mechanisms]. The challenge becomes to redeem the promise of discursive designs in the face of the threats that have been enumerated. As I said earlier, discursive designs exist in the realm of choice, not necessity.

Rescuing Discursive Designs from Political Control

If a claim to collective deliberation and decision through open dialogue is to be taken seriously, then we need to establish a demarcation line between free discourse and social control. This line would recognize both the potential of incipient discursive designs in terms of free and equal political interaction and their vulnerability to exploitation by state and corporate actors interested in bureaucratic control or profit maximization.

Such exploitation would involve extending instrumental, efficiency-oriented, and maximizing rationality into nominally discursive domains. This subtle extension of social control cannot be overt. Rather, it constitutes manipulation, defined by Goodin (1980, p. 8) as "power exercised (1) deceptively and (2) against the putative will of its objects." It should be noted that such manipulation is a sin that can be committed by any actor, including the least advantaged. Nevertheless, given their general predilection for purposive rational action, one should distrust government agencies and corporations more than other actors here (on the likely motivations of state actors, see Evans, Rueschemeyer, and Skocpol, 1985).

To live up to their promise, discursive designs should reflect what Parsons (1971) calls the "collegial" type of social formation (other examples of the collegial type include professions in their internal workings, local communities, and informal networks). This kind of formation can only be secured by actors' fidelity to the norms that maintain the integrity and quality of communal social interaction. These norms should restrain pursuit of self-interest and in so doing resist the encroachment of bureaucratic or market imperatives.

What should the content of these norms be? One answer that fails to fully convince is provided by Sciulli (1986, pp. 753–5), who applies Fuller's (1969, pp. 46–84) eight principles of procedural legality to the definition of collegial formations. To Sciulli, a setting is collegial and nonauthoritarian, and the instrumental pursuit of interest is restrained, to the extent that rules, duties, or prescriptions (Sciulli, 1986, p. 754)

1. are comprised of general statements, rather than ad hoc dictums;
2. are publicized or made available to all affected;
3. are (with few exceptions) prospective, rather than retroactive;
4. are clear and understandable, at least to those trained in rule-making;
5. are free from contradiction or demanding opposite actions from the citizenry;
6. are possible to perform by the citizenry;
7. are not frequently changed;

8. and, finally, are congruent with the actual administration of the rules.

As applied to discursive designs, these principles could function as both standards of collegial interaction and as criteria for the evaluation of any collective decisions. However, the applicability of these eight principles is limited to the extent of their vestigial ties to law, rule making, and administration. Fuller's own purpose in enumerating them was to delineate what may properly be called a *legal* system. The application to collegial social formations is entirely Sciulli's. In the context of discursive designs, the qualifier in principle 4 about "those trained in rule-making" would have to be dropped as elitist. And principle 8 should be eliminated altogether inasmuch as it connotes enforcement through legal or bureaucratic structures.

These criteria could be applied to the evaluation of particular cases. Thus principle 1 would be violated to the extent discretionary judgments were being made about individual actors (e.g., if one miscreant were granted special privileges). Secretive proceedings would be in violation of principle 2, as would systematic exclusion of interested parties. Principle 4 directs our attention to the possibility of subtle and manipulative use of language to placate or confuse opponents.

As presented by Sciulli, the list of eight principles constitutes a minimal set of criteria according to which a collegial formation can be recognized. This minimalist approach does have the advantage of drawing a demarcation line that can be used to sort (or at least argue about) real-world cases. Its associated disadvantage is that situations that meet the eight criteria might still be in substantial violation of the precepts of communicative rationality (if to a lesser degree than situations that did *not* meet the criteria). For example, the criteria might be satisfied in a forum with highly restricted participation, in which special interests produce an agreement to their mutual advantage whose costs are imposed on a broader public. This scenario is far from a remote possibility, for it is consistent with the interest group liberalism Lowi (1979) claims already dominates the U.S. political system, much to the disadvantage of any public interests.

Very different from Sciulli's minimalism are approaches that evaluate real-world arrangements by some counterfactual standard. One such standard is the ideal speech situation discussed in Chapter 2. Forester (1985) applies the precepts of ideal speech to public planning, which he believes should be conceived of as communicative action rather than instrumental action. As such, contributions to planning discourse should be comprehensible, sincere, legitimate (given the individual's role, e.g., as a planning professional), appropriate to the context and topics under discussion, and truthful (Forester, 1985, pp. 209–10). Aside from evaluating contributions to discourse, these norms can also be extended to the evaluation of planning processes. So, for example, sincerity translates into an unrestricted ability to advance sincere arguments.

In terms of the categories developed in Chapter 2, Forester's approach combines pure and indirect critique. That is, he both compares existing planning practices with the precepts of ideal speech and reconstructs the planning process as it would be if it were informed by these same precepts. Forester's reconstructed planning would involve careful listening, community education about the process, the cultivation of poorly organized groups, and the like. This reconstructed planning discourse can then be deployed in the criticism of existing planning practices.

Kemp (1985) applies a similar strategy to public inquiries by way of calling them to account as purportedly open and democratic means of collective decision making. In particular, Kemp criticizes the 1977 British Windscale Inquiry. This inquiry involved a proposal to construct a thermal oxide reprocessing plant (THORP) for nuclear waste at Windscale (whose name was later changed, in the interests of linguistic deception, to Sellafield) in Cumbria. The distortions that pervaded the Windscale Inquiry worked systematically to benefit the particular interests of THORP's proponents, most notably British Nuclear Fuels Ltd. (BNFL), a government-owned corporation. To begin, the objectors (including several environmental groups and the Town and Country Planning Association) had little in the way of financial resources and research capabilities compared to BNFL. Mr. Justice Parker, who presided over the inquiry, ruled out economic evidence against THORP while admitting economic evidence in its favor (Kemp, 1985, p. 191). The legalistic rules of the inquiry were familiar and congenial to the proponents but not to the objectors. And BNFL could hide behind the Official Secrets Act at key points. Justice Parker's summary in favor of THORP – against the continued opposition of the objectors – was therefore systematically distorted toward the interests of state and capital.[4]

The most obvious problem with the "maximal" approach to the

evaluation of institutions and practices as articulated by Forester and Kemp is that, unlike Sciulli's minimalism, it identifies no cutoff point at which approval can be registered. Whereas Sciulli's criteria allow too much, Forester and Kemp can approve of nothing.

However, the fact that an ideal is unattainable does not preclude its use for evaluative purposes; one might say the same about economic efficiency or social justice (however one defines them). As noted in Chapter 2, the precepts of communicative rationality can be used as critical standards to distinguish degrees of departure from the ideal. (This use can involve pure direct comparison or it can entail indirect construction of context-specific counterfactuals.) So although the THORP inquiry is easily condemned as a major departure from these precepts, its sins are not as blatant as the secretive and deceptive acts associated with the early years of the Windscale complex in the 1950s. For example, a 1957 fire released quantities of radiation known by Windscale's operators and the government of the day to be highly dangerous. But the danger was played down and subsequent control and cleanup operations minimized to avoid a public relations disaster. In particular, the British government did not want to jeopardize its credibility in the context of the nuclear cooperation it was pursuing with the United States. This information only came to light in 1987 as a result of the thirty-year rule on the release of British government documents.

The general point here is that we shall always need a critical theory directed toward particular institutions, be they systematically repressive ones or potentially discursive designs. The precise content of this theory will vary with context. Discursive designs do not just constitute an element in the critical theory program for political organization sketched in Chapter 2. Incipient discursive designs are themselves potentially problematic and need to be held up to the standards implicit in the idea of public discourse by individuals acting as critical theorists.

Given time, a succession of discursive exercises held up to critical scrutiny could create and reinforce norms of free discourse, and the critical aspects of modern consciousness more generally. In so doing, such exercises would strengthen the realm of choice in its contest with the realm of necessity and so help constitute a world increasingly hospitable to truly discursive designs and to the participatory *process* of discursive design. Institutional reconstruction would flourish in such a world.

Discursive Community

The zenith of collegial social interaction may surely be found in the idea of community, though the community in question should obviously be communicatively competent and nonhierarchical rather than the traditional kind celebrated by classical conservatives. That is, in the language of Habermas, its everyday lifeworld should be communicatively rationalized and free from myth, illusion, deference, and domination. This requirement does not mean that relationships and norms should be fully transparent to participants; a transparent community would be no community at all because it would have no *distinctive* norms. Similarly, a transparent lifeworld would be no lifeworld at all, as its sterile homogeneity would allow no disagreement about, and hence no contemplation of, the substantive content of values (White, 1988, p. 103).

Community may be defined in terms of recurrent, direct, reciprocal, and many-sided relationships among individuals with some degree of common interest. Participants in real-world discursive exercises typically are located in some kind of community, be it a neighborhood or the network of a new social movement.

It has long been noted that applying legal adjudication to intracommunal disputes can disrupt the community in question and shatter its latent internal conflict resolution capabilities. Herein lies one argument on behalf of informal justice, which may reinforce and reconstitute community (see Adler, 1987, p. 21). Aside from reproducing existing communities, discursive designs could also function as channels through which the style of social interaction that defines community can strike back at the instrumental and hierarchical designs of state and market actors. In other words, incipient discursive designs exist on a battleground. This battle is not between particular actors and interests (such as environmentalists and polluters) but rather between instrumental social control and discursive social and political interaction.

If the latter style can prevail, then discursive designs may help effect social and political transformation on behalf of community and nonhierarchical, discursive political interaction. This process need not just operate through existing communities expanding their bounds at the expense of state or corporate actors. New communities (though possibly overlapping with existing communities) can constitute themselves as products of the process of discourse. It is in this sense that communicative rationality can recreate the world.

Conclusion

Discursive designs at their degenerate worst could act as just another avenue for social and political control, a way for dominant political–economic institutions to postpone the consequences of their contradictions. On the other hand, to the extent their collegial claim is redeemed, they can prevent and reverse encroachment by state or market imperatives upon nonhierarchical social and political interaction and upon discursive community.

Though there are forces at work conducive to the development of discursive designs, the liberal bureaucratic state, itself entrapped by the imperatives of capitalist production, imperils such institutional innovations. This peril constitutes a further reason to emphasize the notion of a public sphere separate from, and confronting, the state. Fortunately, there is one arena of collective choice where there is no state. This arena, the international system, is also where many of today's most severe, intractable, and complex social problems may be located. Herein surely lies a golden opportunity for discursive designs. The next chapter will take advantage of this opportunity.

CHAPTER 5

International Discursive Designs

with Susan Hunter

The International Condition

The absence of any overarching state or state analogue in the international polity is a decidedly mixed blessing. As suggested in the previous chapter, this absence is indeed one less obstacle to discursive democracy. But the concomitant vacuum in central authority has always meant endemic conflict. It hardly need be said that such conflict can be terribly destructive and that the very annihilation of humankind has become one possible outcome.

The chronic pathos of the international anarchy results from largely autonomous actors (nation states and others) pursuing their particular ends in an uncontrolled environment.[1] As Ashley (1980, pp. 205–6) notes, this condition is truly tragic, for it can only be made worse to the extent actors are aware of its dynamics but nevertheless continue to pursue their interests in instrumentally rational fashion. A Henry Kissinger may be smart and aware, but he does not help. In this sense, international affairs are even more poignant than classical Greek tragedies, where at least the audience is allowed to see through the misconceptions of the actors and imagine a better outcome.

The fact that international tragedies result from a combination of instrumental action and a lack of central authority suggests two general kinds of solution. The most popular advocates strengthened authority at the system level, perhaps even some kind of world government (see, e.g., Mendlovitz, 1975; Soroos, 1977). The trouble is that any such solution would reproduce on a grand scale the instrumental rationalization and other nefarious effects of expanding national states and bureaucracies. Centrally administered systems of this sort are also extremely clumsy when it comes to dealing with complexity, uncertainty, variability, and value conflict (see Chapters 2 and 3). Such conditions are ubiquitous when it comes to international security, economic, and ecological problems.

An alternative solution would change not the decentralization of the international polity but the instrumental rationality pervading it. Now, instrumentally rational action in an essentially anarchic system is not unambiguously destructive. As Axelrod (1984) and Taylor (1987) demonstrate, tit-for-tat strategies on the part of instrumentally rational, self-interested actors can secure a large measure of cooperation without central authority. Keohane (1986) applies this argument about reciprocity to the international system. But despite such possibilities, it is obvious that war does often break out, that economic relations of dependence and exploitation persist, that structural violence (chronic repression) is endemic, and that crucial international problems such as those relating to the threat of global nuclear war, nuclear proliferation, desertification, Third World debt, or the greenhouse effect go unsolved.

The theme of this chapter is that the international polity would benefit to the extent the instrumental rationality of its component actors were brought to order by communicative rationality in their interactions. Institutionally, this move would imply the establishment of international discursive designs capable of resolving conflicts, coping with complex problems, and supplying public goods. The international arena presents an acid test for discursive designs, for it is here that many of the world's most conflictual, complex, and intractable problems are found. But however ambitious it may seem, this approach is clearly less utopian than the program for strong authorities at the system level required by the centralized solution to international tragedy.

This chapter will pursue the theme of communicative rationalization with a stress on international environmental problems. A parallel, if more abstract, argument for a similar kind of rationalization in the context of international security issues has been tendered by Ashley (1980, pp. 205–30), who does, however, stop short of institutional proposals.[2]

The focus on ecological concerns is not rigid or exclusive. Indeed, it could not be, for problems in the international system (no less than elsewhere) tend to be complex and interconnected. So problems related to environmental deterioration can strain cooperative capacities in the international anarchy (see Orr, 1977). For example, transboundary pollution and scarcity of natural resources or agricultural land cause conflict, which can turn violent. Note the "cod wars" fought over a natural resource by Britain and Iceland in the 1970s and the battle between India and Pakistan for control of the waters of the Indus (this latter dispute also had economic and strategic dimensions). Moreover, ecology is not just an issue area in international politics; it is also a perspective on international relations in their entirety. This perspective is widely associated with the work of Harold and Margaret Sprout (1965), who were among the first to establish the pervasive importance of man–nature relationships in international affairs.

This chapter will argue that discursive designs could retain the decentralized character of the contemporary international system (and thereby avoid the repression and problem-solving pathologies of administrative structure) while simultaneously promising conflict resolution, coordination, and, by implication, effective problem solving. The special features of the international system can actually facilitate effective communicative rationalization, which may indeed be suited to the unique structure of this system. International discursive designs may even prove applicable to cases in which actors exhibit profound value differences.

Discursive designs can also be related to the notion of international regimes, which constitute one kind of response to demands for institutional structure to provide public goods and overcome collective action problems in the international system (Keohane, 1983). Regimes may be conceived of as devices for promoting cooperative behavior transcending short-run self-interest (Krasner, 1983, p. 3). Aside from "principles, norms, amd rules," international regimes require "decision-making procedures" (Krasner, 1983, p. 1).

Discursive designs could play three complementary roles in emerging international regimes. First, they could function as the decision-making components of regimes. Second, they could be instrumental in creating regimes. Regimes may be conceived of as another kind of public good that discursive designs can supply. This is not, of course, the only way regimes can be constructed; as Young (1983) points out, they can also be instituted through imposition by a hegemon, spontaneous development, and formal negotiation. But voluntary reasoned consensus constitutes one of the most secure conceivable foundations for any international regime. Spontaneous regimes are vulnerable to decay in a dynamic environment, and imposed regimes will last only as long as the hegemon's enforcement capabilities (Young, 1983). Regime stability can be further enhanced by the third potential role of discursive designs, as transformation mechanisms once a regime is in place. In a dynamic environment a regime needs a capacity to adjust its structure in response to changing demands, constraints, and opportunities. Discursive designs offer adjustment in a manner that maintains and reinforces any reasoned consensus underpinning a regime.

International Conflict Resolution

Third-party intervention of the sort often associated with incipient discursive designs is no stranger in the international arena. However, most applications to date have been confined to two-sided crises in the relations of nation states, in which violence is a live possibility (see, e.g., Young, 1967). In light of the pressing need to pull adversaries away from each other and prevent further hostilities, most such interventions have not proceeded with communicative rationalization in mind.

More recently, though, a "problem-solving" approach has gained currency in the context of international conflict. Exponents of this approach seek resolution of conflicts at a level more fundamental than superficial settlement of the disputes in question. Indeed, they argue that effective conflict resolution requires collaborative problem solving. In this light, agreements such as the Camp David Accords between Israel and Egypt are mere dispute settlement, allowing underlying tensions to persist. Dispute settlement may be facilitated by sidestepping or fudging controversial issues. Although it is not always entirely clear what the problem-solving alternative really involves, it is certainly more than instrumental or purposive consideration of means to the end of resolving the conflict at hand. Instead, the approach requires that all the actors involved scrutinize the nature of their relationships and analyze the ultimate roots of their differences in the interests of extinction of the causes of conflict (see, e.g., Kelman and Cohen, 1976; Burton, 1979; Fisher, 1983). Ideally, these actors proceed to reconceptualize the situation away from conflict between their strategic (particular) interests and toward a reconsideration of the underlying interests and needs of one, a subset, or all of the parties.

Proponents of the problem-solving approach have sponsored workshops to bring together representatives of the sides in various conflicts. For example, British and Argentinian parliamentarians have been engaged in informal discussions about the Falkland Islands in the wake of their 1982 war. Although these discussions proceed in the context of deep differences, a degree of reciprocal understanding has been reached. So the British participants came to understand what the word "sovereignty" really means to the Argentinians, and a consensus over norms of process for subsequent negotiations was reached (see Anonymous, 1985).

International Environmental Issues

Environmental problems in the international system do not have quite the same attributes as international security issues. In particular, any lack of resolution is less likely to lead to large-scale violence or immediate system breakdown (though exceptions are possible here, as we noted earlier in the cases of the cod wars and the Indus). More likely than outright breakdown is progressive deterioration or, at best, perpetuation of an unsatisfactory status quo. The consequences might involve gradual attrition in environmental quality of the sort that occurs with desertification, ocean pollution, and climatological change.

Despite their lack of urgency in comparison with security issues, international environmental and natural resource problems have occasionally hosted discursive exercises. One highly localized case occurred in connection with a U.S.–Canada transboundary dispute between the city of Seattle and the Province of British Columbia. Seattle wanted to raise a dam on the Skagit River in order to supply itself with electricity. British Columbia objected on the grounds that land in the Skagit Valley on the Canadian side of the border would be flooded if the dam were raised. Mediation of the dispute under the auspices of the U.S.–Canadian International Joint Commission began in 1982.[3] A settlement was reached in 1983 and ratified in 1984, under which British Columbia promised to supply Seattle with the electricity it needed and Seattle agreed not to raise the dam high enough to back water across the border (see Stein, 1984).

On a more broad-ranging and significant issue, Quaker and Methodist religious groups organized informal seminars for participants in the United Nations Conference on the Law of the Sea in the 1970s (see Raiffa, 1982, pp. 283–7). And at least one international environmental agreement, the Baltic Convention on Marine Pollution, explicitly provides for the possibility of mediation (see Stein, 1982, p. 6).

Dispute Settlement

As we have noted, incipient discursive designs in the international system (and for that matter elsewhere) can be construed as (a) devices for settling particular disputes or (b) means for resolving the problems facing the parties to disputes. These two conceptualizations yield different perspectives on the potential content, role, and function of such institutions. Communicative rationalization will benefit only to the extent a problem-solving emphasis is pursued.

Existing accounts of mediation and other kinds of third-party intervention in international conflicts tend to stress settlement as the primary goal of the process. Thus agreement is indicative of success, even if an underlying hostility among the parties remains. Now, in some kinds of conflicts, settlement by itself is of prima facie value; in an international crisis, it may be important to pull the sides away from each other's throats. Beyond this immediate consideration, there are several benefits effective discursive settlement by itself *can* yield.

First, discursive interaction may settle disputes and generate determinate outcomes at transaction costs lower than those of alternative forms of social choice, such as positional bargaining, coercive diplomacy, or litigation (which is often unavailable in the international arena). This kind of dispute settlement can be achieved in a manner that retains the essential decentralized character of the international system.

Second, discursive interaction can facilitate Pareto-better moves toward the utility frontier of the set of actors involved. Welfare economics tells us that free competitive markets achieve such outcomes automatically, guided only by the invisible hand. A third party can, in effect, function as a very visible hand in facilitating a joint search for Pareto-better outcomes in a negotiating (i.e., non-market) context. For example, negotiations beginning with a single issue that admits of no mutually beneficial solution might profit from a third party introducing other factors or problems. Haas (1980) refers to this strategy as "tactical" issue linkage. The number of potential trade-offs that can be made across problem boundaries is thereby extended, facilitating an overall outcome of net benefit to each of the actors involved (Raiffa, 1982, p. 131). This capacity to produce outcomes involving mutual gain accords well with Stein's (1983) explanation of why self-interested actors rationally renounce a measure of independence in constructing and participating in international regimes.

A conceptualization of discursive interaction in terms of dispute settlement means that any third party convening the forum should take pains to ensure that the content of proposals and style of interaction involved should be sensitive only to the current strategic interests of each party. That is, instrumental rationality should continue to dominate the proceedings. It has long been noted that in debate and dispute over public policies it may be possible for partisans of different positions to agree on an action without agreeing upon the reasons for that action, or indeed upon the nature of the problem to which the action is a response (Lindblom, 1959, pp. 83–4). Think, for example, of the Camp David Accords, mediated by the United States. The governments of Israel and Egypt could sign the same text while holding to very different and inconsistent normative positions. If dispute settlement is all that is being sought, then debate and dialogue are best kept at a superficial level and underlying issues of values scrupulously avoided. In practice, as noted in Chapter 4, mediators and other third parties often suppress moral discourse by viewing outcomes in terms only of compromise between equally valid positions.

If dispute settlement is the primary goal, then the content of any agreement is important, but only insofar as it responds to the immediate concerns of each party in a way that promotes the likelihood of their assent and compliance. Tactical linkage of issues may be expedient here. Further, agreements that function through the co-optation and neutralization of the relatively powerless by the powerful are acceptable in a dispute settlement light.

Doubtless, many international problems can be encapsulated in terms of potential efficiency gains going unrealized as a consequence of rigidities in bargaining positions, perhaps over international trade issues or international transportation networks. And some problems are clearly crises. In these cases, conceiving of discursive interaction in the superficial terms of dispute settlement may be defensible.

However, international problems can involve concerns more

basic than efficiency gains or crisis management. These concerns include chronic structural violence, the danger of nuclear war, and threats to the integrity of ecosystems and their life support capacities. Clearly, such cases require something more than bloodless, inexpensive, and decentralized dispute settlement.

Problem Solving

Required in the latter kind of instance is an effective form of collective problem solving. Raiffa (1982, pp. 219–20) notes that a discursive forum enables actors who in isolation have only partial information and control to pool information and coordinate actions. Similarly, Keohane (1984, pp. 220–40) argues that a major reason for the formation of international organizations (such as the International Energy Authority) is the desire of self-interested actors to pool information resources and hence further their particular ends more effectively. Such recognitions remain grounded in instrumental rationality and so tell but a small part of the story.

Discursive designs ideally operate in a cooperative, nonhierarchical manner. Now, approximations to such institutions are not always *established* as rationalistic, collegial, brainstorming groups with problem solving in mind. However, effective problem solving can arise in conjunction with conflict resolution. To this end, any third party can discourage articulation by actors of their *positions*, between which one can at best only split the difference. Instead, actors should be encouraged to focus on their *interests* (see Fisher and Ury, 1981, chap. 1) and thus facilitate the identification of solutions better than any conceivable difference splitting.

Any such refocusing on interests would involve the exploration and development of means to ends held by one, some, or all of the actors involved. However, beyond this continued pursuit of instrumental rationality, discursive designs also allow for the exercise of reason about normative judgments: interests, goals, values, and problem definitions (see Chapter 2). If it can be attained, intellectual consensus extending beyond empirical knowledge to value judgment forms one of the more stable bases for international regimes (see Haas, 1980). Thus the strenuous effort this kind of consensus formation demands may be time well spent.

Perhaps, as noted in Chapter 2, such consensus could reflect generalizable rather than particular interests. Ashley (1981) applies this taxonomy to the interests of international actors, arguing that all actors have a generalizable interest in the survival of the human species. Hence they would do well to subordinate their pursuit of particular advantage to this shared concern, even if ultimately they adhere to the canons of self-interest.

This distinction is especially important for international environmental problems. Many, if not most, of these problems concern common-property resources. The actors making use of these resources – be they individuals, corporations, or nation states – typically have both particular and generalizable interests in the resource. Take, for example, an ocean fishery. Each actor has a particular interest in the size of its own catch and a generalizable interest in the quality of the fishery as a whole. Or consider the global atmosphere. Actors have a particular interest in the atmosphere as a sink for their airborne pollutants and a generalizable interest in its life-sustaining capabilities. A generalizable interest will, in an environmental context, often refer to the quality of a common-property resource (or the provision of a public good such as ecological integrity). It is noteworthy that parties who are at each other's throats on other issues may agree to sit down and reason together if they believe it is truly a public good they are discussing. So, for example, the Mediterranean Action Plan, negotiated under the sponsorship of the United Nations Environment Program, managed to bring together Israeli and Arab states in a forum that addressed the pollution problems of the basin. Britain and Argentina participated in negotiations over Antarctica at the height of their 1982 confrontation over the Falklands.

Discursive designs may further ameliorate common-property problems because, as pointed out in Chapter 2, they facilitate compliance with agreements. Compliance is problematical in the decentralized international system as free riders have many incentives to subvert agreements (see Young, 1979). Procedures involving nominally authoritative judgment, such as arbitration and legal adjudication, do not always help, for they are inconsistent with the decentralized character of the international system. Thus their nominal judgments are subject to de facto noncompliance. Discursive designs, in contrast, promote compliance because actors freely consent to accords.

Some Necessary Conditions

A number of conditions must be met for any exercise in international discursive design to proceed. First and perhaps most obviously, some problem must exist in the eyes of one or more significant actors within the system, though consensus on the nature of the problem is not required.

Second, a willing, competent, and credible intermediary must be available. Possible sources include the United Nations, a third-party national government, academic institutions, and specialized mediation services.

Third, all the parties to a dispute should have roughly equal capabilities. These capabilities might refer to political power, veto power (e.g., through access to a legal system; it is noteworthy that groups of Canadian citizens have brought suit in U.S. courts against transboundary pollution), information resources, the capacity to hurt the other parties, or the ability to give the other parties something they want. Rarely will the powerful agree to sit down on equal terms with the powerless.[4] Unequal capabilities do, of course, pervade the international system. Perhaps the most striking asymmetry is that between the strength of the North and the weakness of the South. But recent sporadic successes of the South in moving international regimes away from the market and toward more authoritative allocation (e.g., in the Law of the Sea negotiations) suggest such asymmetry is not insuperable (Krasner, 1985, pp. 227–64). Unfortunately, international trade regimes tell a different story.

Fourth, it is crucial that each potential participant regard the others as legitimate participants of equal standing. Hence a degree of consensus as to which actors have a rightful place at the table is essential (this condition does not require that each participant have equal legal or diplomatic standing).

An additional set of conditions must be met if an exercise is to produce determinate outcomes and thereby effectively settle conflicts or achieve Pareto-better moves. First, no party with substantial influence should be excluded, for any such party may subsequently sabotage any agreement reached. This consideration might suggest the inclusion of as many actors as possible, for fear of leaving out potential saboteurs. On the other hand, including too many actors may produce a situation in which each finds it hard to regard the others in terms distinct from an undifferentiated environment (see Young, 1972, p. 55). Free riders will be inconspicuous in such an environment. Hence a second necessary condition here is that the number of parties involved be kept at a manageable level (see Talbot, 1983, p. 94).

A third obvious necessary condition in this context is that the outcome of discussion will have a tangible and significant effect. Although one might expect international agreements to receive legal force less readily than their domestic counterparts, compliance mechanisms for both formal and informal agreements clearly do exist in the international system. Examples include fear of reprisal, felt obligation, socialization into systems of norms, and the convergence of expectations around rules (Young, 1979, pp. 31–4). In practice, most actors comply with most international agreements most of the time.

A fourth condition applies only insofar as instrumental rationality persists all round. There must be a contract zone, a set of outcomes that all parties will prefer to the absence of an agreement. If that zone is large, agreement will be easy, indeed, so easy that third-party intervention may be unnecessary (Young, 1972, p. 53). If that zone is apparently small or even absent, a skilled third party may still be able to uncover a contract zone by generating a large set of alternatives from the interests of each party.

If international discursive designs can, via communicative rationalization, promote problem resolution beyond dispute settlement and the identification of Pareto-better moves, the second and third conditions in this second set can stand restatement. For if actors can engage in discourse about values, then a "contract zone" can be created where none previously existed. Any such process will be facilitated by potential or incipient generalizable interests. Alternatively, actors must be amenable to contemplating and questioning the normative bases of their positions.

Now consider in a problem-solving light the desirability of a manageably small number of parties. Whereas this condition clearly enhances the likelihood of a determinate outcome, with an increase in the number of actors involved, the particular interests of each are likely to receive less attention, and so generalizable interests can come to the fore.

Generalizable interests, and the collegial style of social and political interaction more generally, can be expected to come to the fore to the extent *community* flourishes, though of course the kind of community in question should be nonhierarchical and communicatively competent (see Chapter 4). At first sight, the prospects for community of any kind in the international system might seem dim (despite oxymoronic misnomers such as the "European Economic Community"). However, community does sometimes spring up in the surroundings of prolonged negotiations, such as those over the Law of the Sea and Antarctica. Their membership is drawn from states, international governmental and nongovernmental organizations, and so forth. Both Law of the Sea and Antarctic communities generally pursue decision through consensus, one characteristic of collegial interaction. Their nonhierarchical style is facilitated by the absence of any governmental authority for the international system as a whole. Obviously, if any such community is to be constituted, then some common or generalizable interest(s) need to be either discovered or created in the negotiation process. For example, in the Antarctic case, such interests include continued demilitarization of the continent, scientific values (e.g., with respect to the influence of Antarctica on world climate), and the very demonstration that peaceful and productive transnational cooperation is possible.

Community created as a by-product of negotiation is not the only kind available in the international system. Also possible are the following kinds of community:

1. Border communities, which develop an identity separate from that of the relevant adjacent nation states. A good example exists along the U.S.–Mexico border. Such communities could obviously come into play on transboundary pollution issues.
2. Partisan communities, committed to a broad normative principle. Examples would include the international human rights community and the global environmental movement (composed of activists from organizations such as Greenpeace, Friends of the Earth International, and Green political parties and perhaps even officials from governmental organizations such as the United Nations Environment Program).
3. Professional communities, composed of specialists in fields such as earth sciences, political science, or medicine.
4. Ethnic communities. Obviously, some transnational communities defined by ethnicity would be special cases of border communities. But some ethnic communities are more dispersed, for example, the Inuit of the Circumpolar North and Jewish and Palestinian diasporas.

A Site-specific International Case: Garrison Diversion

The conditions outlined in the previous section can be readily approximated in site-specific disputes with a substantial history of interaction and conflict. Many of the incipient discursive designs in domestic politics are found in such settings. A transboundary dimension should add no insuperable complications. The only international environmental dispute that has received formal mediation, the Skagit River case mentioned earlier, was one particularly straightforward U.S.–Canada site-specific transboundary issue. One of the more prominent and intractable U.S.–Canada site-specific transboundary environmental problems concerns the Garrison Diversion Project in North Dakota, a plan to divert Missouri River water northward. In so doing, the project would introduce, by way of externality, unwanted water and biota into watersheds draining into Canada. This diversion has been a live issue in North Dakota for almost one hundred years. Large areas of central and eastern North Dakota are semiarid; Missouri water could both improve agricultural productivity and provide a secure water supply to industrial and domestic users. The project, generally popular in North Dakota, is less attractive to the people and government of Manitoba, who perceive a threat to commercial and sports fishing, especially in Lake Winnipeg. Garrison is also of considerable interest to Canadians with no direct concern, inasmuch as it is an example of the southern leviathan riding roughshod over Canadian interests (see Carroll, 1983, pp. 175–6).

The current state of the project is impasse. Construction began in 1968, but following a 1976 recommendation of the International Joint Commission that was subsequently endorsed by the U.S. Senate, no work has yet taken place on the parts of the project that would affect Canada.

The eight necessary conditions previously enumerated would all seem to be met in the Garrison case. First of all, there is universal recognition that a problem exists. The problem to Garrison supporters is delay of the project, the cost of which is an estimated $111 million annually to the economy of North Dakota (Garrison Conservancy District, n.d., p. 8), and a concomitant possibility that the project may never be completed. The problem to the Canadians is that work on the project is proceeding even in the absence of their consent. The problem to environmentalists, notably the Audubon Society, is actual and potential loss of wetland habitat for waterfowl and other wildlife.

A willing and competent third party should be easily located. The current impasse attests to the roughly equal capabilities of the parties involved. The candidate participants are easily identified: the two federal governments, the State of North Dakota, the Manitoba provincial government, the Garrison Conservancy District, the Manitoba Indian Brotherhood (concerned about Lake Winnipeg), the Audubon Society, and the Committee to Save North Dakota Wetlands (the major Dakotan opponent of the project). Clearly, this is a manageable number. Moreover, agreement on the legitimacy of participants is already present.

A contract zone clearly exists in the Garrison case. Elements of a positive-sum solution might involve closed wasteway systems that eliminate all direct water connections between supply and drainage systems (to allay Canadian concerns); compensation for losses to the landholders who support the Committee to Save North Dakota Wetlands; the artificial replacement of lost wetland habitat; and perhaps even a federal guarantee to North Dakota of rights to Missouri water irrespective of whether the project is undertaken.[5] Overall, it would seem that the Garrison case – in common, one suspects, with most site-specific transboundary issues – is highly amenable to discursive resolution. There might even be some incipient generalizable interests that could surface, such as the ecological integrity of the Red River basin, which straddles the border. A border community may be less readily identified here. A community of interest is less evident than in the case of the U.S.– Mexico border. However, there are signs of community emerging around the operations of the International Joint Commission.

The Garrison case does, in fact, bear a strong resemblance to some of the site-specific domestic cases in which discursive exercises such as mediation have proceeded. The international dimension appears to add no insuperable complications. Let us now turn to a very different kind of case.

Global Dispute: Whaling

The whaling issue presents at first sight a hopelessly complex and intractable situation, replete with many actors, irreconcilable differences of perceptions and values, no obvious widely acceptable solutions, and little possibility of enforcing any collective decisions that are made. This issue is not atypically complex as far as international problems are concerned.

Unlike many international common-property problems, the whaling issue has a history of concern and response (and hence provides more lessons than most other cases that could have been chosen for illustration). Whaling has been on the international political agenda since 1925, when the League of Nations, in response to steadily declining stocks of great whales, issued a report recommending international protection. However, the decline of stocks continued unabated, leading eventually to the establishment in 1946 of the International Whaling Commission (IWC), whose decisions are made through votes by member nations. Despite the continued presence of the commission, four species of great whales have been brought to the point of extinction since 1946, and several other species are threatened (see Friends of the Earth, 1978). Membership of the IWC and compliance with its decisions (such as quotas) are entirely voluntary. So, for example, though in 1983 the commission passed a resolution calling for a moratorium on commercial whaling to begin in 1986, Norway and the USSR withheld their compliance. After initially indicating it would defy the moratorium, Japan then agreed to discontinue whaling after 1988. But this declaration came in response to the threat of U.S. sanctions and leaves open the possibility of future conflict and noncompliance. At the time of writing, Norway and Japan engage in commercial whaling under the guise of a "scientific" catch (Iceland has just announced its intention to cease this practice). And the moratorium is due to expire in 1990. The record of the IWC is not very impressive.

Actors with a stake in the whaling issue include national governments (both whalers and nonwhalers), environmental groups such as Greenpeace and Friends of the Earth International, aboriginal whalers (in Alaska and Australia), commercial whalers, commercial whale watchers, consumers of whale products, scientists (especially ocean ecologists and marine biologists), and international organizations such as the IWC and the United Nations. The number of potential participants would seem to bode ill for any discursive resolution, especially given a lack of consensus on the legitimacy of participants; Japan and the Soviet Union would not readily consent to reason on equal terms with Greenpeace or Californian whale watchers. Further, there is a clear difference between the capabilities of (say) the governments of the United States or Norway and the Inupiat whalers of Alaska or the activists of Friends of the Earth International.

However, all the actors involved agree that a problem exists. To neutral observers, the whaling issue presents a classical example of the tragedy of the commons: The high seas are owned by no nation, and migrating whales ignore any national boundaries that do exist. To some environmentalists, the problem is one of inhumanity toward magnificent and intelligent creatures. To more ecologically minded environmentalists, the problem concerns disruption of oceanic ecosystems. Japan and Taiwan face an economic problem of overcapitalization in their whaling industries (caused by short seasons and striving for competitive advantage; see Heck,

1975) together with the sanction of world public opinion and the threat of economic reprisals.

Difficulties arising from the absence of consensus on the legitimacy of participants could be sidestepped by interested nongovernmental actors using nation states to press their concerns. Whereas Greenpeace might not readily forego its demonstrations and harassment of whaling ships, it is already the case that some national delegations to the IWC have been effectively captured by environmentalists, and the whaling nations have not refused to negotiate with these delegations.

The use of nation state proxies for nongovernmental actors would make the number of parties manageable. Further, there are some obvious possibilities for coalition formation – and communities of interest and expertise – among actors. The whaling nations clearly have interests in common, and environmental groups could cooperate with each other, with aboriginal whalers (Friends of the Earth already does this to a degree), with the scientific community, and with whale watchers. The number of participants might still remain large, though; currently thirty-four nations belong to the IWC, and another six to eight nations engage in whaling.

The capabilities of actors are more equal than would appear at first sight; whaling is an area where the seemingly powerless can have some success against the seemingly powerful. Consider, for example, the success of Inupiat whalers in battles with the U.S. federal government over aboriginal whaling, achieved by astute political tactics and exploitation of sympathies for aboriginal rights.

Would a discursive resolution of the whaling issue produce decisive results? The likelihood of decisive results is enhanced because the content of any such agreement could not be overturned by any parallel or competing institutions because none exists. This situation is in stark contrast to domestic politics, where courts, legislatures, and other institutions stand ready to frustrate or undermine accords. Moreover, one would expect greater compliance by participant actors to accords to which they have freely consented than to IWC resolutions against which they may have voted.

The boundaries of a potential contract zone cannot be predicted in advance. Speculatively, though, elements of a solution to the whaling issue might involve U.S.-financed compensatory benefits to whaling nations to alleviate economic distress in whaling communities (see, e.g., Totten and Schmidhauser, 1978, pp. 257–75) coupled with preservation of whales through highly restricted quotas and a confinement of whaling to certain groups (such as subsistence whalers).

Given that whale populations are common-property resources, there are a number of candidate generalizable values. The possibilities here would include scientific interests (especially given that scientific knowledge of the life history and ecology of whales is currently highly limited) and the integrity of oceanic ecosystems.

Upon closer examination, then, it is apparent that most of the conditions for international discursive design to occur and succeed *could* be met or approximated in the whaling case. One stumbling block might prove to be the location of a willing, competent, and credible third party. Candidates here might include government representatives or professional mediators from nations that are neutral both politically and with respect to the whaling issue (e.g., Mexico, Switzerland, or Argentina). Any third party would have to be acceptable to the very different perspectives of the USSR, the United States, North Korea, Taiwan, Iceland, and Japan, all of which engage in some form of whaling.

The Prospects for International Discursive Designs

Most interesting international problems are not site specific, clearly defined, or limited to a small number of actors. Hence the whaling issue is more representative than the Garrison Diversion Project.

According to the conventional wisdom, discursive exercises should be especially problematic, if not futile, in cases such as whaling characterized by high degrees of complexity and conflict. After all, such exercises are a form of order, so surely one would not expect them to flourish in the anarchical international polity (in contrast to more well-behaved domestic political systems).

However, the expectations of Hobbesians to the contrary notwithstanding, effective authority need not be accompanied by coercive institutional structure. Discursive designs promise authority based on consent and voluntary compliance. As such, they are ideally suited to the highly decentralized international system. Indeed, the very absence of central authority facilitates their operation, for no competing repositories of authority stand ready to undermine any accords reached. Moreover, discursive designs may be attractive to actors in the international system precisely because they retain a respect for sovereignty – to a much greater extent than arbitration, international administration, or legal adjudication.

The general lesson here is that at least some of the forces that frustrate discursive designs in domestic politics are less obtrusive at the international level, precisely because the international polity lacks any state ever ready to impose and extend its imperatives. However, international discursive designs are not thereby freed from impediment. For though there is no international state, there is an international market system complete with punishment mechanisms. Currently, the world's international trade regime features a renewed emphasis on free movement of goods and capital. Institutions such as the World Bank, the International Monetary Fund, and major private banks stand ready to make life difficult for those – especially debtor nations – who might try to violate this regime. Paradoxically, though, the global trade regime may impose more constraints on the internal politics and economics of these countries than it does on relations among them.

One further obstacle to communicative rationalization is sometimes seen as especially problematic in an international context. International discursive designs would necessarily involve individuals from different cultural backgrounds, perhaps with deep-seated differences in world views. Returning to the whaling example, to a Soviet official or Japanese whaler the word "whale" refers to a resource. To a Greenpeace activist, the same word refers to an intelligent creature with an inherent right to existence. To marine biologists, some environmentalists, and aboriginal whalers, the term "ecosystem" and associated concepts such as homeostasis and equilibrium make sense and indeed may organize a worldview; to a U.S. State Department diplomat or a Taiwanese whaling captain the term may be meaningless. These differences are not merely semantic; they involve a lack of agreement on the very existence of certain objects. Incompatibilities across worldviews exist too in domestic disputes (see Robinson, 1982; Hunter, 1984); the extent to which the problem is more severe at the international level remains an open question. Such incompatibility is not fatal to domestic discursive designs, and there is no reason why it need be any more problematic in international discourse, especially in this increasingly cosmopolitan age. For communicative rationality appeals to standards implicit in human communication wherever it occurs, whoever it is between, and whatever language it uses. And discursive designs do not seek the bland uniformity of perfect agreement across individuals; continued differences and compromises are permissible.

In sum, the forces frustrating discursive designs are weaker at the international level than in domestic politics. Correspondingly, though, the forces favorable to discursive designs are also less powerful here. For of the developments conducive to discursive democratization discussed in Chapter 4, only approaching ecological crisis is likely to be felt in international politics. Certainly, the contradictions of the Keynesian welfare state or reactions against the colonization of the lifeworld have little relevance. The weakness of the structural forces favoring and frustrating discursive designs at the international level means that here, still more than elsewhere, discursive democratization is a matter of choice, not necessity.

There is much to be said on behalf of international discursive designs. They may, like their domestic counterparts, have their difficulties. Yet their alternatives are not particularly attractive. Coercive diplomacy, positional negotiation, international law, and armed conflict – the major forms of collective choice in the contemporary international polity – have done little to ameliorate some of the more severe international problems and promise little more in future. Discursive designs could improve upon this unsatisfactory status quo.

PART III
Public Policy

CHAPTER 6

Policy Sciences of Democracy

If the past belongs to material production and control over the means of physical coercion, then arguably the future belongs to information. Economy and society are becoming increasingly organized around the production, transmission, reception, and transformation of information rather than around material goods. Material production itself is now largely coordinated by informational technology. The ultimate political consequences of this informational revolution are decidedly uncertain. The new technology and its associated ways of life may remain thoroughly under the control of experts and manipulators, one more agent for instrumental rationalization. But more democratic outcomes are conceivable, especially if control over information and knowledge can be decentralized to a competent citizenry (Barber, 1984, pp. 273–9; Luke and White, 1985).

In this chapter and the one that follows I shall address one particular kind of knowledge-based activity that has made some headway in the world's polyarchies in recent decades, the idea of a policy science. Although professional policy analysis now plays some part in the governance of liberal democracies, it is among their social scientists that the aspiration toward a successful policy science has really taken root. Aside from a simple desire to apply social science expertise to policy problems, this program has been advanced as a means of organizing the various social sciences around a problem-solving focus that would both end their identity crises and improve their prospects for attracting government grants (Charlesworth, 1972; Horowitz, 1981). Although the desire for lucre is hard to defend, no apology is necessary for a problem-solving focus in social science and politics as long as war, inequality, poverty, structural violence, and ecological crisis exist.

In terms of the contemporary intellectual division of labor my main concern in this chapter is with the field of policy analysis, which may be defined as "an applied social science discipline which uses multiple methods of inquiry and argument to produce and transform policy-relevant information that may be utilized in political settings to resolve policy problems" (Dunn, 1981, p. 35). But for the sake of continuity with some classic expressions about policy sciences of democracy and tyranny (introduced in what follows), I will use the terms "policy analysis" and "policy science" interchangeably in this chapter. I attach no further connotations to the word "science" in this context and profess only agnosticism on the actual or potential scientific status of policy analysis.

Why this amount of attention to policy and its analysis in a book on discursive democracy? To begin, the rise of the Keynesian welfare state in the second half of the twentieth century has rendered public policy pervasive and important. Among Western industrial societies, between 35 and 55 percent of national income is accounted for by government. Laws and regulations further extend the reach of government and policy. Public policy really can have a major impact on peoples' lives, from prenatal care through early education to employment to prison to old-age pension. And just like many other areas of individual and collective life, public policy is becoming increasingly subject to expert cultures. I interpret the field of policy analysis broadly as that knowledge-based culture concerned with the process and content of public policy. Increasing complexity is likely to add to the demand for such analysis in public policy. In short, policy analysis is an important political force, for better or for worse, and that is why I attend to it.

Although policy analysis is a knowledge-based culture, is it an *expert* culture? Need it be? Should it be? Or is a more truly democratic policy science possible?

If indeed policy analysis has to be an expert culture, then it can be nothing more than another force for the impoverishment of the lifeworld and the obstruction of discursive democracy. I shall suggest that most policy analysis as currently taught and practiced involves exactly this kind of technocratic disposition. The irony is that, aside from reinforcing technocratic consciousness, this kind of policy analysis fails to deliver on the promise that is its very raison d'être, enhanced rationality in social problem solving.

On the other hand, I shall argue that a coherent, defensible, and democratic policy science is indeed conceivable, but only to the extent it proceeds hand in hand with communicative rationality and discursive democracy. And if this argument holds, policy science cannot do much for the problem-solving rationality of existing liberal democracies despite the best efforts of some contemporary analysts. The fate of policy science therein is either to undermine any democratic pretensions or to reinforce ordinary liberal and pluralistic political interaction. Thus policy science in liberal democracy proves either subversive and authoritarian or impotent; in no way does it point to the reconciliation of democracy and problem-solving rationality.

I shall claim that such reconciliation can only be achieved by policy science combined with participatory democracy. But not just any participatory democracy will do; it must be a communicatively rationalized one. And not just any policy science will do; it must be guided by, and well placed to reinforce, the precepts of discursive democracy.

My argument in this chapter is therefore intended to undermine a technocratic view of policy and so help demolish one particularly threatening expert culture. To the extent this demolition succeeds, policy analysis might cease to be an agent of domination and become a material force for emancipation in what might seem a particularly surprising location. So in the language of critical theory, policy analysis becomes a disputed area in the contest between system and lifeworld.

The idea of seeking to combine democracy and problem-solving rationality through policy science is not a novel one. A "policy science of democracy," which would, at least by the sound of it, reconcile the two principles, was in fact proposed by Harold Lasswell (1951) almost four decades ago. However, the most widely accepted characterization of Lasswellian policy science remains a technocratic one. Initially, Lasswell allowed that any democratic commitment was merely a matter of preference about the ultimate goals of policy and as such "the place for nonobjectivity" (Lasswell, 1951, p. 11). This commitment is thus no more or less defensible than subscription to a "policy science of tyranny," to use another of Lasswell's expressions. But Lasswell's prolific output, in particular his later work, also contains intimations and examples of critical dialogue and meaningful participation as integral parts of the analytical process (Torgerson, 1985; Bobrow and Dryzek,

1987, pp. 172–4). Though my intent here is not exegetical, I will suggest that these latter aspects of Lasswell's program can indeed contribute to a defensible policy science of democracy.

Throughout the remainder of this chapter, I shall add flesh to theoretical bones with some illustrations from policy making in and about Alaska.

A Policy Science of Tyranny?

Max Weber's concern that efforts to solve ever more complex social problems will advance bureaucratization and authoritarianism finds many echoes. For example, Dahl (1985a) worries that the technical complexity of problems such as those pertaining to the control of nuclear weapons effectively disenfranchises the bulk of the citizenry, not to mention public officials, lacking the expertise necessary to make intelligent contributions to policy deliberations. Lovins (1977) raises the specter of vital, yet vulnerable centralized energy systems controlled by experts necessitating centralized and authoritarian political control. In the Third World, dictators can excuse their authoritarian proclivities on the grounds that elections and other democratic paraphernalia introduce dangerously short time horizons (see Goodin, 1979, pp. 35–6).

One rather heavy-handed solution to this ubiquitous tension between democracy and rationality would simply dispense with democracy in the name of (instrumental) rationality. The days when Comte and Saint-Simon could not believe society would oppose the progress attainable under rational central administration are long gone. Nevertheless, whether by accident or design, the field of policy analysis now seems poised to reinstate the idea of unencumbered central control, thus constituting one more agent for the takeover of the lifeworld by expert cultures. As such, many of its efforts are consistent with an (albeit subtle) policy science of tyranny. By tyranny I mean not the authoritarian dystopia feared by Lasswell but any elite-controlled policy process that overrules or shapes the desires and aspirations of ordinary people.

A great deal of contemporary policy analysis is microeconomic in inspiration: Analysts seek solutions to social problems that are efficient in terms of their allocation of scarce resources to welfare-generating policies (see Stokey and Zeckhauser, 1978, for a compendium of techniques). A second current of policy analysis is equally beholden to exclusively instrumental rationality but less objectivist in its value judgments than microeconomics. This second current works in what Dunn (1981, pp. 75–80) calls the explanatory mode: Analysts seek generalizations (however local) about the causes of valued policy outcomes, which may in turn be informed by a broad range of goals.

One possible goal that could be incorporated in such analysis is democracy itself. In this light, one uncharitable interpretation of Lasswell's own policy science of democracy stresses the manipulation of policy to thinly democratic ends and away from antidemocratic threats such as that posed by the garrison state (see, e.g., Horwitz, 1962, pp. 300–1).[1]

Criticisms of the antidemocratic implications of microeconomic and explanatory policy analysis are by now widely known, and so there is no need to discuss them at length (for further details, see Tribe, 1972; Fay, 1975, pp. 22–9, 49–64; Paris and Reynolds, 1983, pp. 14–165; Torgerson, 1986a; Bobrow and Dryzek, 1987, pp. 27–43, 122–135). In brief, the relevant charges are that mainstream policy analysis

- preempts political debate with the imposition of dubious value judgments, such as economic efficiency;
- treats ends in simplistic form, as capable of being fixed prior to contemplation of a problem and action upon it;
- conceives of politics in terms of the technological manipulation of causal systems by an elite composed of, or advised by, analysts;
- reinforces hierarchical and bureaucratic notions of the control of human beings; and
- posits an unproblematic consensus on values, and so slides too easily into stands on behalf of some ideological status quo.

Mainstream policy analysis fails to allow that the value positions surrounding any interesting policy issue are typically complex, controversial, conflicting, and fluid. Their content, and the trade-offs between them, may be best worked out in the context of attempted problem resolution, during which stakeholders can explore normative dimensions and the links between different goals (Lindblom, 1959, pp. 81–83; Schultze, 1968, pp. 37–42). As Wildavsky (1987) argues at length, preference formation is endogenous to social interaction.

Mainstream policy analysis would undermine democratic debate most effectively in the unlikely event that its findings were accepted as correct and informed by an unproblematic consensus on values. All that is left would be the Saint-Simonian "administration of things." As Arendt (1977, pp. 227–64) argues, the interplay of opinion at the heart of free democratic discourse is jeopardized to the extent any would-be correct position is advanced or accepted. The tendency of officials in some Marxist regimes to argue in terms of correct and incorrect theoretical stances toward political issues highlights the potential for repression on the basis of purported truth.

The good news is that nowhere have the (instrumentally) rationalistic aspirations of mainstream policy science come close to realization. This failure could arise because the very idea of manipulation of social systems toward uncontroversial goals through a knowledge of causality is incoherent (Fay, 1975, pp. 51–2; Bobrow and Dryzek, 1987, pp. 131–4). The intentional actions of human agents, including those of policymakers themselves, interfere such that manipulations change the character of the alleged laws on which they are based. But even if the mainstream, instrumental rationalist's conception of policy analysis is coherent, its offerings are typically not well received in the real world of public policy, as the burgeoning literature on research utilization attests (see, e.g., Weiss, 1977).

In what sense can we label mainstream policy analysis tyrannical if it is nowhere directly complicit in tyranny? One answer is that tyranny is implicit in its (unrealized) antipolitical aspirations (for an explicit statement, see Stokey and Zeckhauser, 1978, p. 151). But acceptance of this answer would imply that policy analysis just is not very important in the larger political scheme of things, and certainly not important enough to warrant a chapter in this book.

More significant may be the degree to which antidemocratic values are advanced along with the day-to-day production of analysis. Edelman (1977) notes that the most important output of government social service agencies may be a particular perspective on the causes, consequences, and inevitability of poverty. This perspective convinces agency clients and the general public that the professional knows best. Analogously, the main political function of the cumulative weight of technically sophisticated policy analysis may be to promote the idea that public policy is properly the prerogative of experts. Policy analysis that emphasizes causality may even help reify the idea that social processes proceed through a lawlike logic beyond the control of ordinary people who can therefore only resign themselves to the inevitable (Fay, 1975, pp. 58–61; 1987, pp. 92–3). So although mainstream policy analysis rarely has the kind of impact sought by its practitioners, it is nonetheless important as a political force, especially in its legitimation of social engineering.

Following Foucault, one might also argue that policy analysis helps constitute subjects in particular ways, as clients or spectators rather than as citizens or participants. A relevant personal experience in a public bar of an English village inn[2] occurred the summer of 1989. I listened as a lorry driver gave an eloquent, informed, and persuasive argument, contrary to majority opinion in the village, as to exactly why a planning application for a major gravel extraction project in the nearby countryside should be approved. He concluded his speech with the comment "But it's not for the likes of you or me to decide what should be done. It's up to the planners."

I shall now try to illustrate these criticisms of mainstream policy analysis through reference to the Alaskan case. I cannot offer an example of the connection to policy-making sought by the mainstream because, as I have noted, its products are rarely well received by the political powers that be, and Alaska yields no exception. What I can offer, though, is a case of tyrannical policy informed by analysis.

Congress passed the Alaska Native Claims Settlement Act (ANCSA) in 1971 with the best of intentions and with the failures of Indian policy in the lower forty-eight states (especially with respect to the reservation system) in mind. The act transferred 43.7 million acres (11 percent of Alaska) and $962.5 million to Alaska's Native peoples (Inuit, Indian, and Aleut) in order to extinguish unresolved claims upon the land. The institutional recipients of this largesse were the thirteen regional corporations and numerous village corporations created by the act. There was a seemingly unproblematic consensus in Washington that some kind of for-profit corporate form was appropriate. The ANCSA received analytical input from the executive branch and from congressional staff (if not in the fashion mainstream policy analysis would specify).

The ANCSA has produced some major negative unforeseen and unintended consequences in Alaska. The details need not concern us here (for a comprehensive account, see Young, 1981, chap. 2). What they boil down to is the impossibility of establishing what Berger (1985, p. 46) calls "Main Street on the Tundra" in a culture with no experience of corporations (let alone their management) and a setting with precious little in the way of business opportunities. But more important for present purposes is the (manifestly unintended) tyrannical aspect of the act.

One purpose of the act was to instill American values in Native society. The intent was not to repress but rather to expand the options available to ordinary Natives, allowing them to take advantage of the material rewards that corporate America can offer. In short, the idea was to create a "new Native" less beholden to traditional ways (Martin, 1976). This goal was thoroughly insensitive to the culture, abilities, and concerns of the Natives on the receiving end of the act. There was no consultation with the traditional tribal governments, though the weak statewide Native leadership that did exist in 1971 acquiesced in the act.

From the perspective of Capitol Hill, William van Ness, a former aide to Senator Henry Jackson, avers that "the act was . . . a very radical effort at social engineering and it was done on a very, very calculated basis" (quoted in Berger, 1985, p. 21). From the perspective of the tundra, it looked like social engineering too. So Bigjim and Ito-Adler (1974, p. 82) state, "We don't want to be better white men or beat them at their own game . . . AN ACT is forcing us into new ways of organizing ourselves and doing things before we really understand what is happening." They complain that "the experts can write a complicated legal document like AN ACT, but it is the far simpler and humbler folk who will have to live with the consequences" (p. 8). But all was not lost for Alaska's Natives, and forms of policy science more consistent with democratic principles eventually appeared on the tundra, as we shall see in what follows.

In sum, the most widely practiced kind of policy analysis aspires to rationality, but this proves to be at the expense of democracy. One reason for this result is that the policy analysis mainstream can conceive of rationality only in instrumental, technocratic terms. Yet even the efficacy of this kind of rationality is suspect when it comes to social problems of any complexity, as Chapter 3 should have made clear.

Although the continued lack of direct impact of mainstream policy analysis embarrasses its practitioners, the literature on policy research utilization does sometimes disclose a less overt penetration of the perspectives of decision makers (see, e.g., Weiss, 1980). This process is more consistent with less antidemocratic aspirations for policy analysis, to whose character I now turn.

Enter Democracy

The policy analysis mainstream would jettison democracy in the name of a highly suspect claim to rationality. An alternative reconciliation of democracy and problem-solving rationality might be sought by starting with liberal democratic political institutions pretty much as they are (however imperfect) and exploring policy analysis as it might be, a rational activity consistent with these arrangements. The discussion here will begin with the widely popular liberal model of democracy, which also corresponds roughly with the weight of existing institutions laying claim to democracy in Western political systems. After exploring its possibilities and identifying its limitations, I shall turn to the participatory model of democracy, which is less entrenched but more in tune with the ideas about institutions and their rationality developed in earlier chapters.

Contemporary liberal democracy may be characterized in terms of representative government, competitive elections, substantial but not unlimited opportunity for popular pressure upon the state, freedom of association in pursuit of political influence, and a familiar range of individual rights against government. Liberal democratic theory generally interprets politics and policy-making in terms of the pursuit of essentially private interests by voters, entrepreneurial politicians, and other political actors. Recognized dangers inherent in the use of public channels for the pursuit of private interest range from the monopolization of policy-making by iron triangles to the tyranny of majorities. Thus government must be constrained, preferably by constitutional limitations.

The liberal and participatory models can be thought of as the two major variations on a theme of democratic possibilities.[3] In moving from the liberal to the participatory possibility, politics becomes more pedagogical, discursive, concerned with public rather than private ends, and demanding in terms of active citizenship. Conversely, the participatory possibility is less readily captured in terms of bargaining, exchange, strategizing, voting, and representation.

The choice between liberal and participatory models is not, then, an either–or decision. As Barber (1984, p. xi) puts it, with a moderation belied by the rest of his book, "There is little wrong with liberal institutions that a strong dose of political participation and reactivated citizenship cannot cure." However, for the sake of brevity I will address only the ideal types that define the two models. Little violence is thereby done to liberal democracy. Liberal democracy has occasionally flirted with the participatory possibility, especially under the influence of John Stuart Mill and twentieth-century theorists such as John Dewey. Both Mill and Dewey tried to graft a developmental component of political education through citizen participation onto liberal democracy (MacPherson, 1977, pp. 44–76). Both are praised for their efforts by contemporary participatory democrats (see, e.g., Pateman, 1970, pp. 28–35; Barber, 1984, passim). But the last few decades have witnessed a retreat from this developmental project, partly under the influence of findings by opinion researchers concerning mass political incompetence (see Chapter 8 for further discussion of this influence). The resulting "empirical" models of liberal democracy (associated with names such as Schumpeter, Dahl, Eckstein, and Sartori) are happy if ordinary people are spectators in the game of politics. Elections and interest groups offer suitably limited channels for popular influence. Thus the more popular contemporary normative theories of liberal democracy have strong pluralist overtones. As we shall now see, proponents of a policy science for liberal democracy focus upon this pluralist aspect.

A Policy Science of Liberal Democracy

One of the counts against microeconomic and explanatory policy analysis is that in trying to be comprehensively calculating they preempt the interplay of interests cherished by liberal democracy (see, e.g., Wildavsky, 1966, pp. 307–10). Some of the critics here have sought a role for policy analysis congruent with the pluralism of liberal politics. One well-known such presentation is that of Wildavsky (1979). Wildavsky suggests policy analysts throw in their hats with political actors and generate proposals that are essentially consistent with the interests of an actor and feasible within the prevailing constellation of political forces. More radically, Palumbo and Nachmias (1983) argue that the key to success in policy analysis is a thorough accommodation between the analytical and normative perspectives of the analyst and some key political actor. Knowledge would still serve power, but power would be plural.

Perhaps the most systematic policy science of liberal democracy has been developed, though not with that name, by Paris and Reynolds (1983). Paris and Reynolds argue that analysis can never

transcend ideology in political interaction and that policy outcomes will always reflect some balance of ideological forces. However, all ideologies are not equal. They range from the pure dogma
of "irrational" ideologies to more defensible (if ultimately un-
provable) "rational" ideologies. (The terminology comes from
Paris and Reynolds; the quotation marks are to distinguish their
use of the word rational from mine.) In these terms, an ideology is
"rational" to the extent of its internal coherence, its congruence
with empirical evidence, its ability to yield cogent warrants for
policy actions, and its practical utility in facilitating achievement of
its adherents' goals (Paris and Reynolds, 1983, pp. 207–13). The
task of analysis here is not to devise or evaluate policy options but
instead to enhance the "rationality" of ideologies by clarifying and
testing their empirical beliefs and metaphysical commitments.
Hawkesworth (1988) proposes a similar approach to policy analysis, though she speaks in terms of theories rather than ideologies.

The development of an increasingly "rational" ideology can be
found in the Alaskan case. The ideology may be termed indigenist,
as it asserts the rights, culture, and distinctiveness of Alaskan
Natives. Its roots may be found in an incoherent and often nostalgic protest against the effects of ANCSA and other intrusions upon
Native society (see, e.g., Bigjim and Ito-Adler, 1974). But this
ideology soon crystallized in a political movement, encompassing
organizations such as the Alaska Federation of Natives, the North
Slope Borough (an Inuit-controlled local government), the Inupiat
Community of the Arctic Slope, Yupiktak Bista, and the Inuit
Circumpolar Conference. For the most part, these organizations
pursued conventional strategies in the liberal democratic arena.
The "rationality" of the indigenist ideology was refined with contributions from both Native leaders and policy analysts (see, e.g.,
Yupiktak Bista, 1975; Alonso and Rust, 1976; Clocksin, Jeffery,
and Curtis, 1979). This ideology came to stress locally controlled
models of community development, protection and assertion of
Native access to subsistence resources (fish, game, and marine
mammals), renewable resource development, cultural renewal, and
opposition to large-scale oil and mineral exploitation. In short, the
core ideology became increasingly congruent with empirical evidence (e.g., about marine mammal stocks), cogent in its ability to
provide Native leaders and advocates with good political and legal
arguments, and practically useful as a medium for the pursuit of
Natives' goals.

Successful projects along such lines would promote a "polity of rational ideologies" (Paris and Reynolds, 1983, pp. 255–71). In the Alaskan case, ideologies stressing conventional notions about economic development or environmental preservation could supplement the indigenist outlook. The result would ideally be a liberal democracy purged of dogma, presumably producing better policies. Herein lies a claim to rationality in the larger sense of enhanced problem-solving power for the polity as a whole.[4]

On closer examination this claim proves suspect. When ideologies and interests compete, liberal democracy allows two kinds of resolution. The first is compromise, of the sort hammered out daily in the checked and balanced U.S. political system. Unfortunately, any compromise between positions advanced by two or more "rational" ideologies may not itself prove truly rational in the problem-solving sense, as an example from the Alaskan case will attest. The indigenist ideology just outlined has achieved political influence both in Alaska and Washington, D.C., checked of course by other ideologies (and baser concerns). Thus in 1980 Congress amended the ANCSA in response to concerns that control of Native corporations and their land could pass into non-Native hands in 1991 (when shares can be sold for the first time). The 1980 amendments enabled the corporations to restrict voting rights to their Native stockholders and to give the corporation itself, along with the shareholder's family, the right of first refusal to any shares offered for sale. This compromise advances nobody's concerns. From the perspective of indigenist ideology, the most likely result is the creation of class divisions within Native communities, between those who possess shares and those who have none (Berger, 1985, p. 103). From the vantage point of conventional economic development ideology, the amendments render the Native corporations even less capable of operating in and contributing to corporate America. It would be hard to muster a "rational" ideology to back this compromise.

As long as liberalism downplays collective reasoning toward public ends, there is little hope of reasoned resolution of the clash of inevitably partial ideologies or rationalities. Even the integrative encounters discussed in Chapter 3 are ruled out. Indeed, the likelihood of reasoned resolution may be diminished to the extent the "rationality" of ideologies is enhanced by projects of the sort Paris and Reynolds commend. Thus strengthened, such ideologies would meet like medieval knights in battle, secure but incapable of penetrating one another's armor.

The second kind of resolution liberal democracy allows when ideologies and interests clash is for one side's position to prevail, perhaps by carrying a legislative majority. The trouble here is that in liberal democracy any resolution is always temporary. Defeated parties can always return to fight again, be it in policy implementation or in subsequent policy formation (perhaps another legislative vote). If convinced of the "rationality" of their ideology, then presumably they will redouble their efforts in this respect. The consequent vacillation in policy content can produce results far worse than if one of the competing positions were chosen at random and given a long-term commitment. For example, the consistent failure of British macroeconomic policy since 1945 can be traced in part to the fact that no one doctrine was ever given the time to work, before rejection in favor of another as crisis followed crisis. Arguably, persistence with any one of the doctrines would have produced better results (Bacon and Eltis, 1976).

One possibility remains for rescuing problem-solving rationality in liberal democracy. Policy outcomes in real-world liberal democracies are highly sensitive to the relative power of different interests. The "political rationality" of allocating rewards to interests in proportion to their political power has its defenders, notably Diesing (1962, pp. 169–234) and Wildavsky (1966, pp. 307–8). Allocation on this basis minimizes the alienation of key actors from the political system and hence promotes system stability. Unfortunately, a policy can be politically rational without solving any of the problems confronting a polity, except of course the problem of stability. The problem-solving rationality standard is therefore violated; in this sense, political rationality is an oxymoron. And recent ballooning U.S. federal budgetary deficits suggest that series of politically rational allocations can in fact endanger stability. Moreover, it is far from clear what place a smoothly functioning, politically rational system has for policy analysis, beyond modest niches for advocates and feasibility strategists. As Lindblom and Cohen (1979, pp. 19–27, 88–9) argue, interaction can be a complete substitute for cogitation in political decision processes of this sort. It should be noted that the kind of interaction of which they speak has little to do with communicative rationality, for it tolerates deception, distortion, manipulation, and exclusion.

This search for a policy science of liberal democracy leaves us with politics, and democracy of a sort, but rationality and perhaps even policy analysis have now fallen by the wayside. Can discursive democracy do better?

Participatory Democracy

The fusion of rationality and democracy suggested by the idea of a policy science of democracy is, it seems, problematic in a policy-making process driven by the pursuit of private interest, expedient compromise, and representative government.

The alternative participatory vision of democracy emphasizes debate and reasoning about and toward public interests and actions in political communities of citizens who govern themselves, as opposed to liberalism's agglomeration of private individuals governed by their representatives (Pateman, 1970). Most presentations argue that such direct democracy (without representatives) is possible only in small-scale, geographically specific units such as neighborhoods or workplaces, though I shall argue later that the process can indeed operate on a larger scale. The quality as well as the quantity of participation is at issue here if what Barber (1984) calls "strong democracy" is to be pursued.[5] Although Barber does not use the term, communicative rationality goes a long way toward putting the "strong" in his strong democracy. Universal participation, on the other hand, is not required. Participatory democracy strives for consensus, but it accepts the inevitability of conflict. The key to conflict resolution is the reconstruction of private or partial interests into publicly defensible norms through sustained debate (Barber, 1984, p. 135). No bland uniformity of the kind that frightens liberals need be sought, for discursively rational consensus and action can rest upon the mutual recognition of ultimately different perspectives and concerns (see Chapter 2; also Fay, 1987, pp. 174–90). Thus, contra Mansbridge (1980), the "unitary democracy" (to use her expression) of face-to-face, discursive politics may indeed flourish without predetermined overarching common interests.[6]

Substantial departure from liberal democratic precepts occurs here. Having failed in their objectivist quest for transcendent moral principles, liberals generally celebrate the irreducible plurality and ultimate arbitrariness of normative positions (see Williams, 1979), except, of course, those pertaining to the principles of liberal democracy itself. They disparage the idea of any public interest beyond the sum of individual interests.

Participatory democracy as sketched can stake a first claim to problem-solving rationality on the same grounds as discursive designs. That is, public communal reasoning toward policy positions via consensus on normative positions moves the quality of decision to the center of debate, downplaying the influence of strategic interaction or the preferences of temporary majorities. As long as this focus is sustained, a rational whole may emerge from rational parts, a process that is deeply problematic in the "muddling through" and expedient compromise of liberal democracy, though islands of public communal reasoning are not necessarily inconceivable in a liberal democratic setting.

The arguments of Chapters 2 and 3 suggest that problem-solving rationality in public decision is facilitated by the communicatively rational discourse central to strong participatory democracy. For any community of problem-solving inquirers focusing directly on the quality of decisions is effective only to the extent that obstacles to reasoned dialogue are removed.

To the extent obstacles such as hierarchy, inequality in the ability to make and challenge arguments, political strategizing, deception, the exercise of power, manipulation, entrenched ideas, and self-deception persist in the policy-making process, that process resists revealing itself to any would-be communicatively rational community of policy analysts or ordinary political actors seeking to understand how a polity is or could be making decisions. Thus any such community is implicitly committed to the extension of free and open dialogue in the policy process, which is one object of its investigations (Torgerson, 1986b). In this light, acceptance of constraints and distortions in the polity at large undermines the claim to communicative rationality of any smaller community of inquirers. Moreover, as long as such obstacles persist, members of this smaller community will have difficulty finding a hearing in the larger process. In sum, a commitment to communicative rationality in the smaller community implies a commitment to strong participatory democracy in the larger polity.

In short, the problem-solving rationality of a polity in which collective decisions are reasoned toward (rather than emerging as a by-product of strategic interaction) is enhanced by communicatively rational participatory democracy. Thus the fusion of rationality and democracy sought by a policy science of democracy begins to seem plausible.

Some proponents of participatory democracy might, however,

regard such a policy science (and, for that matter, communicative rationality more generally) as thoroughly unnecessary or undesirable. The participatory strand of democratic theory has strong historical associations with Rousseau, who thought its aspirations could be achieved only in societies unencumbered by complex problems. Although policy analysis as a facilitator of problem-solving rationality in public deliberation would be superfluous in Rousseau's own rustic vision, it could redeem that vision in today's more complex world of severe social problems and strongly held differences of opinion. The incipient discursive designs discussed in earlier chapters are indicative of the possibilities here. But what, then, is the appropriate role for policy analysis in discursive designs and participatory democracy?

A Policy Science of Participatory Democracy

Two Lasswellian ideas are suggestive here. His "decision seminar" would be a small group of highly committed individuals engaged in direct communication in an information-rich environment (Lasswell, 1960). Interaction would be uncensored, as participants would be encouraged to freely disclose their ideas and freely criticize the ideas of others. Each seminar would constitute a long-term project, and Lasswell envisaged a global network developing. "Prototyping" would involve the participatory and experimental development of communities (Lasswell, 1963, pp. 99–120).

However, decision seminars and prototyping do not constitute a policy science of participatory democracy. As noted in Chapter 3, decision seminars fall short because they are confined to experts. And only local leaders participated in the most well-known example of prototyping, the Chilean Vicos project. One suspects these designs are hamstrung by Lasswell's residual elitist and technocratic leanings. But if one takes seriously the notions about a communicatively rational community of inquirers sketched in the preceding section, there is a participatory *telos* implicit in these Lasswellian innovations.

What, then, would a policy science of rational participatory democracy involve? First and perhaps foremost, the analyst's role would lie in the creation and sustenance of conditions and institutions for free democratic discourse. This is more of a "meta" role than analysts are used to. It bears some relation to the role of the third-party facilitator of incipient discursive designs discussed in

Chapter 2. Such an analyst is well placed to engage in critical scrutiny of incipient discursive designs in light of the ambiguities introduced in Chapter 4, especially with respect to the danger of subtle political control.

This kind of creative and sustaining role is exemplified by a recent Alaskan case. In reaction to the negative fallout of the 1971 Settlement Act, in 1983 the Inuit Circumpolar Conference (a non-governmental organization of Inuit from Greenland, Alaska, and Canada) created a body called the Alaska Native Review Commission. Thomas Berger, a Canadian judge and lawyer, was invited to head the commission. Over the next year the commission conducted an inquiry into the effects of the 1971 act with the intent of recommending policies to deal with any problems identified. Berger took the commission to sixty villages and numerous fishing camps throughout rural Alaska, a prodigious achievement given the logistical difficulties of Alaskan travel. The idea was to give every Alaskan Native a chance to participate in the inquiry, and 1,450 of them (from a total population of around 60,000) chose to speak. But Berger did not just listen, for his staff provided informational and educational materials in conjunction with each hearing, and he argued with witnesses with whom he disagreed (see, e.g., Berger, 1985, pp. 101–2).

Berger therefore created a public space in which ordinary Natives could develop, express, and share their views. This space existed outside the institutions of government; the commission was not financed or endorsed by state or federal government. Its funding came from foundations, churches, some of the Native regional corporations, and one Native-controlled local government.

This kind of public space between individuals and the state is where the institutionalization of a policy science of participatory democracy might best be sought. Such a policy science involves discourse and holistic experimentation, which, as noted in Chapter 2, are also the model practices inspired by the idea of a public sphere. If the activity were confined to the community, it would be impotent – hardly a *policy* science. On the other hand, any institutionalization within the state of the kind sought by both mainstream and liberal democratic policy analysis is hard to envisage.

Amy's (1984) explanation of why ethical reasoning currently makes little headway in American policy analysis is relevant here. Ethical reasoning involves applying general moral principles to specific policy choices. Amy points out that this kind of argument always raises uncomfortable questions. Just like a critical policy science of participatory democracy, ethical reasoning does not respect privileged analyst–client relationships, the taken-for-granted legitimacy of the values of policymakers and bureaucrats, politicians who prefer to evade questions about basic values, bureaucrats who wish to cultivate an illusion of neutral technical competence, liberal capitalist assumptions, or an incremental political culture.

A policy science of participatory democracy can therefore expect resistance from government institutions. It can flourish only by creating, operating within, and confronting the state from an autonomous public sphere (where one also finds the incipient discursive designs introduced in Chapter 2, if in somewhat compromised form). Here, too, the case of the Alaska Native Review Commission is exemplary. The commission helped to constitute a political community capable of charting its own future, perhaps redeeming the promise implicit in Lasswell's prototyping idea, but on a grand scale. It provided a forum for conflict resolution within that community through the kind of mechanism postulated earlier, the transformation of private into public norms through sustained discussion. Thus Berger (1985, pp. 104–5) relates events at one village hearing where Natives who declare they want to sell their shares to outsiders are persuaded against this idea by arguments from other villagers that the community as a whole will suffer if they do so.

The commission concluded with a challenge to state and federal power. Berger's policy recommendations centered upon the strengthening of the subsistence economy of Native Alaska and the transfer of Native corporation assets and land to rejuvenated tribal governments. Berger's (1985) report did not just represent his own summary opinion. As one witness put it, "He can only rephrase what, ultimately, all of us as individuals and collectively decide is going to happen next in how we view our world" (quoted in Berger, 1985, p. 118).

Although it remains to be seen how much state and federal policy will change as a result of the commission's work, some similar challenges under Berger's auspices have influenced public policy in Canada. Berger has presided over Royal Commissions concerned with family and children's law in British Columbia, the construction of oil pipelines from the Arctic to southern markets, and Inuit and Indian health care. The most spectacular success of the three was the MacKenzie Valley Pipeline Inquiry (Berger, 1977), which helped to persuade the federal government of Canada that no pipelines should be constructed prior to strengthening of the northern renewable resource economy and settlement of Native land claims. The process of the pipeline inquiry formed a model for Berger's later Alaskan effort (for discussion of the pipeline inquiry's exemplary nature, see Dryzek, 1982, pp. 324–5; Torgerson, 1986a, pp. 46–51).

One practical obstacle to the removal of policy analysis from the state and into a separate public space lies in the professional interests of policy analysts themselves. Government bureaucracies offer them employment, finance, and political acceptance. But analysts based in universities or independent think-tanks can more easily shun the state in favor of the public sphere (though there is no reason to suppose these institutions might actually constitute a public sphere). These analysts have nothing to lose but their government grants and contracts and their corporate sponsorships. The intellectual rewards of a Lasswellian network of decision seminars contributing to, but not dominating, the public sphere might help compensate for these losses.

This last possibility suggests that policy scientists of participatory democracy can make contributions within public spaces as well as facilitate their creation. Thus Berger (1985) made good use of a small staff ready to provide information to participants in his hearings and of his own extensive legal and historical knowledge. His better-funded pipeline inquiry involved much more in the way of contributions by anthropologists, engineers, ecologists, economists, and other analysts to community hearings.

Any contributions analysts do make must, though, be tentative (if a lapse into the policy science of tyranny is to be avoided). They can be offered as hypotheses whose corroboration can only be secured by the reflective assent of a broader public. The analyst would have to be sensitive to the political context into which his or her contributions are offered – and help constitute (Torgerson, 1986a, p. 41). Analysts should bear in mind that there is an essential equality in democratic discourse and that their ideas should be presented in a form intelligible to the ordinary political actors with which they are dealing. The code of communicative ethics commended by Forester (1981) is appropriate here: Covert manipulation of agendas, concealment and distortion of information, attempts to distract attention from key issues, and strategic exercises of power should be exposed. Reflexively, policy analysts can turn this searchlight on themselves to ensure that any leadership they

not just career problems, but intellectual as well

exercise is in the interests of facilitating dialogue rather than in exercising undue influence over others (cf. Barber, 1984, pp. 240–1). The general point here is that any instrumental activities the analyst undertakes should be regulated by the principles of communicative rationality.

The precise content of analytical contributions could take several forms. The analyst might be an individual with special technical expertise. Consider, for example, Dahl's (1985a, pp. 75–89) proposed "minipopulus" for policy-making about the control of nuclear weapons, which was introduced in Chapter 3. Assigned to this body would be a group of independent specialists whose task would be to inform it about the technical dimensions of nuclear issues, not to offer or evaluate policy alternatives. The minipopulus should then reason through policy proposals sensitive to the intertwined moral and technical issues involved. Incidentally, it is noteworthy that Dahl's proposal – similar to that made by Burnheim (1985) in a book published in the same year – also confronts the problem of scale stressed by many critics of participatory democracy and to which participatory democrats themselves are acutely sensitive.[7] This criticism is raised by Dahl himself in an earlier work, where he utilizes the "criterion of economy" (the idea that citizens' time is limited and valuable) to defend representative democracy against more participatory alternatives (Dahl, 1970, pp. 40–55). Another solution to the scale problem is implicit in Berger's Alaskan commission, which operated in a physical environment truly inhospitable to large-scale participation: Define an issue area, hit the road, and welcome interested parties at each stop.

The analyst may have access to a number of analytical frameworks that could prove of broader interest to participants in decision. In the Alaskan case, these frameworks would pertain to resource economics, ecology, constitutional law, and cultural dynamics. Such frameworks can have normative as well as empirical dimensions. Hence the analyst need not take the normative position of the audience as given and immutable. Normative arguments do have a place in policy analysis even if, as Amy (1984, p. 581) suggests, they might constitute more nails in the coffin of the technical aspirations of a policy analysis profession.

Though ultimately the audience's judgment is conclusive, the analyst, like other actors, can provide critical contributions to policy discourse that challenge established and entrenched ways of thinking. So the analyst might point to subtle forces of socialization that distort actors' perceptions and presuppositions in the interests of some dominant force (e.g., large corporations) or high-light possibilities and threats of which actors were unaware (e.g., possibilities for small-scale technology in economic development or the threat of control of family life by government bureaucracies). Democratic policies and policy-making can have a substantial ped-agogical aspect, from which policy analysts need not shrink in the name of their equality with other actors. Indeed, policy analysts are well placed to extend the axioms of a community of rational inquirers into the polity at large. Any restriction of free discourse to a community of specialists, as in the integrative approach to problem solving discussed in Chapter 3, is simply unfaithful to the idea of unrestricted discourse. Policy analysts could thus act (ra-tionally) as a spark for democratization of the political system. Ashley (1980, pp. 224–8) makes a similar point about the potential role of social science intellectuals in the international system.

However, there is a residual threat to participatory democracy in the role for policy analysis just outlined. For the mere fact of expertise, or even job description, can constitute the basis for un-obtrusive domination of the laity, no matter how much the expert disclaims such intentions. This danger constitutes a further reason why a policy science of participatory democracy should avoid pro-fessionalization. Professional mystique is a clear source of domina-tion, most obviously when it is tied to "tyrannical" policy analysis (Torgerson, 1985, pp. 254–5). The tension here is not between democracy and science (however one defines it) but is rather be-tween democracy and expertise. Science speaks with both an elitist voice that claims authority on the basis of expertise and a demo-cratic voice that proclaims free debate in the scientific republic.

Lasswell's solution to the residual threat of expertise was a profes-sional commitment to democracy and extraordinary self-under-standing and responsibility, but this noble aspiration bears little relation to what we know about how professions actually operate, not least the policy analysis profession.

Perhaps the surest answer to anxieties about subtle domination would be for policy scientists of discursive democracy to succeed to the extent they rendered themselves unnecessary. Based on his reading of Dewey, Kaufman-Osborn (1985, p. 847) argues that the goal of rational policy inquiry should be "the generation of a com-munity capable of taking political action" on a particular social problem.[8] Generalizing this point, one might argue that political education, participatory action, and successful social problem solving could together help constitute a community fully capable of steering its own course into the future. The distinction between citizen and expert would lose its force. Pending such a dramatic change in the conditions of political life, a policy science of discursive democracy can at least point to the productive reconciliation of rationality and democracy and so help undermine the technocratic disposition of the modern world. But this reconciliation is possible only if policy is more than instrumental action, if science is more than the expert's cogitation, if problem-solving rationality is more than technocratic manipulation, and if democracy is more than liberal interest accommodation.

CHAPTER 7

The Ambitions of Policy

with Brian Ripley

The policy science of discursive democracy sketched in the preceding chapter is a material force for emancipation that also helps to reconcile aspirations to political democracy and collective problem-solving rationality. This chapter attempts to demonstrate that such a policy science, in conjunction with the discursive institutions introduced earlier, enables a degree of confidence in social problem solving that is unwarranted under more established conceptions of public policy and policy analysis. Specifically, we shall argue that communicative rationality in discourse about public policy releases policy analysis and design from some otherwise well-merited inhibitions. This release in turn allows more ambitious attempts to resolve or ameliorate social problems. To the extent this argument holds, there is less excuse for complacency in this world of severe social problems. Our case proceeds through an encounter with some prominent critics of overambitious public policy.

Certainly, there has been no shortage of cautions against excessive ambition in consciously pursued public policy. And contemporary perceptions of widespread (if not wholesale) failure in public policy add force to these warnings. Our contention is that the critics here have missed the target. Based on a correction of their aim, we will suggest there is little reason to eschew ambition in policy design, provided only that one attends closely to the degree of communicative rationality in policy formation. This is not to say that ambition should be pursued for its own sake or that it is always appropriate, merely that fear of ambition should not act as a constraint.

Warnings against Excessive Ambition

A first warning against excess would have policy designers bridle their ambitions due to the inadequacy of weak social science theory. If effective policy design requires a theoretical base, then the more ambitious the design, the greater the demands on social science theory. The trouble is that social science knowledge is dispersed, incomplete, and frequently contradictory. Policy based on such theories is clearly a risky business.

In this idiom, the more prominent critics of overambitious policy include Popper (1966, 1972a) and von Hayek (1944). Von Hayek (1978) argues that "scientistic" movement from theoretical abstraction to practical application inevitably loses sight of the weakness of the theory on which any design is based.

Both Popper and von Hayek warn against utopian planners informed by comprehensive, highly abstract theories. Such visionary blueprints call for radical "canvas cleaning," which translates into the destruction of existing tainted social institutions. Thus the way is paved for authoritarian rule, since any theory for reconstruction is going to be mistaken, tempting its guardians into coercion of an apparently recalcitrant reality. Both these authors and their followers direct their arguments against policy based on any social theory assumed to be true and beyond criticism, whether it pertains to the construction of urban highways or an ideal state (see James, 1980).

Skepticism about the ability of social science theory to inform policy is frequently (if not necessarily) coupled with a more general distrust of public bureaucracies and their component officials, which constitutes a second warning. There is no need to posit motivations of greed, malice (von Hayek, 1944), or low self-esteem (Lasswell, 1930) on the part of public officials in order to doubt the efficacy of public institutions. Ordinary self-interest will suffice. Economistic critics of public decision making such as Friedman and Friedman (1979) assume that bureaucrats are rationally self-interested, like everyone else in society. Thus a sizable public choice literature predicts public organizations will try to expand their size and budget to the exclusion of all other concerns (see, e.g., Niskanen, 1971).

A third barrier to ambitious policy design stems from the political divisions inherent in plural societies, which can rarely achieve a durable political coalition to support any particular social remodeling (at least outside extraordinary circumstances such as depression and war). The prospect here is that exasperated planners may be tempted by the maxim that desperate times call for desperate measures. Thus the rise of authoritarianism in Latin America has often been linked to ambitious economic stabilization policies (Collier, 1979). More generally, overambitious policy can create a situation where programs are created on behalf of citizens but not at their behest. Dissent can expect the whip of a cruel state apparatus.

Antidotes to Excessive Ambition

The discussion of the previous section might seem ample warrant for modesty in policy design. However, there are several antidotes to the dangers of excessive ambition, each of which requires its own distinctive kind of conscious public policy.

Perhaps the most well-known such antidote, especially in the context of weak social science theory, is incrementalism. A thinking person's incrementalism is forcefully articulated in Popper's (1972a) notion of piecemeal social engineering (see Chapter 2) and developed into a methodology of systematic trial and test in public policy by Popperians such as Campbell (1969). In this light, any public policy should simultaneously ameliorate a social problem and yield clear inferences about the veracity of the theory informing the policy. If the theory is corroborated, then policies based upon it should be adopted somewhat more extensively; if that theory is falsified, then alternative directions for policy should be sought. It is crucial, at least in Popper's own formulation, that maximal opportunity be provided for criticism of the policy, the theory on which it is based, and its effects. Criticism should be admissible from all quarters, both expert and lay, for policies based on weak theories inevitably produce unanticipated effects in surprising locations.

A strategy of incrementalism or piecemeal social engineering does little to offset the second warning, pertaining to the self-interest of politicians and bureaucrats. Moreover, if large administrative systems are too cumbersome to pursue any conception of the public interest systematically and effectively, there is little reason to expect the sensitivity, critical spirit, and flexibility necessary for successful experimentation.

Two options present themselves here. The first, in vogue for a decade now, involves privatization and minimization of the scope of government (see, e.g., Friedman and Friedman, 1962, 1984). If we cannot do away with government, a second option is available, that is, make government as decentralized as possible. A perennial theme in the public choice literature would have governmental jurisdictions as small and specialized as possible on the grounds that public officials are visible and accountable to the extent they produce a limited range of services for a small number of people (see, e.g., Ostrom, 1971; Bish, 1978).

The last obstacle to ambition we noted in the previous section, that of political conflict, can be approached in at least three ways.

First, though classical liberals believe consensus on the features of an ideal society is impossible, at least one strand in contemporary liberalism believes consensus is attainable with respect to the content of the worst ills afflicting society. Like the lawmen of the Old West, public policy should try to "clean up the town." More formally, this stance is known as negative utilitarianism (see O'Hear, 1980, pp. 157–8), which restricts public policy to pursuit of the elements of utility functions presumed held in common by all (or at least most) members of society. Such common elements might include eradication of extreme poverty, bringing down the inflation rate, and so forth.

A second, superficially similar means for coping with dissensus in public policy is provided by the "politics of prevention" associated with Harold Lasswell (1965a). But Lasswell is less concerned with ameliorating existing social problems than with anticipating and preventing future ones. Lasswell argues for the articulation of developmental constructs, projections of likely but unwanted future states of affairs (e.g., a militarized garrison state), about which consensus should be possible. Such constructs should function as self-denying prophecies by stimulating policies to prevent their actualization.

A third, perhaps more nebulous approach to dissensus would simply recognize its inevitability and thenceforth seek the identification of any minimal policies around which a broad coalition could be mobilized – or broad acquiescence obtained.

On the other hand, the politically astute policy designer may be able to capitalize on problem complexity in order to at least partially overcome dissensus. One way of apprehending complex problems (dismissed in Chapter 3 as not terribly effective) is through their decomposition into a set of smaller, interconnected problems, each with a potential solution. Along these lines, Hirschman (1973) advises "reformmongers" to entice disparate political groups into problem-solving efforts by framing the issues involved in parochial terms attractive to each of the respective audiences. Having co-opted these diverse groups, the skilled reformmonger can nudge them toward further contribution. Each political group feels it has obtained a victory, some progress is made in resolving a searing social problem, and the shrewd policy analyst's agenda is furthered.

Why the Antidotes Fail

The critics of excessive ambition in public policy would seem, then, to have made a number of remedies available, all of which salvage the possibility of consciously pursued public policy, if in modified form. We will argue in this section that these measures generally fail to serve as the remedies envisioned by their proponents.

The purported virtues of incrementalism are undermined upon closer examination of its central concept. Although Dempster and Wildavsky (1979) tell us "there is no magic size for an increment," the problem here is less the lack of any scale by which to measure size than it is the demands on theory, dismissed by incrementalists as weak and unreliable, to help us distinguish incremental from nonincremental adjustments. An intervention may turn out to be too big and prove to be the first step on a slippery slope from which there is no escape (see Goodin and Waldner, 1979, p. 4). For example, deciding to construct a short stretch of freeway may effectively commit a government to a larger network of freeways in order to eliminate the congestion on roads leading to the first stretch. On the other hand, an intervention may prove too small to either make any difference to its target or yield any inferences about the theory on which it is based. Schulman (1980) notes that projects like the NASA space program require large commitments of resources if they are to produce any results at all.

Aside from being unable to tell us much about the actual size of an increment, weak theory cannot tell us how to construct an experiment for testing itself, especially with respect to the influences that need to be controlled (see Goodin and Waldner, 1979, pp. 13–16). Nor can it indicate how long we should wait before adjudging an experiment a success or a failure.

Strategies involving privatization and a concomitant expanded role for market allocation hardly constitute a panacea for the ills of policy. Galbraith (1967) and others have long warned that large private institutions are subject to the same behavior (and the same problems) as large public institutions. Moreover, it is abundantly clear that market systems are unable to supply the values economists call public goods, at least to the degree such systems are competitive and decentralized. To the extent they are oligopolistic and centralized, the ills of large-scale organization appear.

Both market and piecemeal social reform are planks in the classical liberal platform, articulated forcefully by Popper and von Hayek. There is a clear inconsistency here. Although Popper and von Hayek both stress the limitations of any theory of society, a belief in the power of the market rests on just such a theory – and a fairly comprehensive, macrolevel one to boot.

Of course, not all market advocates share the caution of Popper and von Hayek. Some see market theory as strong enough to use as a base for radical reconstruction (see, e.g., Friedman and Friedman, 1984). These bolder classical liberals suffer an inconsistency of their own, though, for it will require drastic, purposeful, but unmistakably *governmental* action to bring their utopia into being. But governments, they tell us, inevitably go astray in their actions. One of the few escapes here seems to be the one advocated by Friedman and Friedman (1984), a grass-roots mass movement to shrink government headed ideally by a charismatic leader. The use of such totalitarian means to lead society toward a market system is highly risky.

Governmental decentralization proves no more compelling than privatization as a means for promoting efficiency and accountability. The counterargument to the public choice decentralizers is of course that economies of scale can make large organizations more efficient than smaller ones, which in turn suggests consolidation of governmental units.[1] When two theories predicated upon different assumptions predict opposite results, clearly an appeal to empirical evidence is necessary. The available evidence is equivocal (see Lovrich and Neiman, 1984, for a survey).

Turning now from "positive" utilitarian market and public choice advocates to negative utilitarian problem solvers, it is clear that their requisite unproblematic consensus on what constitutes the worst ills in society is rare. Even when such a coalition can be patched together, it may prove short-lived. Consider, for example, the fate of New Deal liberalism (Reich, 1985). The twin perils of economic collapse and global war forged a consensus built on a spirit of solidarity through shared sacrifice. Postwar affluence allowed expansion of social welfare programs without any immediate or obvious costs to groups within the coalition. The economic ills of the 1970s exposed the underlying fissures, and the lack of a coherent unifying philosophy left the coalition open to collapse.

Moreover, even if the requisite coalition and consensus is conceivable, it is by no means obvious that policy designers should await its arrival before proceeding. Take the history of the civil rights movement in the United States. One would presume that a social evil such as massive racial discrimination would engender the rational consensus negative utilitarians predict. But when the issue of civil rights finally did reach prominence during the 1960s, there was certainly no immediate consensus on the nature of the problem. Race riots and heightened racial tension were perhaps symptomatic of a lack of agreement, but they certainly did not suggest inaction pending consensus.

In fact, most policy debate results from competing definitions of searing social problems. There turns out to be little difference between negative and positive utilitarianism on this score.

One further distinction that loses its power upon closer examination is that between avoiding dystopia and pursuing utopia. For example, von Hayek's (1944) *Road to Serfdom* both explicitly warns against an authoritarian dystopia and implicitly describes a market utopia. Just as people disagree about utopia, so can they differ over dystopia. And any strenuous avoidance of dystopia can also involve coercion and repression of individuals who demur. Consider, for example, some of the implications of the British Conservative government's efforts to avert "serfdom" in the years following 1979. In that period Britain gained a de facto nationally organized police force constructed to confront organized trade unions. Trade union activities have been further restricted by governmental prohibitions against sympathy strikes and secondary picketing.

The remaining means for coping with dissensus discussed in the previous section is the minimalist strategy. This approach has all the familiar defects of "muddling through" when it comes to circumstances of severe policy problems, rapid social change, and changing social values (see, e.g., Dror, 1964). Martin Luther King's eloquent "Letter from Birmingham Jail" offers a stinging critique of white moderates who repeatedly urge blacks to be patient and cautious in their reform efforts. Willingness to accept slow, gradual reform may in fact prove to be a direct function of one's place in society rather than a commitment to risk aversion in public policy. Hirschman's attempts to accelerate and direct muddling by manipulation on the part of the policy analyst is perilous inasmuch as it relies on trickery. One suspects that if this trickery were exposed, then the analyst would indeed achieve a social consensus – against his or her agenda. If such a fate is to be avoided, then the policy analyst needs synoptic vision and consummate political skills, which hardly constitute an antidote to excessive ambition.

Recasting the Distinctions

The more widely prescribed antidotes to excessive ambition in public policy turn out to be placebos, effectively obscuring the spread of the diseases they purportedly cure. But we have still to determine the appropriate ambitions of public policy, or more precisely, the conditions under which one can confidently commend what kinds of policy design.

Our approach to this determination rests on a conjecture, which we will attempt to substantiate, that the principal detractors of excess in policy have erred in the distinctions they make and hence have all hit the wrong target. Based on a correction of their aim, we will develop some distinctions of our own, thereby generating some guidelines as to when policy design may be embraced and when avoided.

Consider, first, the misplaced distinctions of piecemeal social engineers and incrementalists outlined in the preceding section. The irrelevance of the piecemeal–holistic distinction should draw attention to the other, more convincing plank in the Popperian policy platform, the need for maximal criticism of policy proposals and effects.

Turning now to laissez-faire critics of large public organizations, let us suggest they redirect their ire at *hierarchy* rather than size or publicness. For private organizations are quite capable of malfunctioning, and small governmental units are not immune to subversion of their ends by self-interested officials. As we have already noted, the limited available empirical evidence suggests that small size is not necessarily correlated with effectiveness or accountability.[2] On the other hand, a substantial literature on organizational and administrative structure points to the informational problem-solving pathologies of hierarchical systems (see, e.g., Lindblom,

1977; Thayer, 1981). Aside from the problems associated with its ties to exclusively instrumental rationality (see Chapters 2 and 3), hierarchy can obstruct the free dissemination of information, conjecture, and criticism essential to effective problem solving. The incentives are such that individuals use information as a resource in intraorganizational struggles rather than as an aid to joint problem solving (see Wilensky, 1967). Those at higher levels use their privileged command of information to solidify claims to authority. For their part, subordinates release and slant information in a manner designed to put a positive gloss on their performance. In short, hierarchy inevitably fosters distorted communication and communicative irrationality. Hierarchical systems may be adequate for routine decision making and simple tasks (Inbar, 1979) but not for problem solving in a complex and variable environment (see Chapter 3). Although hierarchy may be more likely in large organizations, size itself is no guarantee; nor will small scale necessarily dispense with hierarchy.

If laissez-faire critics were indeed to channel their energies into a critique of hierarchy, they might even get tactical support from participatory democrats (who would, unfortunately, violate the canons of *discursive* democracy by engaging in such expedient action). Thus Barber (1984, pp. 293–8) cautiously endorses quasi-market voucher schemes for education and housing, provided they proceed in tandem with community control rather than individual choice.

Finally, consider again pluralist warnings against excessive ambition in policy. Surely, the key distinction here is not between boldness and modesty, for imposed *modest* reforms can expect a similar fate in plural society. Rather, it is the fact of imposition that tempts failure, and hence the relevant distinction becomes the degree of imposition.

The common pattern emerging from our correction of the detractors' aim concerns the (variable) conditions of policy formation, pertaining especially to critical oversight, hierarchy, and imposition. Too little criticism and too much hierarchy and imposition tempt failure. These three dimensions converge on a single quality, the openness of discourse about policy. Critical oversight involves openness to challenge and counterargument; hierarchy stands condemned to the extent of its distortion of communication; and imposition means a refusal to countenance weaknesses of a policy. The importance of communicative rationality will now be explicated in our continued quest for the elusive "difference that really makes a difference" in the ambitions of public policy.

The Conditions of Policy Discourse

Designed public policies require the backing of both empirical and normative theory. Empirical theory concerns the effects of policy and normative theory the worth of such effects and the processes through which they are produced (in terms of interests and values met, violated, promoted, obstructed, or ignored). Policy debates, and hence policy design, involve communication about both kinds of theory. In practice, of course, policy arguments generally intertwine empirical and normative propositions. But as we shall see, there are schools of thought that suggest that one or the other dimension should be foreclosed, which is why we retain the two dimensions for our own analytical purposes. Thus we can say that each dimension can vary in its degree of openness. Debate is closed, and communication is distorted, to the extent of hierarchy, suppression of criticism, and imposition of a policy or design scheme upon a reluctant community. We will argue that a focus on the openness of discourse in both empirical and normative dimensions is necessary, that closure on either dimension is perilous, and that closure on both aspects simultaneously can prove disastrous.

Figure 7-1 represents diagrammatically our observation that policy communication has normative and empirical dimensions, both of which can vary from open to closed (or from free to distorted). Dichotomizing these two dimensions gives us four cells. Cell A may be termed "closed society," cell B "open society," cell C "good intentions," and cell D "practical reason." The reasons for these labels will become apparent in the discussion that follows.

Closed Society

Given the thrust of our argument so far, it should immediately be obvious that cell A risks policy disaster. Occasionally, temporarily closed communication may be justifiable, perhaps in some cases of foreign policy crisis decision making. Even here, however, a case can be made for unconstrained communication *within* a closed policy-making group (George, 1972) of the sort that characterizes the integrative encounters among instrumental rationalists discussed in Chapter 3. More generally, the inevitably weak and un-

		Communication over empirical claims	
		Closed	Open
Communication over normative claims	Closed	A	B
	Open	C	D

Figure 7–1. The conditions of policy communication.

corroborated empirical theory informing policy design will yield unanticipated and unwanted consequences. In the first instance any such errors are likely to be suppressed rather than exposed and corrected. Moreover, to the degree intended consequences *are* achieved, they will upset the actors or interests excluded from policy debate, causing subversion of, and opposition to, the policy in question.

Paradoxically, cell A is where the control of any would-be elite of policy engineers seems to be strongest. Those regarding policy design as a technical rather than a political matter would be happy with this location. Clearly, much policy analysis methodology, especially the microeconomic and explanatory kinds discussed in Chapter 6, is cast in this image. But if our characterization of cell A is correct, this situation is exactly what should be avoided. Consider two examples.

First, this style of policy formation characterizes several Latin American cases in which authoritarian governments have faced little in the way of critical debate over their efforts to put economic theory into political practice. O'Donnell (1973) coined the term "bureaucratic–authoritarianism" to characterize regimes in Brazil, Argentina, Chile, and Uruguay that coupled narrowly technocratic policy style with military coercion. In recent years, the policymakers of such regimes have been steeped in neoclassical economic theory at U.S. universities, where they developed a dogmatic view of how an economy and policy system ought to be organized. Upon being let loose on their own economies, they could engage in "experiments in radical conservative economics" (Foxley, 1983) to further their visions.

The case of Chile is instructive but by no means unique. The Pinochet regime emerging from the 1973 coup, which toppled Allende's government, embarked on an ambitious reorganization of the Chilean economy, ostensibly to fight inflation and roll back socialism. This economic overhaul involved austere stabilization measures, such as substantial cuts in social welfare programs and rigid control of the money supply. The shared ideology of regime policymakers quelled debate over the empirical validity of monetarist economic theory. And a well-armed, active state police effectively stifled the citizenry's criticisms of the normative aims and consequences of economic policies.

Turning to the Northern Hemisphere, in the 1980s the United Kingdom has experienced a government uncritically committed to a particular economic theory, paying little heed to criticisms of the theory itself, evidence about its effects, the ends it is intended to serve, and the side effects of pursuit of these ends (see Prior, 1986, for an insider's account). As unemployment mounted and economic growth moved into reverse, the guardians of the policy congratulated themselves on a shrinking public sector borrowing requirement with some manifestations of what Janis (1972) calls "groupthink."[3] Defenders of the British monetarist experiment could always plead that the long term will justify the strategy or that short-term difficulties were a result of factors such as global recession outside government's control. And indeed, an economic upturn in some regions of Britain in 1987–9 lent some support to this defense. But what is at issue here is not the economic theory's veracity, falsity, or even macrolevel ambitions but the immunity to criticism of the process and policies it inspires, their intentions, and the theory itself. Of course, the theory was attacked from outside governing circles and was gently criticized within Thatcher's cabinet. But this critical discussion had little influence on policy formation.

Possibilities for salvaging ambitious policy design in cell A might be sought in the adoption of strong moral restraints by policymakers, perhaps along the lines of the stringent ethical code commended to would-be policy scientists by Harold Lasswell (see, e.g., Lasswell, 1965b, p. 14). This strategy might work if empirical and normative knowledge about complex policy problems could be centralized in the hands of a few. In Chapter 3 it was suggested that the strategies available for any such small group confronted with complexity are ineffective. So we concur with the arguments of Popper and von Hayek discussed previously in commending suspicion of any such centralization regardless of the credentials and intentions of the individuals involved.

Cell A in our scheme promises some rather blatant shortcomings. Cells B and C have more insidious implications.

Open Society

Cell B constitutes the preferred location of Popperian enthusiasts of free criticism of policies and the theories informing them. To liberals and open-society advocates alike, all value positions are of equal validity, except, of course, for the values of free expression, honest use of language, and critical rationality intrinsic to the very idea of an open society. Popper himself treats any other values as mere subjective preferences (Williams, 1989, p. 181). Differences among normative positions are seen as ultimately irreducible,[4] and to this extent the normative dimension of communication is prematurely closed. Obviously, this kind of closure is very different to that obtaining in cell A. Cell B is relativist when it comes to normative positions, whereas A is authoritarian. But irrespective of the source of closure, both cells have little time for normative debate.

Policy design under such relativist conditions can only involve pursuit of essentially arbitrary ends (even if there is a negative utilitarian consensus on these ends). The effective pursuit of arbitrary ends raises once again Weber's specter of triumphant *zweckrationalitat*. This recognition of the dangers of instrumental rationalization of social and political life has been echoed over the years by Frankfurt School theorists such as Horkheimer and Adorno (1972) and Habermas (1984). An especially pertinent connection to public policy has been made by Tribe (1973). Our purportedly instrumental collective choices, Tribe claims, also shape our future preferences and ends and hence our future selves. A drastic manifestation of this process may be found in policy choices about genetic engineering, which may affect who we become biologically. Less extreme examples are numerous. Decisions about resources to be devoted to different kinds of education shape the preferences and personalities of the individuals experiencing that education. Policy informed by market values is itself likely to promote both adoption of such values on the part of individuals who realize they have become increasingly functional for personal betterment (or necessary to avert poverty) and a reaction against market morality by those averse to competitive struggle.

The net result of this victory of instrumental rationality is that society and polity lose control of their destiny as they cast themselves adrift on a sequence of instrumental choices whose ultimate destination cannot be predicted or controlled. Consider, for example, the tide of events set in motion by series of limited instrumental choices about nuclear weaponry.

Good Intentions

If cell B in our diagram represents the hazards of excessive concentration on the instrumental and empirical side of social problem solving and policy design, cell C constitutes a different peril, that is, exclusive focus on the normative aspects of public affairs. In cell C, open normative communication enables free discussion about elements of the right and good life, both individual and collective. Such discussion might even produce a measure of social agreement of the sort that forged the "collectivist consensus" in wartime Britain, which in turn laid the normative foundations for the subsequent development of the British welfare state.[5] This kind of discursive collective life is, of course, found in Arendt's authentic politics (see Chapter 1), which disdains issues of empirical relationships and problem solving. To the extent critical theorists believe social problem solving involves abandoning oneself to the powers of instrumental rationality, they may show similar disdain (e.g., Keane, 1984, pp. 184–6). But critical theorists need not eschew empirical analysis so long as it is regulated by the canons of communicative rationality.

A disdain for the empirical side of social problems may be fine so long as one sits in the faculty club armchair – or perhaps even in one of Arendt's councils. But when this disdain is combined with a casual concern for social problems, it becomes dangerous. Popper and von Hayek would claim that cell C is indeed the road to hell (or at least serfdom), paved as it is with good intentions. Both note that most overambitious social reformers are well meaning. Occasionally, such reformers may even gain near-universal consensus on the desirability of their project. Such was the case over the 1940s vision of a British welfare state. But any neglect of the empirical dimension means that inevitable errors in a project or its execution will not be anticipated or uncovered. As their schemes go awry, the guardians of the project may be tempted to take actions that will further obstruct its fruition, such as coercion, or the identification and repression of scapegoats. The pursuit of the widely held goal of racial desegregation through means of court-ordered busing in the United States is indicative of the possibilities here. Busing provoked opposition even from those who shared the goal of desegregation.

Practical Reason

Cells A, B, and C in our scheme are all hazardous locations for ambitious public policy. It should come as no surprise that we believe cell D is safer. Cell D's free empirical and normative dialogue recapitulates a model of politics that is discursive, democratic, and participatory. The practical dimension of this dialogue is open to the possibility of social reality itself changing as a result of discursive deliberations engaged in by the citizens constituting that reality.

In this scheme of things, it is communicative rather than instrumental rationality that governs the reconstruction of reality that is the essence of policy design. And to the extent governmental structures are inhospitable to communicative rationality, such discursive policy design should once again shun the state in favor of confronting it from an autonomous public sphere.

One implication here is that effective policy, however ambitious, requires that the "objects" of design participate in the design process (see Dryzek, 1982) such that the conjectures of analysts (or anyone else) require validation from a broader public. This conclusion was, of course, reached from a different direction in Chapter 6. Policy design therefore differs from architectural and engineering design in being a discursive rather than a manipulative process. In this light, policy design is inevitably political, for concerned stakeholders as well as policy analysts can make and challenge claims. Thus politics and analysis are integrated, but not in the sense of analysis serving the political powers that be. The policy analyst should provide critical contributions to policy discourse, as suggested at the end of the previous chapter, rather than engineer and effect policies at the behest of the powerful.

This perspective on policy design can be tied to the institutional analysis that preoccupied Part II of this study. Although incipient discursive designs have often focused on conflict resolution rather than policy design, such resolution often requires the creative design of patterns of action reflectively acceptable to participants. And the case of the Alaska Native Review Commission discussed in Chapter 6 indicates how policy design, in the form of concrete proposals for public action, can emanate from free discourse in the public sphere.

Conclusion

Like any ideal, communicative rationality in policy communication functions as a standard for the evaluation and criticism of existing practices and the design of new ones. To the extent it is violated, designed policy can expect to err. To the extent this standard is met, one should not shrink from ambitious schemes for the resolution of social problems.

If purist followers of Arendt and an earlier generation of critical theorists remain unconvinced by these extensions of the classical model of politics and communicative rationality into social problem solving, they would do well to ponder the alternatives. If complacency in the face of the world's pressing problems is ruled out, and if policy-making inspired by exclusively instrumental notions of rationality is both inept and authoritarian, then the only real option left is to coerce the world into becoming a place where one does not have to think so hard. Policy interventions would have pretty straightforward effects in such a world, which would have little need for either instrumental or communicative rationality. Whether rustic and conservative, laissez-faire and classically liberal, uniform and fascistic, or administered and Stalinist, any such world is not a very attractive place.

PART IV

Political Science

CHAPTER 8

The Mismeasure of Political Man

Although the policy orientation addressed in Chapters 6 and 7 has gained popularity in recent decades, most social scientists still regard explanation and interpretation of social phenomena as their first tasks. In keeping with this emphasis, this chapter and the two that follow contemplate the rationality of social science per se rather than of institutions (Part II) or policies (Part III).

In terms of the categories accepted by most Western political scientists, the focus of this study therefore now shifts from normative to empirical inquiry. Not that matters are really quite that simple. For as Taylor (1969) has demonstrated, empirical social inquiry tends to "secrete" normative judgments, if only by identifying the bounds of the possible in social and political arrangements. "Can't implies shouldn't" – it is unreasonable to aspire to that which cannot be attained. In keeping with Taylor's point, I shall attend closely to the normative secretions of empirical social science.

But why should we actually care about social science? Does it really have any material connection, for better or for worse, to the prospects for democracy and emancipation? Or is social science inevitably just a backwater, a safe haven for misanthropes, malcontents, and pedants? I would argue that social science in general and political science in particular do indeed merit three chapters in a book on discursive democracy for the following reasons.

Social and political sciences are more important in contemporary politics than they might at first seem. Public officials occasionally lend an ear to economists; in the 1960s in the United States they even listened to sociologists, much to their eventual regret. Political scientists have always had more trouble finding the ear of the powers that be, except on national security and foreign policy issues (think of Henry Kissinger or Zbigniew Brzezinski). This lack of direct influence is not for want of trying. Leading political scientists have for a century or more sought scientifically informed reform of an antiquated American political system, only to have their hopes repeatedly dashed by the recalcitrance of the very institutions they sought to change (Seidelman and Harpham, 1985).

The actual influence of political science in public affairs has for the most part taken place behind the backs of its practitioners. Moreover, contrary to the reformist hopes of prominent American political scientists from Lester Ward to Theodore Lowi, this influence has generally involved legitimation of the status quo. To use an idiom I shall deploy in the pages that follow, political science draws on and reinforces the dominant discourse of society and polity. In this chapter I substantiate this claim through reference to the most popular kind of empirical political science, opinion survey research.

An equally important justification for attending to political science is the role it could play in processes of emancipation, even though this role bears little relation to the current shape of the discipline. Critical theory must come from somewhere. That somewhere cannot be conventional, hierarchically ordered political organizations whose political products are bound to be of the instrumental kind: platforms, strategies, and the like. A more promising source is an intellectual community that, *if it is true to its own claims to cognitive rationality*, must be committed to communicative rationality in the polity in which it moves. This essential connection between the cognitive and communicative rationality of an intellectual community is established toward the end of Chapter 10.

Whether one calls this intellectual community "political science" is not very important. Nor does it matter whether its activities proceed inside or outside universities. Certainly, the description I have just advanced does not resemble the contemporary discipline, which spends much of its time undermining its claims to cognitive rationality (as I shall argue). Nevertheless, the study of politics as it *could* be – and, I shall argue in Chapter 10, *must* be to warrant a claim to cognitive rationality – is an obvious location for the generation of critical theories of politics. For the community engaging in that study is, by definition, the locus of a polity's interpretation and resolution of conceptual and empirical problems about political life. So if the material forces that render political reconstruction a possibility are indeed abroad, as argued in earlier chapters, this locus is necessarily going to matter in processes of political change. Here I assume, as must any critical theorist, that history does not unfold with an iron necessity.

But in what sense is the activity I have just described and proposed political *science?* Ultimately, this proves not to matter very much, provided the activity in question is cognitively rational. Throughout Part IV I shall occasionally invoke the name of science, which some regard as an exemplary cognitively rational activity. I do this not because I worship in the temple of science but to convince those who do that *even* a commitment to science undermines objectivism, instrumental rationality, a search for general laws of society, large-n statistical studies, and so forth. Conversely, I shall argue that such a commitment points directly toward communicative rationality. Students of politics less beholden to science may still need convincing of the virtues of communicative rationality and discursive democracy in their inquiries, but in different fashion.

In this chapter I undertake a critical scrutiny of the most popular instrument in the "scientific" study of politics, the opinion survey. This instrument will be subjected to a scrutiny made possible by recent advances in the philosophy of science and political discourse analysis. I will argue that regardless of any utility when applied to other questions, such an instrument can produce only a fundamentally flawed account of politically relevant human dispositions. Further, I will claim that extensive use of opinion surveys functions in a particularly subtle and unexpected way to reinforce a prevailing political order of instrumental domination and control, which treats mass politics in terms of individuals who are mostly passive and only occasionally and minimally disposed to participate in political life. Conversely, I argue that this widespread use obstructs the discursive democratization of politics, which would involve more in the way of active dialogue among competent citizens. Given the dominant status of survey methods in political science, this chapter therefore portrays the mismeasure of political man.[1]

I have suggested that social scientists are well placed, should they so choose, to contribute to the discursive democratization of politics. To the extent students of mass politics remain beholden to the opinion survey, they are, however unwittingly, obstructing such democratization. Thus the mismeasure of political man is of more than parochial disciplinary concern.

Measuring Political Man

Speculations as to human political characteristics and capabilities are probably as old as organized politics itself. The diversity of speculations suggests political man may be a multifaceted creature. Bits of evidence selectively adduced can back the dismal view of man underlying Hobbes's bleak political prognosis, the far more cheerful interpretation that informs Rousseau's rustic utopia, and most points in between. Whereas there is clearly more to political theorizing than examination of individual human attributes, a philosophical anthropology underpins every political theorist's conception of actual, possible, and desirable political orders. For example, if substantial numbers of people were not strongly disposed to knavery, there would be no point in "designing institutions for knaves," to use Hume's famous dictum.

Empirical scrutiny of political man was once fairly casual. Only in the last few decades has systematic empirical inquiry been brought to bear. A number of tools rooted in fields as diverse as social psychology, physiology, psychoanalytics, and sociobiology have been utilized. But by far the most popular approach has involved the application of survey research methods, especially in conjunction with the fields of public opinion and voting studies.

At risk of doing violence to a substantial and nuanced body of literature, the principal findings of these last two fields as they relate to the content and distribution of politically relevant characteristics and capabilities may be summarized as follows. Most people are uninterested in and uninformed about politics. When pressed, they express attitudes highly intolerant of unpopular minorities. There is little consistency across any political opinions they do express. Their minimal political behavior is often under the sway of social and psychological forces the individual does not fully understand (in the standard sociopsychological model of voting behavior, vote choice is determined by attitudes, which in turn are affected by social forces). Moreover, they are prepared to adjust that behavior to conform to their perceptions of the opinions of those around them (Noelle-Neumann, 1984). Although some recent American studies have found more in the way of constraint across issue attitudes and issue-oriented voting than in the past (see especially Nie, Verba, and Petrocik, 1976) and substantial retrospective judgment by voters on the performance of governments (Fiorina, 1981), these findings call for but marginal readjustments to an unflattering portrait of political man (Nie, Verba, and Petrocik, 1981; Kinder and Sears, 1983, pp. 664–8; Kinder, 1983, pp. 393–7).[2] For the most part, Blondel's (1981, p. 48) surmise still holds: "Politics is too distant, too complex, too mysterious, and therefore too frightening for the common man to be prepared to be involved."

Such micropolitical contentions have clear macropolitical import. Indeed, just about every study reflecting upon mass political behavior pays homage to the inspirational force of democratic theory in imparting meaning to the empirical quest (see, e.g., Berelson, 1952; Asher, 1983, p. 341). Moreover, contemporary liberal democratic theory has drawn support from this empirical literature in arguing for limited and indirect popular influence in political life (see, e.g., Dahl, 1956; Sartori, 1962; Eckstein, 1966). In this spirit, Almond and Verba's (1963) "civic culture" celebrates liberal democracy but demands enough deference and parochialism to regulate the dangers of excessive participation. Although some unanticipated political developments over the past few decades have seen this contemporary theory lose much of its vitality, the weight of survey findings supports no alternative theory. So Sartori (1987, pp. 102–10) can still deploy these findings to back his unrepentant account of limited democracy. And popularizations of this view may still be found in introductory political science textbooks; for example, in Dye and Ziegler's (1987, pp. 14–17) bestseller the "irony of democracy" is that elites rather than masses are the guardians of democratic values.

Opinion surveys have met with a variety of criticisms since their introduction to political science. Some dislike the method (e.g., Lane, 1962), some the macropolitical implications of the field's findings (e.g., Pateman, 1970, pp. 5–7). Yet the political opinion survey continues to flourish, an enduring legacy of the behavioral revolution that swept the discipline in the 1950s. If political science has a dominant method, survey analysis is it (see Achen, 1983, pp. 69–70). In 1979–80, 35 percent of the articles in the three major American political science journals involved survey research (Presser, 1984, p. 96). Moreover, the conjunction of survey research and voting studies is frequently paraded as the most scientific branch of the study of politics, proof positive that political *science* has arrived [see Beck (1986, p. 241) for a representative statement]. The trappings are evident: covering-law explanations,[3] systematic bodies of theory, cumulative research programs, testable hypotheses, quantitative methods, a community of like-minded practitioners, and "engineering" applications in consultation to political leaders.

Whereas individuals who reject the whole idea of naturalistic explanation in social science (e.g., Taylor, 1971) will find support in this chapter, my own critique is more limited. For I focus here on a single instrument, the opinion survey, put to just one kind of use, the study of the content and distribution of political capabilities. My critique of the instrument as put to this use might be accepted without subscription to grander arguments against the possibility of social *science*. In fact, my account takes at face value the contention that politics can indeed be approached through scientific instruments and that the opinion survey really is such an instrument, though the understanding of science that informs my analysis shares the postempiricist rejection of objectivism.[4]

Cognitively rational rejection of any one research program, such as that encompassing the opinion survey, must await a demonstration that some rival program possesses superior explanatory or problem-solving power (Lakatos, 1970; Laudan, 1977, pp. 106–14; see also Chapter 10). Candidates include intensive ideographic interaction with subjects (Lane, 1962); Popperian situational analysis, which can explore deviations from a baseline of individual rationality (Farr, 1985); the intentional approach to public opinion outlined by Brunner (1977); and experimental work within a public choice paradigm (e.g., Orbell, Schwartz-Shea, and Simmons, 1984). Given that the analysis of this chapter is highly critical of research programs organized around the opinion survey, it suggests the alternatives merit further attention and development. My own preference, which I shall develop in the following chapter, is for an approach that takes the subjectivity of individuals seriously. Unlike the other alternatives just mentioned, this approach is consistent with the ideas about freely discursive political life sketched in Parts II and III.

Understanding Scientific Instruments

Scientific instruments provide access to phenomena for which explanation is sought. So an electron microscope yields access to the molecular world, and large telescopes enable exploration of galactic forces. To be readable, an instrument must embody a theory; for example, interpretation of the readings on a thermometer in terms of temperature is rooted in thermodynamic theory. As Popper

(1972b, p. 107n) puts it, all scientific observations are "interpretations of the facts observed; they are interpretations in the light of theories." Theory-neutral scientific instruments cannot exist.[5] In the early days of an instrument's use this theory of instrumentation will typically be in the forefront of its users' consciousness. With further use of the instrument the theory can fade from awareness, so the instrument can yield seemingly direct access to observed phenomena. In reading a thermometer, one does not need to be aware of how Boyle's law is applying; one simply reads temperature. The instrument becomes like a window through which a room is viewed; the observer can let the instrument slip from awareness. One need be no more conscious of the theoretical underpinnings of the instrument than of the principles of grammar and syntax when reading a book.

The similarities between reading a book and reading a scientific instrument are explored by Heelan (1983), who notes, following Gadamer (1975), that in reading a text we are from the very beginning projecting a meaning for the text as a whole. Otherwise, our reading would be incoherent. This projection is always rooted in the cultural milieu of the reader, which is why such varied readings of classic texts like *Das Kapital* or the Bible are possible. Similarly, in making an isolated reading on an instrument we are always projecting a meaning for the set of readings (on one or more instruments) we will obtain. This act of projection too is culturally conditioned. Kuhn (1970b) was among the first to note that scientific communities can be analyzed in cultural terms (see also Garfinkel, Lynch, and Livingston, 1981). Thus reading a scientific instrument involves the application of culturally acquired capacities (Heelan, 1983, p. 185). A common set of readings can convey different meanings to adherents of (say) wave and corpuscular traditions in optics (in the unlikely event that one set of readings will interest both traditions). The "text" generated by a set of readings of scientific instruments is, then, a cultural artifact.

This discussion of the culture in scientific instrumentation is not meant to disparage particular scientific instruments or research traditions. Heelan (1983, p. 189) notes that transparent, culture-soaked technologies of instrumentation generally characterize the advanced stages of research programs when there is "broad agreement about general outlines of scientific understanding." So analysis of this culture should not take the form of a search for correctable bias and error, for the culture is properly intrinsic to the instrument. Worries about the theoretical grounding of instruments are found only in the early phases of a program. Instruments drop from consciousness as practitioners become more adept in their use.

Heelan's account contains no means for the evaluation of instruments, just a way of understanding their function in the practice of science. I will argue later that we can, at least in social science, use the cultural dimension of scientific instrumentation to develop evaluative questions. But first, let us consider the opinion survey instrument in Heelan's terms.

Theory and Culture in the Survey Instrument

The limiting case of a bad scientific instrument would be one thoroughly opaque to its users. Practitioners could make no sense of stimuli produced by the instrument; think, for example, of an untrained person confronted with the output of a mass spectrometer. Of course, generally only trained people confront mass spectrometers. So how could a community employing an opaque instrument possibly exist?

Confessions of such opacity come from the quarter of survey research itself. Achen argues both that the opinion survey is the major quantitative political science method and that its users do not know what its readings convey: "Bluntly put, political scientists do not know what survey responses are measuring" (Achen, 1983, p. 80). More technically, researchers are unable to choose between competing simulations of measurement error in the absence of a "mathematical theory of the survey response" (Achen, 1983, p. 80). Survey researchers also have no good theory to explain the impact of different phrasing and ordering of questions, while being only too aware that wording and ordering can make a huge difference to responses, having devoted substantial attention to such matters over the years. But if the theory is missing, how can a meaningful instrument exist?

The answer may be that Achen overstates his case, so only the refinement, not the creation of what he calls "theories of data" (i.e., instrumentation), is needed. Perhaps the survey instrument is currently light on theory but heavy on culture. This disparity reinforces the need to attend to the culture of the instrument, which, let me stress again, is not the same as saying that the instrument suffers from bias and error amenable to discovery and correc-

tion by practitioners. Such attention would still be justified if the
theory were better.

Political Discourse in Scientific Instruments

The aspects of a (scientific) culture embodied in an instrument are
not easily assessed empirically, for like any culture, they are unspoken and taken for granted by users of the instrument, who are
typically unaware even of the need for consensus upon them. So
how may one speak of the hitherto unspoken?

The appropriate procedure here begins by treating these unspoken aspects as the underpinnings of a discourse. In these terms,
a discourse embodies a shared set of capabilities that enable the
assemblage of words, phrases, and sentences into meaningful
"texts" intelligible to readers or listeners (see, e.g., van Dijk,
1985). With Heelan's account of the essential identity of texts and
sets of readings on scientific instruments in mind, these capabilities
can also be said to refer to the assemblage of instrument readings
into intelligible wholes (Heelan himself does not make this extension). Similar un-self-conscious, taken-for-granted processes operate in both ordinary language and scientific instrumentation.

Political scientists have rarely attempted to bring such processes
to explicit awareness. One exception is Edelman's (1977) analysis
of the political positions embedded in seemingly clinical and technical discourse among those who administer to the poor on behalf
of the welfare state. Unlike Edelman, the present focus is not on
the discourse of a particular scientific or professional community
but on the discourse implicit in a scientific instrument like the
opinion survey.

However, in common with Edelman, my focus will be upon the
specifically political aspects of discourse. Sociolinguists have not
generated any universally applicable set of questions with which to
scrutinize a discourse. The questions one asks depend upon the
purpose of the inquiry. Given that my purpose has to do with the
study of politics, I will stress the political and hence engage in what
Seidel (1985) and Alker and Sylvan (1986) call political discourse
analysis. The political aspect of a discourse includes the following
four elements.

1. An ontology, that is, a set of entities whose existence is recognized or
   constructed. Examples might include utility maximizers, social class-
   es, or the Hegelian *Geist*.

2. Assignment of degrees of agency to these entities. Some may be granted subject status (e.g., prime movers in political events or the proletariat in the Marxist theory of revolution); others may be categorized as objects (e.g., slaves in the antebellum South or Japanese in American World War II propaganda).
3. Among those with agency, a recognition of some motives (such as self-interest, self-doubt, anxiety, moral rectitude) and a denial of others. For example, Edelman (1977, pp. 20–1) points to professional interpretation of rebellion among the poverty stricken in terms of psychological deviance rather than reasonable assessment of conditions and options.
4. Conceptions of what is natural and unnatural in political relationships. Taken-for-granted hierarchies based on gender, birth, race, professional expertise, or age are possibilities here.

Before proceeding, let me stress that the remainder of this essay does not address the diverse cultural dispositions, ideological aspirations, and political leanings of opinion researchers themselves. Rather, my concern is with the discourse implicit in their instrument; what follows is rooted in the philosophy rather than the sociology of science. What, then, can we make of the discourse of survey instrumentation in terms of the four elements just enumerated?

The Political Discourse of the Survey Instrument

The ontology of this discourse contains, first and foremost, individuals, understood as structured bundles of psychological attributes. Political behavior is interpreted as the product of psychological forces; social factors can affect this behavior, but such factors are mediated by individual psychology. Individuals are seen as capable of possessing beliefs, opinions, and attitudes about politics that have a real existence outside and independent of political discussion or action. Clearly, the survey encounter itself does not involve such discussion or action (beyond minimal and highly constrained invitations to think through responses to open-ended questions); practitioners see any such presence as contamination.[6] So it must be assumed that an individual's beliefs, opinions, and attitudes about politics are invariant across the degree of action or inaction involved in a situation (though of course survey researchers are interested in how attitudes change with time and political history, e.g., between two waves of a panel survey).

Beyond a particular kind of individual, the ontology of the instrument's discourse recognizes but one kind of political world. This world is characterized by competitive struggle between well-defined entities such as issue positions, parties, candidates, and interests. The political behavior of ordinary individuals therefore consists of choosing sides (with varying degrees of commitment) in such a struggle.

Agency is distributed unequally by the discourse of the survey instrument among the individuals recognized. Full subject status is granted only to the investigators designing and interpreting surveys, who are masters of their situation. At the opposite extreme, interviewers are objects. They must behave like automata as they administer the instrument; otherwise the dreaded interviewer bias will affect responses. The respondents themselves fall somewhere between these two extremes. To the degree they autonomously form their opinions and act upon them, they are subjects. But full subjects would be of no interest to opinion research that strives for covering-law explanations of political behavior. Covering-law ambition is intrinsic to any social science instrument that isolates variables from the totality of the relevant characteristics of an individual and proceeds to seek associations between these variables across individuals. The influences uncovered by such explanations (such as peer attitudes, party identification, social class, party propaganda, etc.) must remain mysterious to the respondent. If these influences were not mysterious, one could dispense with the elaborate survey instrument and simply ask people why they act or behave as they do. Thus ordinary people are treated as though they respond to stimuli according to the way they are programmed, such that they are incapable of freely crafting responses to stimuli. In this sense, they may be termed reactive rather than active. Their behavior reflects the causal influences upon them; they are objects.

However, as already noted, the survey instrument allows respondents an element of subjective status. The behavior of subjects requires some motivation. The motives recognized by the discourse of the survey instrument are all instrumental in character in that they involve behavior designed to achieve some end. The end can involve perceptions of material self-interest, sectional interest, or the public interest or a simple desire to see one party, candidate, or issue position prevail or the political system survive. The content of the end and the (ir)rationality of the action can be investigated using the instrument. But it is intrinsic to the discourse that, ontologically speaking, there are such things as ends and instrumental actions and that rationality consists of nothing other than instrumental action.

The point to be stressed here is that political behavior is seen as coterminous with other kinds of social or economic behavior. The very first voting studies were carried out by Lazarsfeld and his associates after he was frustrated by an inability to survey consumer behavior. Whether he turned to voting for the intellectual reason that consumer behavior is too complex to study directly (see Natchez, 1985, pp. 47–53) or for baser pecuniary motives (Berns, 1962, p. 57), he clearly thought the same techniques appropriate to both areas. This original sin of the field was not absolved by the demise of Lazarsfeld, Columbia, and social determinism and the victory of Michigan and social psychology in the 1950s. As Michigan's Miller put it, "we did not have any theory which argued that political behavior was any different from social or economic behavior" (Miller, 1960; quoted in Natchez, 1985, p. 163). The instrument today still does not allow the possibility that individuals may shift gears when it comes to politics. Achen (1983, p. 70) notes that political methodologists have made few original contributions to survey methodology, preferring to "shop for hand-me-down techniques invented by statisticians, psychologists, and economists."

Finally, the instrument's discourse embodies a "natural" political relationship in the survey encounter itself, which is thoroughly structured and dominated by the survey designer. The respondent must not fully understand the purpose of the encounter, for such understanding would affect its results and take us into the realm of the experimenter effect dreaded by experimental psychologists.

Each of these elements of the discourse of the survey instrument should sound quite innocuous and unremarkable to those schooled in mainstream political science.[7] I will argue that in combination they undermine the claim of the instrument to tell us much about politically relevant human characteristics. What, then, renders political dispositions impenetrable to this particular instrument?

The Uniqueness of the Political

To pursue this issue, a more basic question must be asked: What is politics? One popular answer is that politics involves power and the instrumental pursuit of interest (see, e.g., Dahl, 1984, pp. 8–

35). The commonalities between this notion of politics and the discourse embedded in the survey instrument should be obvious (at least to the degree the subjectivity of respondents is recognized in the latter). These commonalities arise not just in terms of the kind of political world recognized in the instrument's ontology but also with respect to questions of agency and motivation. So is not the instrument ideally suited to the study of political behavior? Indeed, if we dig a little deeper, we can trace both the popular definition of politics in terms of power and interest and some aspects of the survey instrument's discourse to a classical liberal conception of man in society. Opinion researchers may be unaware of this connection. Thus Natchez (1985) argues that voting studies have been sundered from the liberal constitutionalist view of democracy that would give them political bite. But any such gaps could be easily bridged at the conscious level, for they do not exist at the unconscious, taken-for-granted level of discourse.

The alternative account of political life introduced in Chapter 1 defines politics in terms of public debate among people deciding how individually and collectively they shall act and interact. This classical conception of politics goes hand in hand with communicative rationality, and I tried to show in earlier chapters how discursive and participatory practices and institutions could be inspired by it. In this chapter I will use the classical model primarily as a critical device, along lines suggested by Ball (1983a), to highlight the partiality of the survey instrument's discourse. Critical perspective might also be provided by Marxism, as indicated by Lindblom (1982a),[8] psychoanalytics, cybernetics, or microeconomics.[9] The classical model is used here not just because it fits the broader emphasis of this book on discursive democracy but also because it is tied to some political alternatives at one end of a continuum of democratic possibilities. Its distance on this spectrum from the conception of politics implicit in the survey instrument makes it well placed to highlight all the key implications of that discourse, of which a reexamination is now in order.

A Classically Political Critique of the Instrument

To begin, an ontology that treats a person as a bundle of structured attributes and conceives of mass politics in terms of an agglomeration of such individuals finds little resonance in the classical model, which sees the production of political opinion as an eminently fluid, collective, and public affair. Hence political processes can proceed and conclude in ways that do not simply reflect and aggregate individual dispositions, be these dispositions fixed and predetermined or flexible and malleable. The survey instrument's recognition of causal social influences upon individuals hardly does justice to such possibilities. It allows that man is a social being, admitting influences rooted in factors such as role playing or social networks. So, for example, the effect upon individuals of the content and distribution of opinions among friends and neighbors can be investigated (Huckfeldt and Sprague, 1987). But the instrument does not allow that man can be a political being in the classical sense. Social man is constrained within or driven by necessity into a web of relationships; (classically) political man is free to create and recreate relationships. These creative possibilities cannot be expressed in the political world recognized by the instrument's ontology, where individuals can only choose sides in struggles.

According to the discursive classical conception of politics, one should not expect any evidence of political perceptions and beliefs outside the context of political action (the second aspect of the instrument's individualistic ontology noted earlier). Such disembodied and constrained beliefs are sought by opinion researchers in the form of ideology or, in recent more sophisticated work, scripts and schemas (see Kinder, 1983, pp. 414–15). By classical lights they are a veritable hindrance to the ideal of free, action-oriented political debate, so we should rejoice if we do not find them and criticize them when we do.

Conversely, one should regard any apparently issueless thinking disclosed by the survey instrument not as a defect of the individual but as a defect of the kinds of discourse in which this individual is engaged. It is only through their expression in political action that (classically) political attitudes and behavior can be discerned. To be called political, cogitation should be related to, and revealed in, action itself or action-oriented debate.[10] The survey encounter fails here because it is artificial, disembodied, divorced from action, and hence nonpolitical. At best, it can only pick up on the echoes of past situations in which people were more engaged politically, which might show up, for example, in reasons given for current party loyalties.

The broad point here is that the kind of interaction between the analyst and the object of his or her inquiry should be capable of generating the kind of information the analyst seeks. For example,

van Dijk (1984, p. 5) argues that his structured discursive interviews do capture what he wants to explore about racially preju-
diced talk precisely because the interview itself is a conversation
with a stranger.

One does find intimations of such concerns in the writings of
opinion researchers. For example, Gant and Davis (1984) argue
that apparently ignorant responses to survey questions indicate
only mental economy in information processing; once individuals
have processed information about issues or candidates into choices,
that information is rationally discarded. In similar spirit, Key's
(1966) attempted resurrection of the issue-oriented voter argues for
a focus on issues only in the context of the judgments people make
about the parties they could vote for and that there is no sense in
looking for any feelings about issues outside this act of choice. In
all other respects Key subscribes to the discourse of more orthodox
opinion researchers. His departure here is minimal. For the kind of
context he (like Gant and Davis) emphasizes – selection from a
predetermined menu of candidates or parties – is only marginally
political in the classical sense. But even this mild heresy was rejected out of hand, rather than argued against, by the mainstream,
which simply could not fathom what Key was up to (see Campbell,
1966). However limited his departure, Key verged on challenging
an element of the survey instrument's discourse; such curt dismiss-
al is exactly what discourse analysis would predict.[11]

Further intimation of the importance of an acting context may be
found in an opinion researcher's concession that "identically word-
ed questions actually have different meanings over time as the social
and political contexts change" (Asher, 1983, p. 348; see also Nie et
al., 1976, pp. 10–12). If one allows that a crucial dimension of
political context is the degree to which it is action related, this
recognition is potentially devastating. Thus the fact that survey
respondents frequently express highly intolerant attitudes toward
unpopular minorities is of little concern from the perspective of
classical politics because people rarely act upon those attitudes (see
Natchez, 1985, p. 112).

More generally, actions are not easily predicted from survey
responses (Niemi, 1986, p. 237). Survey researchers can investigate
this point further by incorporating different scenarios in the instrument in an attempt to represent the genuine dilemmas of real life.
Thus Schuman (1972) demonstrates that the number of people that
can be classified as opposed to racial discrimination depends on the

scenario incorporated in the question. Yet the genuine dilemmas of life take place in the context of interaction with and about real people; nobody suffers from the expression of intolerance in a disembodied survey interview. The incorporation of action scenarios in the instrument can at best capture only expressed dispositions toward action rather than action itself. As Elisabeth Noelle-Neumann, a German opinion researcher of some renown, admits of her own survey scenarios: "But what a weak situation is offered by an interview of this kind – how different it is from life, from experience, from the sensations of reality" (Noelle-Neumann, 1984, p. 18).

It might be countered at this juncture that the opinion survey is designed only to measure attitudes, and at most the expressed intentions that constitute what may be termed the action component of attitudes (Sudman and Bradburn, 1983, pp. 123–5), rather than to predict actions from attitudes. But survey researchers in political science themselves see this lack of predictive power as a serious lacuna in their efforts to develop a science of public opinion directly relevant to *political* science rather than just psychology (Niemi, 1986, pp. 237–8). As long as this gap remains, one should hesitate before applying the results of opinion surveying to macrolevel theories of democracy and politics.[12]

Turning now to the question of agency, here too the discourse of the survey instrument proves (classically) nonpolitical. Recall that this discourse distinguishes between autonomous "subject" researchers and largely reactive "object" respondents. Nothing further from the classical conception of political relationships as discursive and pedagogical can be imagined (short of a system of command). Reactive individuals under the sway of causal influences have no place in classical politics. The scathing reactions to Lane's (1962) departure from the survey instrument and its discourse are instructive here. Lane employs in-depth interviews to investigate individuals' political attitudes and finds more coherent structure than do the survey researchers. Kinder (1983, p. 399) dismisses Lane on the grounds that such encounters create ideology rather than merely report upon it. The survey researcher fears introducing such interactive and productive cogitation into the survey instrument's encounter, for to the extent it occurs, respondents become unrepresentative of the larger population, and the interview experience will differ across respondents (Weisberg, 1986, p. 299). Yet if Kinder's criticism is on target, Lane should be congratulated for inadvertently adhering to the classical canons by seeking cogitation in the context of a more truly political encounter. (In passing, it should be noted that the "ideology" Lane seeks to uncover would be inconsistent with classical principles.)

Now consider again the question of recognized motives embedded in the survey instrument. The idea that motivation is only instrumental is thoroughly consistent with politics conceived in terms of power and the pursuit of interest. But from a classical perspective, such behavior constitutes an invasion of the communicative and discursive rationality of politics, in which individuals publicly and jointly reason toward collective ends and actions (cf. Barber, 1984, p. 151), by an exclusively instrumental rationality appropriate to different aspects of life (such as economic production and exchange or engineering and technology).

Finally, consider once more the "natural" political relationship found in the instrument, specifically its domination by the survey designer. Such domination is absolutely essential, for if the respondent understood that the investigator were trying to discern causal influences upon individuals of which they were unaware, a negative reaction might intrude. If informed of the alleged causal laws governing their behavior, they might even change that behavior, thereby subverting the law. Widespread dissemination of causal knowledge about individual behavior can conceivably undermine the empirical regularities in behavior that alleged laws capture (Gewirth, 1954). Of course, opinion researchers themselves have an interest in maximizing dissemination of their work. But this just highlights once again the difference between the aspirations of members of a community and the inherent characteristics of the instrument they wield. The discourse of the survey instrument has a subtle stake in perpetuating the reactive side of human behavior and suppressing the active aspect. For the generalizations it seeks are meaningful only if behavior is repetitive and regularized across individuals and across time. Such behavior is, of course, inconsistent with the classical idea of politics.

This last criticism applies with special force to the extent the instrument treats individuals as plastic and reactive objects. However, as already noted, the instrument's discourse also admits instrumentally motivated subjects. Laws about aggregates of this second kind of individual can be "agentistic generalizations," which are immune to the kind of subversion just discussed. The best-known agentistic generalizations are found in microeconomics, where the validity of laws of supply and demand depends on the instrumental rationality of large numbers of individuals. The aggregate result does not change to the extent each individual is aware of his or her miniscule contribution to the operation of the law in a particular market. But even such agentistic microeconomic laws apply only as long as the people they are about adhere to particular standards of behavior – such as rational maximization – which in principle they can choose to violate (Wilson, 1984, pp. 231–2). So even if it renounces social psychology and adopts microeconomics, thereafter to seek only agentistic generalizations, the survey instrument still has a stake in perpetuating a certain kind of constrained behavior inconsistent with classical politics.

Democratic Alternatives

It should be clear by now that there is a conception of politics to which the opinion survey instrument is thoroughly appropriate and another version of the political with which the instrument is incommensurable. Why not call a truce at this point, and let each side investigate its own kind of politics in the manner it sees fit? Although this kind of compromise might displease survey enthusiasts who believe their findings should aspire to more universal validity, at least their community would secure a prominent place.

Unfortunately, the truce has already been violated by those with broader ambitions for the survey instrument. This section will explicate the nature and implications of this violation through reference to three models of democracy. Two of these models are recognized by the instrument's discourse. The third is rooted in the classical conception of politics and so cannot be encompassed by the survey instrument.

Opinion researchers have always proclaimed an interest in major theoretical questions about the participatory potential of the masses. Referring to the study of the determinants of vote choice, Asher (1983, p. 341) states, "This research agenda of course reflects enduring questions of democratic theory about the role, competence, and performance of a democratic citizenry." From Berelson, Lazarsfeld, and McPhee (1954) on, this interest led to the debunking of a "classical" theory of democracy. "Classical" theory as portrayed by opinion surveyors for purposes of empirical test posits instrumentally rational, enlightened, politically aware, and issue-oriented voters making independent reasoned choices among candidates and parties. This theory was seemingly refuted, and "contemporary" democratic theorists erected in its stead a version of democracy that allows limited citizen access to political power and applauds widespread political apathy for its functional contribution to democratic stability. This version bears a striking resemblance to politics as actually practiced in the United States.

The results of opinion research that undermined "classical" democratic theory were in fact corroborating liberal constitutionalist democratic theory, as a close reading of Natchez (1985) should make clear. The contemporary theory itself proves just a warmed-over version of liberal constitutionalism (Pateman, 1980, p. 59). More recently, rational choice theorists of the Rochester school have attempted to resurrect the "classical" model, so far with questionable empirical corroboration (Weisberg, 1986). Thus the discourse of opinion research recognizes just two democratic possibilities. One is contemporary, liberal constitutionalist, and essentially identical with the model of liberal democracy introduced in Chapter 6. The other is "classical" and hyperrationalistic.

The curious aspect of "classical" democratic theory as portrayed by opinion researchers is that it never existed prior to its description in the works of Berelson and his successors. It is either myth or caricature, as Pateman (1970, pp. 16–21) makes abundantly clear. Yet despite the exposé of Pateman and others, opinion researchers (even those who want to revive the model) cling to the myth. So Asher (1983, p. 376) equates instrumentally rational prospective voting (with an eye to what candidates actually will do when in office) with rehabilitation of the "rational independent citizen of classical democratic theory." Similarly, Beck (1986, p. 246) states that "voting on the issues (or policy voting) long has been a cherished ideal of democratic theory."

This rational independent citizen, thought to have been debunked by the early voting studies and now revived in the hands of the Rochester school, cannot come from liberal constitutionalist democratic theory's conception of political man. Nor can this citizen come from a correct understanding of classical politics, which has no place for atomistic individuals. So where does he come from? Let me suggest that students of voting behavior invented a "classical" theory within the confines of a discourse of individualism, instrumental behavior, and cogitation outside action. This discourse allowed them to see nothing else, such as the true classical conception of politics.

Perhaps the best way of highlighting the difference between the "classical" theory of opinion researchers and the true classical theory is through reference to the role of ideology. In the "classical" theory, ideology plays a positive role: As Kinder (1983, p. 391) puts it, "interest in the possibility of ideological reasoning was and still is an expression of concern for the quality and very possibility of democratic forms of government." In true classical politics, ideology is despised as an impediment to unconstrained political debate, fit only to be criticized and shattered (see, e.g., Geuss, 1981, pp. 26–44).

Despite the omissions in their enumeration of democratic possibilities, opinion researchers have clearly invaded the territory of classical politics and debates about democratic alternatives. Survey discourse recognizes only liberal constitutionalist and hyperrationalistic "classical" options. The other major strand in theories of democracy may be termed republican, participatory, or (more truly) classical. Pateman (1980, p. 59) refers to this strand as the "neglected classical theory of participatory democracy."[13] The opinion researchers' recognition of two models of democracy seems at first sight able to address the question of mass political competence, but in fact it misses the point of the main democratic debate, which pits liberal constitutionalists against classical participatory enthusiasts (as, e.g., in Chapter 6).

Inasmuch as empirical opinion research calls into doubt mass political competence (by refuting the "classical" model) and corroborates liberal constitutionalism, it implies more participatory democratic options, such as the one sought by the true classical model, are unattainable. A truce between opinion surveyors and the true classical model under such circumstances would merely cover a defeat for the classical.

Some Larger Implications

Such a defeat might be greeted with equanimity in some quarters. Perhaps nothing is lost with the demise of classical politics and the absence of instruments to study it. For is not this classical idea itself lost in the mists of time, along with the Athenian *polis*? Are not those who seek its resurrection romantic dreamers with a normative vision, as opposed to the empirical scientists of opinion research? Is not instrumental, individualistic, reactive, and limited power politics – allowing at best what Barber (1984) calls "thin democracy" – now universal? It is noteworthy that Coleman (1986, pp. 1317–8) explains the midcentury growth of survey analysis in American sociology through reference to the demise of integrated local communities (of the sort that might be hospitable to discursive classical politics) and the concurrent development of national masses of atomistic individuals confronted as audiences by corporate and governmental actors.

Classical politics is a minority interest in today's world, and in the form used for the critical purposes of the bulk of this chapter it may seem utopian. Yet there is growing potential for movement toward a classical style of politics in public life, as earlier chapters should have made clear. Thus the classical conception poses an authentic challenge to the liberal constitutionalist version of politics.

In the light of this choice, the discourse of the opinion research instrument takes a stand on behalf of a politics of thin democracy. Moreover, let me now substantiate my claim that the discourse helps to maintain and reconstitute this kind of politics, thereby contributing to the legitimacy of the political system where such politics may be found.

It should be stressed that my central point here is not that the results of opinion research used instrumentally by the powers that be maintains them (and their system) in power. These results are indeed used by commercial political consultants and image makers to win elections and further contribute to expert administration and instrumental rationalization of political life. But this use is beside the point here. And perhaps the results of opinion research really are of limited value to would-be manipulators. So Butler and Stokes (1971, pp. 529–30) argue that opinion researchers simply do not know enough to advise potential manipulators, and that even as their knowledge increases, it is in principle "accessible to all," advantaging no one unduly. If so, we need not fear a technocracy of those who wield the survey instrument.

Rather, the important point here is that, like any manifestation of any discourse, every application of the survey instrument reproduces the discourse and political vision embodied in the instrument. Each use is a dialectical "moment" in the life of the discourse, both drawing upon and reinforcing the discourse (see Alker and Sylvan, 1986).[14] As Edelman (1977) notes, professional language can enter into and help shape everyday life, even as its dissemination occurs without any other significant or effective actions on the part of the professionals in question. Kelman (1987, pp. 93–4) makes a similar point about the negative effects of the production and diffusion of public choice analyses on norms of public spirit among government officials.

Opinion survey discourse is not just the preserve of a detached intellectual community (as may be the case with the discourse of some scientific instruments). This discourse has many of the same roots as the public philosophy of Western political systems (liberal constitutionalism) and plays a major part in the public life of these systems. Thus survey discourse contributes to the legitimation of the dominant political order and, conversely, stands in the way of a more discursive, democratic, and communicatively rationalized politics.

This function is accomplished solely at the taken-for-granted level of discourse. Every time a survey is designed, or its questionnaire administered, or its results analyzed, or its conclusions reported in textbooks or discussed by students in a class or noted by fellow practitioners, political leaders, or the attentive public, then a conception of politics as properly instrumental, individualistic, limited, reactive, and power oriented is reinforced and furthered, at the expense of a politics of unimpeded discussion and interaction. The mismeasure of political man lies squarely in the path of attempts to promote alternative visions of political life and, if Aristotle is right that man is indeed *zoon politikon*, obstructs man's achievement of his true nature.

CHAPTER 9

The Measure of Political Man – and Woman

If political science and political man are ill-served by the discipline's dominant method, the opinion survey, then what is the alternative? One option is a retreat from empirical study of the content and distribution of politically relevant human dispositions altogether, which would seek comfort in older forms of philosophical speculation (see, e.g., Storing, 1962). Despite the attractions of this venerable alternative, any concern with the prospects for participatory democracy and other political forms really can be informed by systematic empirical work (or so I shall argue). In this chapter I shall outline and illustrate a methodology for the empirical scrutiny of political man that is broadly consistent with the ideas about communicative rationality, critical theory, and classical politics that pervade earlier chapters. In particular, I shall try to show that this methodology can meet all the standards used to judge and condemn opinion surveying in Chapter 8.

It may surprise the more sympathetic reader of earlier chapters that the orientation I have in mind, Q methodology, involves quantification, though any statistical analysis is very much subordinate to the broader analytical and interpretive task. Quantification in social science is often regarded as the preserve of instrumental rationalists, opinion surveyors, and other suspicious characters. The result is that, as things stand, "those who can measure well too often restrict themselves to inconsequential epiphenomena, while those who complain remain steadfastly aloof" (Brown, 1985, p. 1). There is of course no reason to value quantification as such, independent of the uses to which it is actually put. I shall try to demonstrate that statistical analysis can indeed find useful service in discursive democracy and critical theory.

Quantification as such is, then, no evil. It only becomes so in the uses to which it has been put by opinion researchers and others committed to *causal* explanation of social and political behavior. In the interests of further subverting the latter kind of social science, I shall also try to show that research programs organized around Q are more defensible qua science. Indeed, the Q approach is closer to what successful *natural* sciences actually do than are the opinion surveys, regression equations, and other paraphernalia beloved by those objectivists in the social disciplines who idolize what turns out to be a largely mistaken conception of successful natural science. However, the justification for Q offered here is ultimately political rather than scientific: Q can contribute to a program of discursive democratization.

As discussed in this chapter, Q methodology is not an off-the-shelf technique, ready made for discursive democrats. Rather, it provides a set of tools that can be selected and shaped to their purposes. To this end, I shall draw upon the extensions of Q made by William Stephenson, who invented Q in the 1930s (Stephenson, 1953), in his "concourse" theory of communication and by the political scientist Steven Brown to questions of *political* subjectivity. The reader is cautioned in advance that this chapter is only suggestive in terms of Q's contribution to the study of democratic politics and policy rather than exhaustive in its development of that potential. By way of approaching Q's claims, let me build upon the classically political critique of opinion research of Chapter 8 to specify a set of desiderata for any instrument for the empirical study of political man (and woman).

Requirements for a Good Instrument

The critique of the political discourse of the survey instrument developed in Chapter 8 proceeded in terms of four categories: ontology, agency, motives, and relationships regarded as natural. These same four categories can be used to specify the requirements for a good instrument.

To begin, the ontology implicit in an instrument's discourse should recognize the collective and discursive dimension of political life as well as the capacity of the individuals who participate in it to create and re-create relationships. In other words, politics should be treated as more than competitive struggle in an environment of atomistic individuals. In order to meet these ontological concerns, the same instrument that apprehends individuals should also be capable of modeling the discourse and debate that, by classical lights, constitutes their *inter*action as well as their action. That instrument should also allow that revealed capabilities, beliefs, opinions, and attitudes can vary across contexts, in particular the extent to which contexts are action related. Indeed, the instrument itself should involve a (classically) political encounter and action-related cogitation in its very application.

Turning to the issue of agency, a good instrument should allow that those who devise, execute, and respond to it can all be full subjects capable of interpreting the world coherently, organizing their own beliefs and opinions and participating in the re-creation of their political environment. Conversely, the instrument should not depend on the causal influences upon individuals remaining mysterious to them; full transparency in both the instrument and the influences it uncovers should not affect the content and validity of inquiry. In principle, any individuals under scrutiny should be able to turn the instrument on themselves - and upon the erstwhile investigator - with no effect on the validity of results.

As far as motivation is concerned, the instrument's discourse should allow for communicative as well as instrumental political action. Thus the instrument should be able to apprehend intersubjective reasoning, self-disclosure, and debate about collective ends and actions.

Finally, no hierarchies should be entrenched in the instrument. In particular, any encounter necessary to produce information should not be dominated by those who design and wield the instrument.

In keeping with critical theory's concern with systematic distortions of political life (especially on the part of wealth and power), one more desideratum may be added to these four categories. Users of the instrument should be able to distinguish revealed characteristics of individuals and interactions that are constrained, distorted, and dominated from those that represent free and uncoerced cogitation, action, and interaction. And the findings thus generated should promote the latter at the expense of the former.

I shall claim that Q methodology, though far from perfect, can go a long way toward meeting these desiderata. In so doing, Q can not only contribute to our understanding of the communicative dimension of political life but also reinforce the cause of discursive democracy. Before scrutinizing Q in this light, a few words about the essentials of the approach are in order [fuller treatments may be found in Brown (1980) and McKeown and Thomas (1988)].

Q Methodology and Concourse Theory

The hallmark of Q methodology is that it takes the subjective, self-referential opinions of respondents seriously in seeking to model the whole subject as he or she apprehends a particular situation. The subject is assumed to possess a potentially well-organized and coherent orientation that is modeled in terms of his or her reactions to a set of statements. These statements should be expressed in language fully intelligible to the subject, who is then free to make of these statements what he or she wishes.

The subject is confronted with a set of statements (usually around forty to sixty) and asked to order them (for statistical reasons, in a quasi-normal distribution) from those the subject agrees with most (usually coded +5) through those regarded with indifference (scored 0) to those the subject disagrees with most (coded −5). Every opportunity is given the individual to think about his or her ordering, discuss the procedure with the person administering it, and reflect upon and change rankings. The ordered set this procedure yields is called a Q sort. Every ranking within it only has meaning through reference to the rankings of every other statement. Thus the whole subject, or relevant aspects of the self, holds together as one. The ordering a subject produces represents his or her own construction of a particular reality, and Q methodology rests on the principle that the analyst should not seek to impose any other supposedly more "scientific" or "objective" construction upon subjects.

The statements themselves can be generated in a variety of ways depending on the theoretical interests of the investigator. In light of the broader concerns of this book with the discursive and communicative aspects of politics, the most appropriate source of statements is a pertinent area of political discourse. This area might concern a policy issue, or a particular political conflict, or a debate about broad principles. In Q methodology, any such area is referred to as a "concourse" (running together) of statements (Stephenson, 1978). A concourse can be operationalized as the complete population of statements made in or about the area at hand. It is this population of statements that defines the concourse rather than the population of individuals who might engage it. The statements of interest are those actually made by the individuals involved with the concourse, and as such these statements should prove meaningful to these same individuals. Several heuristics are available for sampling the concourse in systematic fashion (see, e.g., Brown, 1986, pp. 58–9, 61–2).[1]

A single Q sort does, then, represent an individual in terms of his or her whole orientation to the concourse in question. Such a single Q sort is of highly limited interest. A picture or model of the concourse as a whole can be constructed by summarizing and comparing the Q sorts of the individuals involved in it. (No representative sample of individuals is required; just a single person from each relevant perspective is needed.) One can begin to paint this picture by correlating individuals against one another. (It is important to distance this interindividual correlation from the more familiar correlation of *variables* undertaken in connection with R-analysis techniques such as opinion surveys.) If the correlation between individuals A and B is 1.0, their opinions are in perfect agreement; −1.0 indicates perfect disagreement. Such correlations are typically not very helpful, and a variety of factor analytic techniques can be used to probe and model the concourse further (again, these seek patterns across individuals, not across variables). No cookbook recipe is available for the application of these procedures; rather, they constitute searchlights, and the direction the beam is pointed depends on the theoretical interests of the observer.

One particular concourse is presented in Tables 9-1 and 9-2. This concourse concerns arrangements for the international management of Antarctica [fuller results from this study are reported in Dryzek, Clark, and McKenzie (1989)]. The Antarctic concourse was sampled by seeking statements pertaining to the environment, resources, sovereignty, the existing treaty system (which has governed Antarctica since 1958), internationalization, the role of the Third World, and so forth. The Q sorts were obtained from twenty-three individuals active in Antarctic affairs from eleven different countries. These Q sorts were then factor analyzed on a judgmental (i.e., not a mathematical) basis. Two significant factors were located: one defined by its concern with environmental preservation, the other by its support for the treaty system status quo. These are not the only factors that can be generated, and so the structure they represent is just one picture of the Antarctic concourse. Other pictures could have been taken. The loadings of the twenty-three individuals on the two factors are presented in Table 9-1.

Table 9–1. *Factor loadings in the Antarctic concourse*

Nationality	Position	Factor loadings	
		1	2
1 United States	Governmental	66	27
2 Brazil	Scientist/governmental	75	41
3 Argentina	Scientist	66	−22
4 Japan	Diplomat	78	41
5 China (PRC)	Scientist/governmental	32	43
6 United States	Attorney, INGO	30	75
7 United Kingdom	Scientist/governmental	67	32
8 Argentina	Social scientist	27	57
9 Australia	Diplomat	48	33
10 United States	Governmental	67	36
11 United Kingdom	Scientist/governmental	70	20
12 United States	Scientist/governmental	36	83
13 France	International law/governmental	48	64
14 United States	Governmental	62	46
15 United States	Environmental INGO	19	75
16 Germany (FR)	Scientist/IGO	89	−03
17 United States	Scientist/governmental	75	35
18 United States	International law, INGO	67	35
19 New Zealand	Environmental INGO	36	76
20 Australia	Scientist/governmental	63	10
21 France	Governmental	47	08
22 Sri Lanka	Diplomat	34	61
23 Brazil	Scientist	40	75

Abbreviations: IGO, International Governmental Organization; INGO, International Non-Governmental Organization.

Table 9-2 further defines this picture of the concourse by reporting the statements whose score differs most substantially across the two factors (these scores are derived from an idealized Q sort that can be computed for each factor). All these representations try to capture the debate and dispute and consensus and conflict within the concourse. (The absence of bipolar factors indicates limited conflict in this case.)

Before proceeding, it should be emphasized that Q is essentially interpretive in its philosophy of social science. As such, it abjures both objectivism and causal explanation (thus departing substantially from opinion research). Instead, Q seeks a "feeling for the

Table 9–2. *Factor scores in the Antarctic concourse*

Statement	Factor scores	
	1	2
10 Commercial exploration and exploitation of Antarctica's mineral and renewable resources should be prohibited. Only physical, biological, and ecological science-related studies should be permitted.	−1	+2
17 Antarctica should become a world park with restricted scientific activity and greatly reduced tourism.	−2	+3
3 The treaty nations know more about the region's mineral and hydrocarbon wealth than they are admitting. They stand to benefit substantially from this wealth, and that is why they do not want the question resolved or even discussed in a larger forum such as the United Nations.	−3	0
31 The Antarctic Treaty System's main value in the international political system is as an exemplar of peaceful international relations. It is a model of international cooperation, and hence its basic framework should be preserved.	+3	0

Note: Strongest possible agreement indicated by +4; strongest possible disagreement indicated by −4; 0 indicates indifference.

organism" (Brown, 1989). It engages in intensive analysis of particular individuals or collectivities in order to apprehend the fullness of their subjectivity in the subjects' own terms. Although Q can be used in causal explanation of macrolevel phenomena (e.g., the content and stability of the existing Antarctic management regime), it does not (and cannot) seek causal explanation of individual actions. That is, Q interprets the actions of individuals in terms of their consistency (or otherwise) with the subjective orientations it uncovers.

As an interpretive methodology, Q studies only particular cases (be they individuals or concourses). Those schooled in mainstream social science methods, in particular survey research, might protest that Q is severely limited in that it offers no possibility of generalization from the microcosm under study to any larger universe. But intensive study of individual cases is, of course, how the more successful natural sciences (especially physics) actually proceed in their empirical analyses. It is a very odd kind of scientism that regards regression and other methods for averaging observations over large numbers of cases as the essence of empirical science. Such averaging means that the observer has little faith in any single observation. In contrast, Q has greater confidence in its individual observations and as such is consistent with a "Galilean" view of science (Brown, 1985, p. 24). That is, any lawlike generalizations – for example, "every individual has a coherent rationale for voting the way they do" – will come from intensive scrutiny of individual cases in all their specificity.

When it comes to extending its results to some larger population, Q does seek generalizations, but of a different order than those sought by survey research. Opinion researchers make general statements such as "vote choice in England is more affected by religion than by social class" or "50 percent of the population identifies with a political party." Generalizations in Q take the form "the environmental factor found in our Q study of Antarctica represents the orientation of a larger number of individuals concerned with Antarctica"; but we cannot determine the size of this larger group, in absolute terms or relative to the size of other groups.

If observation, generalization, and interpretation were all Q had to offer, then from the perspective of the larger concerns of this book its contribution would still be limited. For despite its implicit *telos* of free intersubjective understanding, interpretation per se is entirely consistent with acceptance of the authority of that which is being interpreted, be it an individual, culture, tradition, text, or state (see Fay, 1975, pp. 90–1). Indeed, this acceptance underlies the conservatism of hermeneutic theorists such as Gadamer (1975). Later, I shall show how Q can be turned to more critical use and so meet the fifth desideratum outlined earlier. But first, let me show how Q can meet the first four criteria for a good instrument.

Q and Discursive Democracy

The first, ontological requirement is met rather easily. The concourse theory of communication in Q defines social life in general, and politics in particular, in terms of verbal interchange. This interaction is much more than exchange or agglomeration across atomistic individuals. Each individual's location within it only exists and makes sense by virtue of every other subjective position found in the concourse. But even as it helps define these individuals, a concourse itself is their creation and is modeled in their terms. Therefore, Q apprehends the individual subject and the concourse simultaneously. The parts (subjects) make sense only in terms of the whole (concourse), and the whole makes sense only in terms of its parts. To highlight Q's departure from opinion research in this respect, consider the absurdity of any claim to the effect that the opinion survey could model both the individual voter and the competitive party system. In short, then, it is clear that Q's political ontology is the discursive and egalitarian one of the classical model.

In further contradistinction to the opinion survey, Q does not assume and require that revealed capabilities, beliefs, opinions, and attitudes about politics are invariant across the degree to which their context is action related. In Q it is assumed that the subject is *potentially* well organized in his or her own orientation toward a concourse and that this potential can be realized in the context of action. In terms of the classical ontology, conducting a Q sort *is* a political encounter and as such is well placed to discern politically relevant characteristics and capabilities. The encounter involves cogitation, discussion between subject and investigator, and the production (not discovery) of a coherent profile for the subject. Obviously, as with any instrument, the findings result from an interaction between the instrument and that which is being studied. Heisenberg's uncertainty principle suggests there is little to worry about here. But note how dramatically Q's political encounter differs from the way the opinion survey forces its respondents into a straitjacket.

The second requirement concerns the equal distribution of agency within the instrument's discourse. Recall that in the opinion survey's discourse the respondent is first and foremost a plastic and reactive object; only the survey designer is a true subject. In contrast, Q *begins* by taking the subjectivity of respondents seriously and then gives them the opportunity to talk about and think through their positions in terms of language they understand. Moreover, the investigator can be inserted into a Q study on the same terms as the respondents; that is, his or her own subjectivity can become part of the results. To illustrate, let me now insert myself into the Antarctic concourse introduced earlier. My own personal Q sort of the thirty-four statements about Antarctica gives me a loading of 25 on factor 1 and 76 on factor 2. In principle, then, the roles of investigator and subject can be reversed. So, for example, a Japanese diplomat (respondent 4) could have carried out the study, and I could have been one of his subjects. Any such reversal of roles should have no effect on the study (assuming both of us dealt with the same concourse). Thus, Q's encounter really is egalitarian; not only does it proceed in terms of the language actually used by participants but also it can only benefit to the extent its methodology is made transparent to participants. Again, try to imagine the effects of any such role reversal or transparency on an opinion survey. Once individuals understood the purpose of the survey, any ensuing changes in their own responses would completely undermine the validity of the results in terms of the need to generalize to a larger population.

So far, I have said little about how Q can actually be used to investigate the content and distribution of politically relevant dispositions and capabilities and so inform judgments about the prospects for (communicative) rationality and participatory democracy in particular situations. The Antarctic study does not address such issues (I introduced it mainly because it is a Q study I worked on myself, such that slipping myself into the concourse was easy). Let me now rectify these oversights and in so doing address the third requirement for an instrument, that it recognize a variety of motives on the part of agents.

My illustration here comes from an intensive Q study of a single individual undertaken by Brown (1985). In the Antarctic case, one Q sort was obtained from each of twenty-three participants. In Brown's case, one set of statements was administered eighteen different times to a single individual under different conditions. The statements in question concerned national political issues (ranging from the legalization of school prayer to pressurizing South Africa to eliminate apartheid). The conditions are those listed in Table 9-3. These conditions were specified by the researcher, though there is no reason why they could not have been defined by the subject too. The first is simply what the subject, X, prefers, with no further specifications. The second refers to what would bring most gain to the subject. The eighth concerns what is most moral. The fifth refers to what makes X angry. Condition 17 is particularly interesting; drawing on the idea of Rawls's (1971) original position, it asks X to order the policy positions for a society in which she would be ignorant of her own status. In the language of critical theory, condition 17 should therefore intimate X's conception of generalizable interests, in contrast to the clearly particular interests the second and third conditions capture. Condition 18 is also noteworthy; it

Table 9–3. *The political motivations of Ms. X*

Conditions of instruction	Factor loadings		
	A	B	C
1 Personal preference	83	06	−24
2 Gains (utility income)	15	60	−20
3 Costs	−17	−06	70
4 Happiness	83	−06	−20
5 Anger	−82	−20	04
6 Rationality	67	03	55
7 Informed position	77	−13	23
8 Morality	87	−13	−22
9 Republicans now	−64	40	56
10 Republicans to get elected	61	40	09
11 Republicans in future	−57	36	54
12 Democrats if in office now	48	−12	62
13 Democrats to get elected	50	−15	08
14 Democrats in future	46	−21	68
15 Ideal government	89	03	−06
16 The good society	91	09	04
17 Rawlsian position	94	14	04
18 Personal preference (t_2)	93	00	21

Source: Brown (1985).

seeks X's preferences simpliciter at the end of this prolonged procedure, thus allowing – and in fact demonstrating, when compared with condition 1 – that the encounter has had an educative effect. The eighteen Q sorts were then factor analyzed by Brown in order to uncover patterns among them. The factor loadings of each of the eighteen conditions are as reported in Table 9-3.

Clearly, Brown's analysis can tap a variety of motivations. With the additional piece of information that X votes for Democrats, we can conclude that she is not instrumentally motivated in her voting behavior, for she does not vote her material self-interest. If she did, she would vote Republican. For the positions she ascribes to Republicans (conditions 9, 10, and 11) load highly on the same factor as the position that would bring her most material gain (condition 2). And factor C represents both costs to her and what she believes Democrats will do once they are in office (the fact that C also represents what she feels Republicans will do in office suggests a measure of skepticism about both parties on her part).

The overall preferences of X, the positions she is likely to take on policies, and her voting behavior prove consistent with her conceptions of what is moral (condition 8), rational (condition 6), and generalizable (condition 17). Apparently, X is quite a public-spirited person. Those interested in the public commitments required by communicative rationality and participatory democracy might draw considerable comfort from these results. Here X proves nothing like what opinion researchers or economists tell us the ordinary person is like. Of course, X is just one individual, and one would need to repeat these procedures for relevant others (perhaps in the context of proposals for local discursive designs) to draw any stronger conclusions.

The fourth requirement concerns the absence of hierarchy in the instrument's discourse. From my earlier discussion, it should be clear that the encounter Q contrives is a thoroughly egalitarian one and the roles of observer and respondent are interchangeable. Granted, it may take substantial time and effort to master the technical intricacies of Q methodology. (I know it took me long enough!) But the instrument's discourse contains no obstacle to such an education. And the effectiveness with which the instrument is wielded can only be enhanced to the extent such technical information is grasped by respondents. Again, in contrast to survey research, Q has an implicit stake in promoting the active and competent side of its subjects.

Further movement toward the elimination of any residual hierarchy in Q methodology has been made by Celia Kitzinger (1986, p. 168), who states:

I would like to explore the possibility of "democratizing" Q by, for example, using collective Q sort construction from a group (such as a self-help group or political campaigning group). Debate within the group could be represented in the form of a collective Q sort composed by the group, and the group, as a group, could interpret the factors that emerged. This would be a starting point for attempting to find a way in which control over the research process could ultimately be handed over completely to the participants themselves.

Kitzinger reports that she has already used Q to facilitate and structure discussions in a women's group.

By now I hope I have shown that Q enables the investigation of the capabilities and characteristics of political man and woman in a fashion consistent with the discursive and egalitarian classical conception of politics. If this is true, then every application of Q reinforces (however little) a discourse of free disclosure and communicatively rational democracy, in just the same way every piece of survey research reinforces a discourse of political manipulation and thin democracy (see Chapter 8).

Nevertheless, it remains conceivable that Q taps only misconceptions and distortions in political characteristics and communications. For example, it is possible (if not very likely) that any consensus uncovered in the Antarctic concourse represents only the hegemony of dominant actors such as multinational corporations interested in Antarctic resources. Similarly, it might be the case that X's conceptions of what is moral, generalizable, and rational are conditioned by the subtle domination of wealth and power in her political milieu. These considerations suggest that the next step in this methodological program be critical. How, then, can Q be deployed to distinguish coerced and distorted individual viewpoints and collective consensus from free and uncoerced ones and promote the latter at the expense of the former? In other words, how can Q methodology be used in conjunction with critical theory?

Critical Theory and Q Methodology

Recall that a critical theory strives to interpret the condition of a group of sufferers, make plain to them the cause of their suffering, and by sketching a course of relief, demonstrate that their situation is not immutable. Any such theory is validated by reflective acceptance and ensuing action on the part of its audience. In its standard presentations, then, a critical theory has three aspects: one interpretive, one quasi-causal, and one emancipatory. Whereas Q is largely silent on questions of causality,[2] let me suggest that it can generate major contributions to both the interpretive and emancipatory moments of a critical theory.

A critical theory should begin by ascertaining the "*felt* needs and sufferings of a group of people" (Fay, 1975, p. 94). Q Methodology is uniquely well placed to determine desires, needs, sufferings, and discontent as actually felt by subjects. For Q seeks categories not in the instrument itself or in the theory of the analyst but in the subjects themselves (as such, the application of Q is a kind of reconstructive science). Thus any subsequent analysis based on Q findings, critical or not, is well placed to speak to discontent and suffering as actually understood by subjects themselves.

Obviously, a critical theory needs to ascertain not just the content of deprivation and discontent but also their cause. In terms of this quasi-causal element,[3] Q can do no more than specify the factors for which explanation is sought. To illustrate, a critical theory of bureaucracy (and bureaucrats) could make good use of a Q study directed toward a taxonomy of the self-understandings of bureaucrats and/or their clients. For the moment, one might reserve judgment on whether particular self-understandings so revealed are felicitous or pathological, but one could parse the taxonomy in a search for self-deprecating, distorted, self-defeating, or otherwise problematic self-understandings.

Ideas about the causes of such conditions would have to come from outside the Q study (e.g., in a Weberian account of bureaucratic rationalization). Any such causal theory should be accepted or rejected not on the basis of statistical tests or other empiricist paraphernalia but, rather, on the basis of whether or not it is reflectively acceptable to its audience. Using Q to specify the *explanandum* is a quasi-causal theory does not, of course, guarantee that the theory will pass this test. But let me suggest that any quasi-causal theory that speaks to an *explanandum* that would *not* be revealed if a Q study were conducted can anticipate reflective rejection, for any such theory will not have addressed the felt discontent of its intended audience.

So far, I have emphasized Q's contribution to the interpretive moment of critical theory. An examination of Q's contribution to the emancipatory moment can begin by noting that, in critical theory lights, self-understandings can have both manifest and latent aspects (Fay, 1975, p. 98). If suffering and discontent are the issue, then one can anticipate manifest self-understandings that are to some degree pathological. The results of Q here can demonstrate to subjects that any such pathological self-understandings are not the only ones available and that there are latent, marginal, or suppressed alternatives. If the latter are not available, then there is no hope for critical theory, and one must retreat into the bleak pessimism of an earlier generation of critical theorists (notably Horkheimer and Adorno). Alternatively, the critical theorist would have to appeal to some transcendent standard that does not exist anywhere in the self-understandings of his or her audience, and so confirm its critics' charges that critical theory traffics in the coercive imposition of theorists' blueprints.

To illustrate how Q can be used to identify potentially emancipatory alternative self-understandings, consider the Q study of
lesbian identities carried out by Kitzinger (1986; see also Kitzinger
and Stainton Rogers, 1985). Kitzinger administered a single Q sort
to forty-one lesbian women. Using procedures similar to those
described earlier for the Q analysis of concourses, she factor analyzed these forty-one Q sorts, discovering five factors, each of
which represents an alternative identity. The first she calls "personal
fulfilment" (lesbianism is something the subject comes to, finding
happiness and freedom by so doing); the second "special person"
(lesbianism means nothing more than attraction to a particular
person); the third "individualistic" (lesbianism is just one given fact
of the subject's life); the fourth "radical feminist" (lesbianism is
chosen for political reasons); and the fifth "traditional" (lesbianism
is something about which the subject is apologetic and ashamed).

Though Kitzinger refrains from explicit comparative evaluations,
it is hard for her not to characterize the fifth identity as pathological;
if nothing else, the women who load highly on this fifth factor
indicate their own sense of suffering. To these women, the identities
revealed in the other four factors (except for the second, which is
probably inaccessible) are alternative self-conceptions that might
alleviate their discontent. Of course, it is up to the women in factor 5
to accept or reject these alternatives. But whatever their decision,
these alternatives are actually available inasmuch as they are demonstrated in the self-conceptions of other lesbians; they are not just
theoretical pie in the sky.

The lesson of this lesbian example is that Q can be used to
deconstruct and render problematic what is taken for granted in
identities, discourses, and concepts. A more explicitly political
example may be found in Stainton Rogers and Kitzinger's (1986)
use of Q to deconstruct the concept of human rights. In the realm
of health policy, Stainton Rogers and Stainton Rogers (1988) use Q
to deconstruct the concept of addiction, thereby exposing the
ideological basis of existing policy in one conception of addiction
and suggesting alternatives to this status quo. Brown's study of
Ms. X discussed earlier shows how Q can be used in intensive
fashion to deconstruct what it means to be rational in terms of a
single individual's political orientation. With the content of these
dimensions made plain to her, Ms. X could reflect upon and perhaps choose more explicitly among them.

In so using Q, the analyst can bring to light alternatives to any problematic status quo and so engage in what critical theorists call *ideologiekritik,* or the criticism of ideology. It is in these alternatives that the seeds of liberation may be found.

Critically motivated Q analysis cannot, of course, be used to generate proposals for social change that would render distorted identities and understandings no longer functional or to suggest the actions that would enable individuals or groups to alleviate discontent and deprivation. But critically inspired Q can intimate alternative conditions and identities and so stimulate a search on the part of the audience (or, indeed, the analyst) for actions that would bring these alternatives into being.

It remains conceivable that a concourse is so saturated with distorted communication that Q could bring to light no alternative to a problematic status quo. Indeed, the Q analyst would have no way of even describing this situation as problematic. Michel Foucault, for one, points to the prevalence of such hegemonic discourses related to sex, criminality, mental health, and so forth. Oddly enough, Foucault's personal example points to an escape from the constraints of distorted communication. For in describing hegemony, Foucault implicitly claims personal exemption from it through the very act of description, thus showing that in fact there is no hegemony. The Q analyst can claim a similar exemption. Moreover, he or she also has license to search high and low for individuals who might prove different. If, however, there is true and total hegemony (Weber's polar night?), then it would encompass Foucauldians, critical theorists, and Q methodologists alike. There would be no hope for Q, and no hope for anything else. My own experience in carrying out Q sorts, along with my reading of the Q studies of others, suggests that anything even close to such hegemony is rare.

Conclusion

The classical model of politics and associated notions about discursive democracy have now been deployed in a scrutiny of two social scientific instruments, the opinion survey and Q methodology. Opinion surveying stands condemned, but Q merits tentative approval.

Those beholden to objectivist and deductive–nomological conceptions of social science might, however, remain unconvinced of

Q's virtues as detailed in this chapter. When all is said and done, they might argue, does not Q's picture of political man represent nothing more than the assumptions implicit in its discourse? That is, if Q begins by assuming individuals are potentially well-organized subjects with a coherent outlook that informs their actions,[4] then it is no surprise that Q yields positive conclusions about politically relevant characteristics and capabilities.

Two replies are possible here. The first notes that although Q does not allow for badly organized or incoherent subjects, it does recognize the possibility of subjectivity that is unsavory from the perspective of discursive democracy (e.g., if Brown's Ms. X proved to be motivated solely by her personal material utility).

A second reply would move the issue to the level of competing research traditions (or research programs, or metatheories, or paradigms, call them what you will). Following Kuhn (1970b), one cannot judge a theory in isolation from the paradigm that inspires it. Analogously, one should not judge instruments in isolation from the research traditions that utilize them. How, then, may one judge the merits of competing research traditions in political science? The next chapter addresses this question. I shall argue that the same standards I have applied to the scrutiny of instruments can be brought to bear upon the competition of research traditions. This extension will enable a more global assessment of the practice and progress of political science as a purportedly rational discipline and an evaluation of its potential contribution to discursive democracy.

CHAPTER 10

Progress and Rationality

The activities of political scientists can either frustrate or contribute to human emancipation. That is the lesson of the exposé of frustration in Chapter 8 and the discussion of a potential contribution in Chapter 9. However, even if they accepted the arguments of these chapters to the extent of (say) renouncing opinion surveying, many political scientists might still claim that emancipation is of no proper concern to a discipline whose essential task is explication and explanation of the political world, not evaluation, prescription, or criticism.

In this chapter I shall argue that even if one regards explanation as the sine qua non of social science, one cannot avoid taking sides on issues of domination and liberation. Nor is the matter one of simply choosing sides as one will. For if political science is to redeem its claim as a progressive and cognitively rational explanatory discipline – and dare one say a science worthy of the name – then its practitioners simply must commit themselves to the canons of communicative rationality. My argument commences with a contemplation of what progress and cognitive rationality mean and entail when it comes to social science.

Progress consists of an increasing ability to explain and connect complex phenomena. Progress in science, as in any rational activity, implies choice between competing explanations, theories, or theoretical frameworks based on good cognitive reasons. Good cognitive reasons can take many forms: problem-solving power, predictive success, consistency, simplicity, and the like. Thus a gun at the head may be a good reason for handing over one's wallet, but not a good *cognitive* reason.

Choice based on good cognitive reasons is one aspect of rationality. Given that this is how rationality is generally understood in contemporary philosophy of inquiry, I shall follow this usage in this chapter; so whenever I speak of rationality simpliciter, I mean cognitive rationality. I shall also have cause to mention instrumental and communicative rationality, which will retain both their adjectives and the definitions they received in Chapter 1.

The centrality of rationality and progress to received ideas about science may explain why the specter of relativism raised in the wake of Kuhn's (1970b) account of scientific revolutions was so frightening. Kuhn himself protests innocence of relativism (see, e.g., Kuhn, 1970a, pp. 259–66). But both his admirers (such as Feyerabend, 1970) and his detractors (notably Lakatos, 1970, and Popper, 1970) have argued that Kuhn portrays science as neither rational nor progressive. The specter has now been laid to rest by postempiricist philosophy of science (see Bernstein, 1983, pp. 51–108), but only after considerable modification of the concepts of rationality and progress. In particular, rationality has been divorced from objectivism. My intention in this chapter is to ask, in light of this modification as cast by Laudan (1977), whether *political* science can be rational and progressive. My answer, put most simply, is that the discipline can be progressive, but not in the sense now understood by philosophers of science (including postempiricist ones). And political science can be rational, but only to the extent both the discipline and the larger society in which it moves are *communicatively* rational.

In outline, my argument will proceed as follows. The progress of a scientific discipline as generally understood consists of a series of stable rational choices among research traditions or research programs. Rational comparisons across research traditions can be made in political science too. But any such comparison must be contingent upon the social context, largely external to the discipline, that defines the empirical problems for political inquiry. Historical variability in this context means that research traditions may fall only to rise again – rationally. Hence progress as normally understood cannot occur. However, the progress of political science can be reconceptualized as an increasing capacity to cope with contingency in its empirical problems. This reinterpretation has direct implications for the conduct of political inquiry. In particular, a tolerance of diversity in research traditions is essential to the progress of the discipline.

More important, this reconceptualization of progress calls attention to the circumstances in which socially determined empirical problems are defined. To the extent these circumstances are distorted by wealth, power, or professionalism, political science "progresses" only in the terms established by a communicatively irrational society (and discipline). Only to the degree empirical problem definition is free and unconstrained is defensible disciplinary progress conceivable. And *that* is likely only to the degree the polity, the discipline, and – crucially – their interaction are discursively democratic.

Conceptions of Progress

In one widely held view that owes much to positivism, science progresses by accumulation (for an application to political science, see Riker, 1982). Theories are formulated, verified, and then added to the accumulated stockpile of true theory. This positivist view of scientific progress has suffered enough at the hands of Popper (see especially Popper, 1972b) to render superfluous any punishment I might add. Progress, on Popper's own account, consists of a succession of tentative theories of increasingly corroborated content. Theories can never be conclusively verified or confirmed, only falsified. Theories are corroborated inasmuch as they resist falsification in repeated testing. Falsification is a progressive act, for it leaves in its wake a set of problems demanding resolution, which can only be achieved by some new or better theory.[1]

An exploration of the progress of political science in terms other than those of positivists and Popperians requires some fine distinctions between different kinds of progress. Let me clarify three senses in which I will use the term. I shall refer to the progress of a discipline as global progress. If I use no qualifier, this is the sense of progress intended. Progress inside a research tradition, itself within a discipline, is called internal progress. And the reinterpretation of progress as a capacity to cope with contingency I will term lateral progress.

Kuhn's challenge to both positivist and Popperian views of science is based on his contention that empirical phenomena are themselves interpreted through the lens of the same paradigm containing any theories to be tested. Kuhn's analysis suggests a more complex conceptualization of progress in science. First, Kuhn argues that progress from nonscience to science occurs with the articulation and enforcement of a paradigm. Some political scien-

tists have seized on this idea to contend that the increasing profes-
sionalization of the discipline is indicative of its progress (see, e.g.,
Almond, 1966). An identical application to the policy sciences is
made by Schneider, Stevens, and Tornatzky (1982). Second, internal progress within an established paradigm can be clear and unam-
biguous. Investigators simply solve the puzzles the paradigm defines as interesting. But what of global progress in Kuhn's conception of science?

His critics, notably Lakatos (1970) and Popper (1970), claim
Kuhn believes that paradigms are thoroughly incommensurable
and noncomparable. Hence any choice between paradigms is but
an irrational matter of the "mob psychology" of the scientific community (Lakatos, 1970, p. 178). In this interpretation, Kuhn allows
no progressive succession of paradigms. Kuhn protests that criteria
of accuracy, simplicity, fruitfulness, scope, and consistency can be
applied to the comparison of paradigms. But even one of Kuhn's
most articulate defenders on this point admits that Kuhn himself
has failed to clarify the epistemological status of these criteria, let
alone the details of exactly how they should be applied when paradigms compete (Bernstein, 1983, p. 58). Kuhn has shrouded progress and rationality in a fog bank of ambiguity.

The clearest escape from this fog bank has been charted by
Lakatos (1970) and Laudan (1977). These two authors follow Kuhn
in accepting the existence of paradigm analogues, termed research
programs (Lakatos) or research traditions (Laudan). But like Popper they also specify clear and general criteria for choice among
programs or traditions. Here, rational choice consists of determining which of an array of competing programs or traditions is most
progressive internally. This criterion is more explicitly normative
for Laudan than for Lakatos, who often appears more interested in
the appraisal of scientific history than in principles for actual
choice by practitioners of a discipline, and indeed argues that rational judgments about the relative merits of different research programs can only be made retroactively. I shall follow Laudan in
arguing that the comparative appraisal of research traditions can
and should be undertaken by practitioners to inform the content of
their future work (though such judgments must be informed by
history).

To Lakatos, internal progress consists of a succession of theories
of enhanced explanatory power. More formally, a move from theory T1 to theory T2 is progressive if (a) T2 predicts more facts than
T1, (b) T2 can account for all the prior explanatory successes of T1,

and (c) some of the excess predictions of T2 are empirically corroborated. To Laudan, internal progress occurs with success in
solving significant problems. These comparisons between programs or traditions are essentially dynamic, based on the rate of
theory change or problem solving rather than momentary explanatory adequacy. For both Lakatos and Laudan, global progress in a
discipline, as opposed to a program or tradition within a discipline,
exists to the extent that rational choice across programs or traditions occurs. Thus, for example, Einstein's program rationally re-
places Newton's in physics, Copernicus's rationally supplants
Ptolemy's in astronomy, and neo-Darwinian and punctuated equilibrium programs currently vie for supremacy in evolutionary biology. The internal progress of a research tradition and the global
progress of a discipline are conceptually distinct but logically
related.

How applicable are the standards developed by Lakatos and
Laudan to social science in general and political science in particular? A cursory glance at the discipline reveals a veritable multitude of
theoretical perspectives. But this very proliferation should be cause
for concern: Why do we, unlike natural scientists, fail to recognize
more approaches as degenerating and discard them as such? Could it
be the case, as some admirers of natural science tell us, that the social
sciences are indeed immature? Does our multiplicity of perspectives
and approaches contain no true, well-defined research programs or
research traditions to provide grist for rational comparisons and
progressive choices?

I will argue in the next section that political science is indeed
home to research traditions worthy of the name. However, my
thesis is that there is a fundamental difference between the enter-
prises of natural and social science sufficient to preclude rational
and progressive choices among research traditions in the social
sciences, at least in the sense these choices are made in the natural
sciences. This difference resides in the nature of the problems confronting natural and social science, not in any supposed immaturity of social science. In a nutshell, the problems confronting the
two activities are open to determination outside the scientific community in qualitatively different ways.

Research Programs and Traditions in Political Science

Moon (1975) and Ball (1976) believe that Lakatos's guidelines may
be used to compare research programs in political science in essen-

tially the same manner as in natural science.[2] However, it is clear that none of the existing major perspectives in political science truly meets the standards of a successful Lakatosian research program. That is, none of these perspectives has yielded a series of theories of increased empirical explanatory power, with each theory incorporating its predecessor in the series and predicting novel facts. On the other hand, there is precious little in the natural sciences that stands up to Lakatos's stringent demands (see Grünbaum, 1976; Laudan, 1977, p. 77). The remainder of this chapter will therefore set Lakatos aside and instead employ Laudan's more forgiving analysis as a touchstone.

To Laudan (1977, p. 81), "a research tradition is a set of general assumptions about the entities and processes in a domain of study, and about the appropriate methods to be used for investigating the problems and constructing the theories in that domain." If a perspective is to be called a research tradition, it therefore requires three essential elements: ontological commitments (i.e., principles for the recognition of real entities and relationships), methodological commitments, and a number of theories (see Laudan, 1977, pp. 78–9). If a research tradition is to stand in its own right, this set of elements should not be shared in its entirety with any other research tradition.

In Laudan's sense of the term, there are indeed research traditions in the social sciences. Laudan himself refers to Marxism, behaviorist psychology, Freudian psychology, cybernetics, and capitalist economics. The examples used henceforth in this chapter are of research traditions in Laudan's sense and not mere perspectives or approaches. Where necessary, I shall justify their status as research traditions with footnotes describing their ontology, methodology, theories, and distinctiveness.

Having established that political science can indeed lay claim to the possession of true research traditions, let me now return to the differential character of problems in natural and social sciences.

Problems in the Natural Sciences

The essence of scientific activity is solving problems.[3] Most contemporary philosophers of science can agree upon this much, even as they disagree about much else.[4]

Laudan notes that problems can be of two basic kinds: empirical and conceptual. An empirical problem is "anything about the natural world which strikes as odd, or otherwise in need of explanation" (Laudan, 1977, p. 15). Any other kind of problem is conceptual. A conceptual problem exists if a theory is internally inconsistent, if it employs vague analytical categories, if it has difficulty in specifying how empirical measurements should be made, or if it conflicts with some other theory believed to be well founded (Laudan, 1977, p. 49). Internal progress for Laudan, therefore, resides in the resolution of empirical and conceptual problems by the practitioners of a research tradition. For example, the internal progress of Copernican astronomy consists of steps such as accounting for apparent anomalies in the motion of planets, but also of its ultimately successful struggle with religious views requiring the earth to be the center of all things. All problems are not of equal significance. They can be weighted rationally, if only qualitatively, by such factors as their generality, the degree to which they have been solved by other research traditions, and whether or not they are expropriated from or to another domain of inquiry.

Conceptual problems of conflict with a purportedly well-founded theory leave open questions concerning the origins of any such theory; hence they invite social or cultural determination of the problems confronting natural science inquiry. This kind of conceptual problem can stem from sources external to the scientific community. For example, Einstein's investigations in his later years were informed by his belief that "God does not play dice with the universe." Pre-nineteenth-century geology had to cope with the problem set by the Bible: How can geologic history be accommodated in a time span of less than five thousand years? Darwinian biology has encountered resistance from both Soviet Marxist orthodoxy and American fundamentalist Christianity. Biological theories that predict interracial differences in intelligence offend liberal egalitarian sensibilities.

Thus natural science conceptual problems arising from inconsistencies between competing worldviews can originate outside the scientific community. But what of empirical natural science problems? Can they, too, have external sources? Here, one may usefully distinguish between experimental and observational natural science.

Experimental natural science (exemplified by physics and chemistry) is largely immune to external influence on its empirical problems and, for that matter, upon its conceptual problems of internal inconsistency, measurement, and vagueness of analytical categories. Empirical problem formulation, weighting, and dissolution reside in the logic of a research tradition or in the rivalry among research traditions. Most fundamentally, empirical problems arise through the success or failure of theories in a tradition or in a rival tradition.[5] Empirical problems in observational natural science (such as astronomy, paleontology, and evolutionary biology) generally arise in exactly the same manner as in experimental natural science. However, the door is open to external influence from natural events such as the arrival of a comet, an ecological collapse, or evolution of a new form of life. In addition, human events such as the discovery of a new kind of fossil or celestial object can have a similar effect.

Thus observational natural science is not totally immune to external influence on the content of its empirical problems. Nevertheless, in observational as in experimental natural science, the relevant disciplinary community regards the formulation, weighting, and dissolution of empirical problems as properly matters for the practitioners of the discipline and nobody else. Hence the history of a natural science is amenable to a reconstruction that eliminates external influences (see Lakatos, 1971).[6]

This general immunity to external empirical problem definition will apply as long as science holds to its traditional motive, sheer curiosity about the universe (Laudan, 1977, pp. 224–5). However, if the boundary between science and technology becomes blurred, as may be happening in contemporary genetic biology, then this immunity will be lost. In that event, natural science empirical problems will in some important respects come to resemble social science empirical problems, to whose character I now turn.

Problems in the Social Sciences

The social sciences too are concerned with solving problems that can once more be divided into Laudan's empirical and conceptual categories. However, there are some important differences between the problems confronting natural science and those confronting social science. Before turning to the character of these differences, let me mention two features of social science problems that prove to be insufficient to demarcate social science from natural science.

First, the question of complexity is insufficient to account for any major methodological differences. Social and political phenomena are indeed complex, and they do incorporate teleological components such as human minds and the ends of action that add variability to interactions in the systems under study. But many natural phenomena, for example ecosystems, are complex too. An ecosystem also possesses emergent properties at higher levels of organization sufficient to demand that analysis proceed as if it had teleological elements (see Patten and Odum, 1981). Complexity may add a layer of difficulty to the apprehension of social and political problems, but it does not render them different in kind from natural science problems.

Second, only differences of degree exist between the constitution of conceptual problems in social and natural science. Worldview influences are perhaps more likely to arise in the social sciences due to the pervasiveness of political ideologies of varying stripes addressing the same subject matter, especially in political science (see, e.g., Diesing, 1983). Yet there is no reason in principle, though it may be more difficult in practice, why social science should be any more susceptible to ideological forces than the natural sciences. Marxist or public choice analysis may encounter ideological criticism, but so may Darwinian biology and marine mammal ecology. Thus the special character of social science problems must be sought elsewhere.

The key distinguishing feature setting social science apart is that its empirical problems are in large measure constructed, weighted, maintained, changed, and dissolved by social forces external to the disciplinary community.[7] This external social influence on empirical problem definition is not a defect or an irrational matter of fad or fashion, nor does it introduce noncognitive reasons into the choice of research traditions. Rather, this influence is rooted in the fact that the social conditions and problems requiring explanation or understanding change with time. Changes of this sort affect the content of the empirical problems confronting political scientists.

One might argue that social sciences are susceptible to external influence on their empirical problems simply because they are for the most part observational rather than empirical sciences. Observational natural science is subject to similar, if much less violent, external forces, as noted in the previous section. However, the crucial demarcation is not externality as such but the fact that the constitution and redefinition of social science empirical problems is socially mediated. That is, society's perceptions (and not just the disciplinary community's perceptions) of what is interesting, desirable, and undesirable in social conditions are historically mutable. Empirical problems with origins in social and technological change can be, and are, mediated by public opinion, the activities of interest groups, and the priorities of political leadership. (I shall argue later that the conditions of this mediation are crucial.) Unlike comets or newly discovered fossils, novel social science empirical problems can be constituted by the agents who are the subjects of political science inquiry. Another way of stating the same point is that the very objects of political science are constituted by those agents' beliefs and understandings.

It is not so much that the community defining empirical problems is separate from or external to the disciplinary community but rather that the discipline constitutes part of this larger community. Political scientists do not sit outside the world that is the object of their study; they are at once observers of and participants in this world. As participants in the social world, social scientists can play a role in the definition of empirical problems by society and polity. Think, for example, of the widespread influence of supply-side economics in the United States in the 1980s. As academic administrators and advisors to research foundations, they can mediate the way these problems reach the research agenda of the discipline. As seekers of financial support, they can stress the relevance of their research to the problems of society or to the problems of those who control the purse strings (cf. Ball, 1983b, pp. 147–9). On the other hand, they could choose to criticize rather than pander to the political agenda of the powers that be.

Even their special role as observers of political life fails to set political scientists apart from the larger community. For as observers, political scientists resemble other agents in their subscription to and action upon theories about the social world. They are not immune to the empirical surprises this world often springs upon its members (see MacIntyre, 1973). Political actors as well as political scientists are problem solvers, and both groups confront novel problems in the courses of their lives. The life of political scientists is special only in that their novelty comes in the form of "metaproblems." That is, they are required to explain situations confronted and constituted by agents who are themselves engaged in solving perceived problems (Popper, 1972c, p. 177).

At this juncture, any line between external and internal definition of empirical problems becomes thoroughly blurred. The two influences are really aspects of a single process. This situation is a far cry from natural science, be it observational or experimental.

The perceptions of social scientists themselves as they watch the BBC or read the *New York Times* can of course affect the more precise definition of empirical problems. For example, for Keynes

(1936) equilibrium in a market economy at less than full employment is an empirical problem requiring explanation. For classical economists and modern free-traders such as von Hayek and Friedman, such an equilibrium does not exist, indeed cannot exist, and hence the empirical problem(s) they need to explain is different. Yet the substance of the empirical problems posed by events such as the Great Depression as interpreted by society at large cannot be ignored, even as the details are cast in different form by Keynesians and anti-Keynesians. Social scientists have a say in the definition of their empirical problems, but so does the rest of society, and so does the reality of events such as depression, stagflation, and revolution.

One last difference between natural and social science should be noted. A natural science empirical problem can only be dissolved by its solution or appropriation by another research tradition. In contrast, social science empirical problems can be dissolved by social forces, such as those that have swept away the industrial world's absolute monarchies.[8]

Shifting Empirical Problems in Political Science

Several examples should serve to clarify how empirical problems in political science are socially determined. These examples and those that follow in the remainder of this chapter should be read as rational reconstructions rather than as veridical history.[9] This apology may be muted by a recognition that all accounts of history are reconstructions of one sort or another.

1. The inception of a market order in society, what Polanyi (1944) refers to as "the great transformation," heralds a new set of empirical problems. For example, how does one explain the stability, coordination, and trade cycles characterizing market systems? With what kind of a political system is a market likely to be associated? Does a market order require any particular kind of polity? With time, the market's existence, coupled perhaps with changes in the relative value society attaches to private and public goods, can direct attention to empirical phenomena such as externalities.

2. American domestic political tranquility in the 1950s and 1960s spawned a focus by many political scientists on the determinants of consensus and political stability. Theories of cross-cutting cleavages and functional harmony were part of the product. Elections

stood out as interesting events; hence there was an upsurge of interest in voting studies. The comparative turmoil of the 1960s and early 1970s together with extreme instability in the new nations of the Third World stimulated theories of political change, revolution, and protest.

3. Public choice theory reached prominence in the 1950s (if not initially by that name), though its contemporary exponents ascribe a substantial, if inchoate, prehistory to this tradition (see, e.g., Riker, 1982). The 1950s work in the tradition addressed paradoxes associated with the use of voting systems to aggregate preferences, a fit topic for that decade (see Arrow, 1963). By the 1960s, collective good problems became more apparent to society at large, and the field shifted its focus to free riders and the logic of public goods supply. The widespread perception of the inherent failure of government programs in the 1970s led to the popularity of theories about why governments must fail (e.g., Niskanen, 1971).

4. Diffusion and assimilation models of international and national development give way to *dependencia,* and internal colonial models as Third World countries and, in some cases, the peripheries of developed nations fail to follow in the anticipated developmental footsteps of the industrial core. This failure is eventually interpreted as a general phenomenon by the relevant elites and political scientists who study development. Further impetus to this shift comes from perceived U.S. misbehavior in Vietnam and Latin America and questionable activity on the part of multinational corporations. The empirical problem changes from one of explaining why a relatively benign path occurs to why relations of domination and exploitation persist.

By no means do I wish to suggest with examples such as these that an externally and socially determined shift in the content of empirical problems is a smooth and rapid process. Quite the contrary. Powerful political interests can resist or promote redefinition. And one can expect controversy over the precise definition, if not over the general content, of these problems. For example, is big government really failing wholesale? Can equilibrium at less than full employment exist in a market economy? Or for that matter, what do the terms "failure," "equilibrium," and "full employment" really connote? Moreover, investigators who have made substantial intellectual investments in certain kinds of empirical problems, be they of voting behavior or social unrest, can be expected to offer resistance to any downgrading of their importance.

It should be noted, too, that the social sciences are subject to external social determination of empirical problems to varying degrees. One would expect physiological psychology and archeological anthropology to be fairly immune; social psychology, social and economic anthropology, economics, sociology, and political science to be very susceptible; and clinical psychology and ecological anthropology to fall somewhere in between.

The Impossibility of Progress?

If indeed the empirical problems confronting research traditions in political science are subject to external social forces, then stable and definitive rational judgments as to the relative merits of competing research traditions cannot be made. For it would seem that a research tradition may be judged internally regressive if novel socially determined problems come along about which it is silent. On the other hand, a tradition may seem internally progressive if some such problems come to the fore about which it does have something to say. To adopt Lakatos's terminology, the protective belt of theories surrounding the hard core of a research program can, in political science, be punctured or inflated as a result of social forces. From the perspective of those familiar with the natural sciences, the social sciences must appear to suffer large elements of randomness in the rivalry of research traditions. But this is not randomness as such, just the necessary consequence of the kinds of empirical problems political science faces.

If global progress in a discipline consists of series of stable rational choices among traditions, necessitating that each defeated tradition fall by the wayside in favor of a more internally progressive one, then clearly global progress in political science cannot occur. Social forces can both frustrate the internal progress of would-be victorious traditions and bolster the fortunes of putative occupants of the rubbish bin of discarded traditions.

Illusions of Progress

The illusion of global progress in political science can, however, arise in at least three ways. First, progress can indeed occur internally within a research tradition. For example, the public choice tradition has been struggling for three decades now with the paradox of voting: Why do people vote when the probability of their having an impact on the outcome of an election is so tiny? A convincing resolution of this problem would constitute a giant progressive step,[10] but only so long as the question of why people turn out to vote is an interesting one. This question would cease to be interesting in a polity like Australia with compulsory voting, or one with no voting at all, or one of sufficiently small size that one person's vote clearly could have an impact on the outcome. Internal progress may give its strongest impression of global progress when a tradition is lucky enough to have new empirical problems appear about which it does have something to say.

Second, global progress in political science can appear to occur in times of exceptional social and political stability or, for that matter, permanent turmoil if this stability or permanent turmoil translates into stability in the content of the empirical problems that society sets for social science. But global progress of this sort again proves to be an illusion, as transitions from periods of social stability like the 1950s to periods of turmoil such as the 1960s amply demonstrate.

Third, illusory global progress may occur when a political science disciplinary community defines its empirical problems in terms of a single polity's dominant ideology, thus lending artificial stability to these problems. Some critics of the last few decades of American political science portray its disciplinary mainstream in this light (cf. Lindblom, 1982a), especially in the days when it largely ignored the distinctive political presence of blacks and women in American society. An equally insidious and prolonged example of such systematic distortion of problem definition occurs with the pervasiveness of the liberal discourse of limited, individualistic, and power-oriented politics. This discourse gives comfort to, and draws comfort from, the voting studies literature about the limited prospects for democracy (see Chapter 8).

Illusions of Degeneration

Several philosophers of natural science argue that resuscitation of an apparently exhausted research tradition can be a worthwhile project (see, e.g., Feyerabend, 1975; Laudan, 1977, p. 83; Heelan, 1983, pp. 199–200). As Lakatos (1970, p. 164) puts it, "programmes may get out of degenerating troughs." However, examples of successful revival in the history of science are rare; the record shows that natural science research traditions typically wax and wane but once. Each, in T. H. Huxley's words, "begins as heresy, and ends as superstition." The result is that "science destroys its past" (Kuhn, 1969, p. 407). In contrast, political science research traditions can degenerate or even die, only to experience resurrection. Consider the following examples.

1. Western social scientists for several decades regarded Marxism as an effectively defunct research tradition. Marxism seemed to have trouble coping with the empirical problems posed by events such as Stalinism, the impetus given to fascism by the Great Depression, the apparent resilience of the capitalist system, and the rise of an affluent working class. Yet Marxism arose with renewed vigor in Western social science in the 1960s and 1970s (see Ball and Farr, 1984, pp. 1–3).[11]

2. Classical macroeconomics held sway in academic and policy-making communities from the nineteenth century into the 1930s. The tradition's demise seemed complete by the mid-1940s following its inability to provide a satisfactory account of the massive involuntary unemployment of the Great Depression. Yet the 1970s witnessed a resurgence of classical macroeconomic ideas in monetarist and rational expectations schools. The revival took a political twist with Olson (1982) and an associated spate of studies of the political economy of economic growth rates.[12]

3. Thomas Malthus was widely regarded as passé for over a century. Yet "Malthus with a computer" (Freeman, 1973) appears in 1972 with the publication of *The Limits to Growth* (Meadows et al., 1972), followed eventually by calls for his rehabilitation as a political theorist (Wells, 1982).[13]

4. The idea that political institutions have autonomous influence on collective outcomes formed a major organizing principle of early twentieth-century political science. In midcentury this tradition was thoroughly displaced by approaches that stressed methodological individualism and saw political life as under the influence of forces originating elsewhere in society. Political institutions came to be viewed as arenas for the pursuit of interest, their structure reflecting social influences, and politics itself came to be defined in terms of resource allocation. However, the 1970s and 1980s witnessed a "new institutionalism" that again treated institutions as independent variables in their own right and individual political action in terms of role and obligation rather than pursuit of preference (see March and Olsen, 1984, for a survey).[14]

It would be hard to find parallels in the natural sciences to such wholesale revival of research traditions. Let me suggest that resuscitation in each instance occurred as a result of changes in the socially determined content of empirical problems. With the latitude granted by rational reconstruction, I would claim:

1. Marxism as a Western social science research tradition made a comeback because it had much to say about social protest and industrial conflict in the developed world and the apparent inability of the Third World to develop smoothly along Western lines.

2. Classical macroeconomics regained popularity in the 1970s because inflation and stagflation replaced depression as the macroeconomic empirical problems of prime social concern. The latter-day classicists offered better explanations of inflation than the Keynesians. Olson's variation of the classical tradition is especially attractive because its introduction of political "distributional coalitions" into the picture can explain the coexistence of inflation and large-scale involuntary unemployment.

3. The revival of the dismal parson (Malthus) was a direct response to perceptions of overpopulation, resource scarcity, and environmental decay that attended the environmental and energy crises of the 1970s.

4. To quote two prominent new institutionalists (March and Olsen, 1984, p. 734):

   This resurgence of concern with institutions is a cumulative consequence of the modern transformation of social institutions and persistent commentary from observers of them. Social, political, and economic institutions have become larger, considerably more complex and resourceful, and *prima facie* more important to collective life. Most of the major actors in modern economic and political systems are formal organizations, and the institutions of law and bureaucracy occupy a dominant role in contemporary life.

The Reality of Progress

The rationality of any choice among competing research traditions in political science must, then, be contingent upon time and place and a given set of sociopolitical circumstances. Empirical problems in the social sciences are externally defined, socially mediated, and historically situated in the way those of natural science are not. The history of political science must therefore be bound up with the history of society. Political science is a historical discipline.[15] To understand the discipline's component traditions, to reflect intelligently upon their successes and failures, and to choose rationally among them, one needs to know the social and historical contexts that shaped them and to which they responded (for more extensive argument along these lines, see Dryzek and Leonard, 1988).[16]

Though informed by this history, judgments across research traditions can and should be prospective.

But the choice among research traditions in political science is no less rational for being historically contingent. Chronic flux in the rivalry of research traditions in political science should not be attributed to irrationality, mob psychology, or any supposed immaturity of the discipline. And against those in the sociology of science who believe social influences fully determine the content of intellectual inquiry, political science can respond rationally to its social and historical contexts (cf. MacIntyre, 1988, p. 390). Hence political science can be a rational discipline. But it cannot be progressive in the same sense as the natural sciences, for stable and definitive choice among research traditions is impossible.

Still there is a sense in which political science can progress, though only on a reconceptualization of progress. Stating the thesis at its boldest, political science is progressive to the extent that its ability to cope with contingency in the character of its empirical problems (scarcity or plenty, stability or revolution, etc.) grows with time. At issue here is not the capacity of a particular tradition to cope with contingency but the capacity of the discipline as a whole. This adaptive capacity is enhanced to the degree that a large number of potentially useful research traditions exists. Metaphorically, political science can be said to progress laterally rather than vertically. The vertical progress of natural science, a succession of research traditions chosen and eventually discarded on a rational basis, is not the only kind of progress that can occur.

A capacity to cope with contingency may be illustrated by the fortunes of the Hobbesian research tradition. At least on one (contested) reading of Hobbes, the Hobbesian ontology contains self-interested individuals and pressing absolute material scarcity of total resources relative to the needs and desires of populations. Hobbes's own work has of course been one of the staples of political philosophy since the seventeenth century. On the other hand, little internal progress in the Hobbesian tradition's applicability to empirical problems pertaining to scarcity is evident in the centuries following his death in which scarcity, at least in the Western world, was held at bay by continuing expansion of frontiers in the New World.

A global social perception of absolute scarcity suddenly reappeared around 1970. The initial response in some quarters was a recollection of Hobbes's analysis by avowed Hobbesians such as

Hardin (1968) and Ophuls (1977). Their prescription was borrowed, with acknowledgment, straight from Hobbes: a powerful sovereign to prevent a disastrous "war of all against all," now redescribed as the "tragedy of the commons" (see Orr and Hill, 1978). After the work of Hardin, Ophuls, and others appeared, a number of anomalies became apparent. For example, it is clear that there exist communities living under conditions of scarcity that manage to hold the tragedy of the commons at bay while retaining extreme decentralization in their political organization. Empirical problems of this sort have been addressed by an outpouring of work that stresses the possibility of conditional cooperation in the rational and self-interested choices of individuals (see, e.g., Taylor, 1976; Axelrod, 1984). Such work has shown that political arrangements other than extreme centralization can cope with absolute scarcity. This latter kind of work is clearly an advance on Hobbes's own analysis of scarcity, in the way that the work of Hardin and Ophuls is not. Yet the success of conditional cooperation studies was made possible by the existence of the Hobbesian tradition, which could be called upon when the content of empirical problems shifted in a direction that made the tradition relevant.[17]

A similar illustration of an ability to deal with contingency can be found in the history of classical macroeconomics, to which I have already alluded. After the general demise of the classics in the wake of the Great Depression, the tradition's flame kept burning only inside the walls of the University of Chicago and in a few isolated outposts elsewhere. The inflation of the 1970s yielded empirical problems the tradition could address, and its flame spread like wildfire throughout the academy and into government. Again, the initial 1970s applications, in this case monetarism and rational expectations, were no improvement on pre-1940s classicism, for they shared an inability to explain large-scale involuntary unemployment. Olson (1982) both pays homage to the classical tradition and constructs a clear advance within it, for his theory can explain involuntary unemployment and its anomalous coexistence with inflation. Olson traces stagflation to the political power in stable societies of distributional coalitions such as cartels and labor unions. His concurrent extension of the research tradition into empirical problem areas traditionally of more concern to political scientists than economists, such as political rigidities and the determinants of public policy, is further evidence of renewed progressiveness.

One implication of these stories of decline and revival in research traditions is that disciplinary history is central to the appraisal of competing traditions and their component theories. This history need not be one of ideological influence on theory, on the one hand, or a history of accumulated stockpiles of scientific truths, on the other. But a full reconstruction of the history of political science as a rational, historically grounded, and (laterally) progressive discipline remains to be written [see Dryzek and Leonard (1988) for some suggestions on how to write this history].

How Much Diversity?

The general lesson of the two examples in the preceding section is that an apparently exhausted research tradition can eventually exhibit renewed problem-solving power. Hence research traditions should not be buried lightly. At the very least, traditions that have shown some past successes merit technicians to keep them in good order. Tenacity by adherents of a research tradition is generally commendable.

However (contra Lakatos, 1970), too much tenacity might lead to irrational discrimination against both the resuscitation of old traditions and the inception of new ones. Those who see a single approach as legitimate, be it public choice, the behavioral persuasion, or Marxism, are among the worst offenders here. A middle path between slavishly following a tradition and discarding it forever should be sought. The somewhat imprecise judgment we can reach at this point is that the rationality and progress of political science, properly understood, rule out two extremes.

On the one hand, any desire for disciplinary homogeneity should be abandoned. Misinterpreting Kuhn (1970b), many political scientists came to believe that enforcement of a single research tradition (paradigm) is required for global progress in the discipline. In contrast, the demands of rationality and a conceptualization of progress in terms of a capacity to cope with contingency require a tolerance of diversity, not its suppression.

On the other hand, an attitude of "anything goes" in research traditions is not defensible. This slogan was proposed by Feyerabend (1975). Later, he asserts that "the history of science is full of theories which were pronounced dead, then resurrected, then pronounced dead again only to celebrate another triumphant comeback." Thus "it makes sense to preserve faulty points of view for possible future use" (Feyerabend, 1987, p. 33). But exhausted research traditions really may have to be discarded sometimes, if only to prevent the kind of irrational discrimination against novel and revived research traditions I just mentioned. For a decision to cling to a "faulty point of view" is simultaneously a decision not to countenance potentially more successful alternatives. There just are not enough of us in the discipline to justify the idea that we should all cling to our old favorites. So if practitioners continue to enforce outmoded traditions in the face of changing empirical problems, then we may require the likes of Senator William Proxmire to come to our rescue. Any such practitioners who receive or disburse public funds are worthy recipients of golden fleeces, which might pressure them to cast their eyes in new directions.

This elimination of two extremes leaves a sizable territory in which the conversation between different research traditions as they confront socially determined conceptual and empirical problems can proceed. And as long as there is political debate and dispute in the larger community, which affect the definition of empirical and conceptual problems, one can expect a lively disciplinary conversation. No single voice should ever gain even temporary hegemony. But one should not regard all voices as equally reasonable. How, then, can we distinguish among these voices? Are the criteria ultimately intellectual, or political, or both?

The Conditions of Problem Definition

Any finer distinctions among research traditions can be approached by examining not their comparative success rates in resolving empirical and conceptual problems but the social context that provides their empirical and conceptual grist. The conditions of empirical problem definition are pathological to the extent they are distorted by factors such as political power, wealth, and professionalism. Success in resolving empirical problems so defined is illusory and ultimately indefensible.

Consider, to begin, how political power can distort problem definition. In illustrating the uses to which his famous three conceptual models of foreign policy-making can be put, Graham Allison (1969, p. 717) argues that all three can be used to answer the question "Why will North Vietnam surrender when?" That North Vietnam *will* surrender seems not to be in doubt. Allison would appear to be accepting the empirical problem as presented by administration policy-makers in Washington. That he would still do so as late as August 1968 (the date identified in his text) is mildly surprising, for by that time, of course, official accounts of the war were being called into question. The section is reproduced in the book-length version of Allison's argument that appeared two years later, though it is qualified by his recognition of "the risks of seeming dated, and being in error" (Allison, 1971, p. 261), and he takes pains to stress that the section is reprinted verbatim from a 1968 conference paper.

The fact that protest against the Vietnam war combined with the battlefield successes of the North Vietnamese shattered this particular empirical problem shows that there are limits to the stranglehold of political power on problem definition. Social science in the Soviet bloc, pre-*glasnost*, was less fortunate. Thomas's (1979) description of Soviet sociology shows how ideological hegemony translates into homogeneity in problem definition and hence into orthodox and sterility in social science. It is no surprise that one finds a paucity of social science in authoritarian regimes.

This recognition of pathological problem definition in blatantly authoritarian regimes should not, though, translate into complacency on the part of Western social scientists. Though not as stultifying or restrictive as official Soviet Marxism, the liberal tradition too can impose restrictions of its own, especially in the United States. In this light, one should be skeptical of the agenda for public opinion research proposed by Natchez (1985), who wants liberal constitutionalism to set this agenda precisely because it is the seat of political power in the U.S. polity. And in an era in which liberal democratic governments dispense largesse to social scientists, it is instrumentally rational and self-interested for the latter to pander to the interests of government officials. It is in these terms that leading social scientists appealed to Congress to restore the cuts made in the social science operations of the National Science Foundation in the early 1980s.

This question of financial support for research brings me to the influence of wealth on empirical problem definition. Aside from advertising, corporate control of the media, and business influence on legislative, electoral, and bureaucratic politics, the most direct avenue for such influence is through foundation grants. These monies do, of course, come with strings attached to the foundation's research agenda. For some, such as the American Enterprise Institute or Heritage Foundation, this agenda is fairly blatantly ideological. Russell Sage, Rockefeller, and Ford may seem to have less overt leanings, but perhaps only because they can be more comfortably situated within the mainstream of American political life (which they have helped constitute). Though they do not determine the results of research, the interests of these foundations do help determine the kinds of questions research addresses (Ball, 1987b).

The influence of aspirations for professional respectability on empirical problem definition is perhaps more insidious still. To Ricci (1984), the tragedy of political science in the United States (and so the world) has always been that intellectual and administrative acceptance within U.S. universities demands the trappings of science. This imperative in turn dictates a focus on tractable empirical problems, however trivial, to the exclusion of participation in the "great conversation" of democratic development.[18]

In this context, it is noteworthy that National Science Foundation grants (financed by the U.S. federal government) are largely administered by social scientists themselves. Nor are these administrators necessarily representative of their disciplines. At least in political science, they were once scientistic zealots, keen to promote technologies such as survey research and large-scale computer modeling of foreign policy and international politics.

Problem definition in political science cannot secure autonomy from external social forces. Hence the discipline can never exhibit vertical progress of the form with which we are familiar in the natural sciences. Its prospects in this respect may be as poor as supposedly softer disciplines, such as art history or literary criticism. Yet political science can be rational, even if that rationality is context bound. To the extent this context is free from distortion by power, wealth, and professionalism, political science can progress in a way requiring no apologies, for with lateral progress comes an ever-increasing capacity to answer the questions in which we are interested or might become interested.

However, political science can only be a rational discipline, and its practice and progress can only be defended, to the extent the circumstances of the definition of its empirical problems are felicitous and uncoerced. And *that* is only possible to the degree society and polity are themselves communicatively rational. It follows that if social science is true to its (cognitively) rational foundations, then it *must* criticize any distorting agents in society and polity. This critical necessity does not mean that all political scientists should be critical theorists all of the time. But all of them should probably be critical theorists some of the time. And if the research traditions to which they subscribe do not allow such criticism, these traditions should be discarded, amended, or suspended. For to the degree social science accepts or ignores distortions affecting its agenda of empirical problems on the part of wealth or power, then its explanatory, problem-solving efforts are misdirected.

If political science as a whole must be critical of society and polity in this fashion, then so must its component research traditions and instruments. Thus any tradition or instrument that reinforces discourses of domination, control, or limited democracy stands condemned. Conversely, any tradition or instrument that substantiates discourses of free communicative interaction merits approval.

In judging, comparing, and making choices across traditions, we can distinguish between a tradition's success in resolving conceptual and empirical problems and its contribution to emancipation. For example, public choice has recently shown great problem-solving success but done little for emancipation. So to answer my earlier question, when it comes to evaluating and comparing different voices within the discipline, both intellectual and political criteria are appropriate.

The political criteria may sometimes seem to produce more stable results here than the intellectual criteria. I noted earlier that the success of a tradition in resolving conceptual and empirical problems may wax, wane, and wax again. But a tradition's emancipatory potential may be more constant, at least when that potential is pretty much nonexistent to begin with. Thus although the Malthusian tradition has had its ups and downs in terms of problem solving, it has had nothing but downs in terms of emancipation. However, this contrast in stability between the two kinds of criteria should not be overdrawn. For if critique, too, must be contextually and historically specific, then different traditions may also wax and wane in their emancipatory potential. Thus although Marxism as a critical theory may have been quite appropriate to nineteenth-century capitalism, it is of questionable relevance to contemporary postindustrial society, which is subject to different agents of domination.

Nor are the two sorts of criteria entirely separable. The intellectual criteria cannot stand apart from the political, for ultimately it is politics that sets the agenda for intellectual inquiry. And if practitioners are willing to accept a systematically distorted set of problems – and the kind of society that defines problems in this fashion – then their efforts must be condemned as misdirected and *intellectually* dishonest. If this is true for our evaluation of particular traditions, then it is true for political science as a whole. To be rational, political science must be critical. This basic critical commitment is not a matter of ideology or of the investigator's preference; it is a matter of cognitive rationality, and it is one matter that does not change with historical circumstances.

PART V

Conclusion

CHAPTER 11

On Extending Democracy

The public face of politics as the twentieth century draws to a close affirms the triumph of at least two broad principles. The first is democracy, understood as the collective construction and application of political authority. The second is rationality, whether understood in terms of making choices for good cognitive reasons or as the capacity to resolve problems effectively through individual cogitation and social interaction. In practice, of course, these principles may be honored as much in their violation as in their observance. But at least on the plane of public justification, conservative suspicion of reason, fascist anti-intellectualism, and authoritarianism of the left and right have all been vanquished. Yet the intellectual demise of their erstwhile opposition has not left democracy and rationality secure. At best, they rest uneasily in tentative accommodation. At worst, there is outright conflict between these two principles.

This conflict arises in many different forms. Max Weber believed rationality entails bureaucratization, which strangles democracy along with the rest of the congenial aspects of human society. Even if Weber's scenario has proven overdrawn, it remains arguable that needs for effectiveness and coordination limit the possibilities for democratizing public organizations (Pollitt, 1986, pp. 180–1). Hannah Arendt, for her part, believes in the inevitability of conflict between the authentically "political" and the inescapably "social." To Arendt, the latter, concerned as it is with mundane issues of problem solving, can only corrupt and destroy authentic politics. To prevent this corruption, she endorses the classic (but unattainable) separation of politics and administration. Postmodernists and deconstructionists take a critique of rationality far beyond Weber and Arendt. They argue that rationality can only constrain and repress human spontaneity and diversity. But beyond their condemnations of hierarchy, it is not clear that they endorse any particular kind of politics, let alone democracy.

In all of these accounts, and many others, it is the authority claimed by expertise that leads rationality to confront, corrupt, and perhaps even destroy democracy. I have tried to show that this claim is unfounded and that the rational activities in which "experts" are engaged point to democracy, not hierarchy. I have argued for the democratization of expertise in politics, public polity, and political science. But this reconciliation of democracy and rationality only makes sense if it proceeds under the banner of communicative rationality. In the discursive democracy that results there are places for rationality in the senses of choice based on good cognitive reasons and effective social problem solving. There is even a place for instrumental action, provided that it is unceasingly regulated and governed by communicative rationality. (There is, alas, no place for objectivism.)

Why, then, has the kind of reconciliation of which I speak failed to occur in social science theory, let alone political practice? The answer may be that choice based on good cognitive reasons is often equated with objectivism and effective social problem solving with instrumental action. Reconciliation between democracy and rationality requires that these associations be decoupled. And democracy, for its part in this reconciliation, must show its participatory and discursive face rather than its protective and strategic aspect.

Discursive democracy does, then, combine democracy and rationality, politics and policy. But what happened to the political science in my subtitle? The answer is that, like rationality, it has been barking up the wrong tree.

Seeking respectability in the American university, political scientists in the United States have for the past century or more tried to ply their trade in self-consciously scientific terms. In this endeavor, their model has been a (mostly erroneous) objectivist conception of the "harder" natural sciences. In terms of Ricci's (1984) telling metaphor, political scientists have tried to build an ordinary column in the temple of science, renouncing any Aristotelian claim to the temple's roof. The effects are not confined to the United States, for American political science sets the tone for the activity worldwide.

Contra Ricci, I have argued in Part IV that there is nothing wrong with an aspiration to political *science*. The fault lies not with science per se but with objectivist misconceptions of it. Indeed, if political scientists want to be scientific in terms of making good, cognitively rational choices across research traditions, then they must also be critical. That is, as I argued at the end of Chapter 10, political science must criticize society and polity to the extent they violate the principles of communicative rationality. To reject this point is to be untrue to the cognitively rational foundations of political inquiry.

The principles of discursive rationality to which these scientific commitments lead are essentially identical with those of the classical model of politics. And I have argued, too, that these principles are the key to effective problem solving in political institutions, to the realization of participatory democracy, and to defensible policy analysis. These arguments suggest that ultimately there is no difference between the rationality appropriate to politics and the rationality appropriate to political science.

I have sought to establish this essential identity in several different ways. The discursive designs sketched in Part II are hospitable to communicatively rational social science in the form of critical oversight and discursive metadesign. In Part III I concluded that the only defensible kind of policy analysis proceeds in terms of contributions to, and facilitation of, free discourse within the public sphere. In Chapters 8 and 9 I argued that political science instruments and methods should be evaluated by the extent to which they embody discourses of uncoerced communication – and reinforce these discourses in the larger polity. Chapter 10 extends this analysis to research traditions. Discipline and polity are joint participants in conceptual and empirical problem construction. To the extent this process is felicitous, so enabling cognitively rational political science, discipline, polity, and – crucially – their interactions must be communicatively rational.

In short, the rationality and democracy of politics and political science run together. I have tried to show that this joint program outperforms its rivals in domains as diverse as congenial and meaningful political community, effectiveness in resolving complex social problems, harmonious and productive international relations, democratic development, and effective social science.

There are, of course, additional domains I might have addressed. I have said little about the internal workings of political parties, industrial democracy (Dahl, 1985b), local community control, the politicization of personality, identity, and culture advocated by contemporary feminists (e.g., Rowbotham, 1986), the democratic control of technology, and the prospects for democratizing the organs of the state, even bureaucracy itself (Pollitt, 1986).

My own preferred location for discursively democratic institutions, discursive designs, and new social movements in particular is a public space where individuals can congregate and confront the state. But if the state, bureaucracy, private enterprise, and family are always going to be with us, then perhaps they merit democratization too. Recognition of the likelihood, if not inevitability or necessity, of the persistence of these institutions leads participatory democrats such as Poulantzas (1980), Held (1987), and Gould (1988) to advocate democratization on a broad front, in civil society *and* the state. All I would add here is that this democratization should be discursive in character. Nor is there any reason to stop at the boundaries of the human world; discursive democracy might even extend into the biosphere, but that is another story altogether (Dryzek, 1990).

There are, though, domains of life where discursive democracy does not belong. Communicative rationality finds its grounding in the linguistic interaction of collective life. It does not speak to theater, wit, religion, music, visual arts, play, poetry, or private experience, unless of course these activities enter into the constitution of collective choices.

The pursuit of discursive democracy on a broad front entails major risks. Flirtation with the state of the sort discussed in Chapters 2 and 4 raises the possibility that discursive designs will be coopted and henceforth used as instruments of state power. Similarly, the involvement of corporations with incipient discursive designs means devaluation of citizen concerns and their compromise by base motives such as profit. And if it is hazardous for discursive democracy to even flirt with the state and capital, how much more dangerous is the pursuit of democracy within the organizational structure of government and private enterprise. Industrial democracy, for example, may be used as a managerial tool to increase worker productivity and profits; indeed, this is the point of the human relations school of management. Or tenant control of public housing may enable a government bureaucracy to devolve some of its more intractable problems, reduce its outlays, and evade larger structural problems in the organization of society.

Such hazards explain why discursive democracy should remember its essential connection with critical theory. Multifaceted and relentless democratization should be matched by multifaceted and relentless critique. The need for critique applies as much to putatively discursive and democratic practices and institutions as it does to systematically repressive ones. As I noted in Chapter 2, critique can be metatheoretical, pure, indirect, or constructive. If I have stressed the last of these types, it is because critical theory is in great need of a constructive moment in order to redeem its *practical* promise. But this emphasis is not intended to disparage more uncompromising kinds of critique. Critical theory should not sleep in its quest for a rational and democratic world it knows can never be attained.

Notes

Chapter 1

1. "Technical" rationality is synonymous with instrumental rationality. And Elster (1983, pp. 2–15) describes a "thin theory of individual rationality" that is also essentially identical with instrumental rationality as characterized here.
2. This definition of objectivism follows the usage of Bernstein (1983), who notes that the term sometimes refers more narrowly to the philosophical doctrine that there exists an objective world whose nature is independent of the subjects trying to apprehend it (Bernstein, 1983, pp. 8–9).
3. For the sake of brevity I shall often use "instrumental rationality" as shorthand for "instrumental–analytic rationality."
4. See Schnaedelbach (1987–8) for an outline and critique of neo-Aristotelianism in German conservatism. This sort of conservatism in truth owes much more to Edmund Burke than its does to Aristotle. So "the fact that neo-conservatives have appropriated some elements of Aristotle's political philosophy for their own politically motivated purposes does not, *ipso facto*, disqualify the principles and categories of Aristotelian practical philosophy" (d'Entreves, 1987–8, p. 238). Habermas (1989) is also guilty of the unfortunate confusion of neo-Aristotelianism with Burkean conservatism.
5. It should be noted here that postempiricist philosophy of science has more recently established the noninstrumental character of science.
6. Deductive–nomological explanations involve causal laws, which are tested through experimental or statistical means. Critical theories, in contrast, are tested by action on the part of the audience to which they are addressed and are confirmed to the extent this audience thereby liberates itself from any supposedly causal influences upon it (see Fay, 1975, for further discussion of these differences).
7. Note, though, that a few liberals – beginning with John Stuart Mill – have advocated a kind of "developmental" democracy consistent with the pedagogical aspect of political reason associated with the first set (see Held, 1987, pp. 85–104).

8. MacIntyre refers specifically to the reflections of Stephen Toulmin (1981) upon his work for the National Commission for the Protection of Human Subjects of Biomedical and Behavioral Research.
9. Arendt grounds this claim in her interpretation of classical politics. It should be noted that Leo Strauss interprets classical politics (which he associated with Plato as well as Aristotle) in terms of a search for truth and moral certainty (e.g., Strauss, 1959).
10. See Bernstein (1986, pp. 238-59) for a critique of Arendt's elitism and tortuous distinction between the political and the social.
11. Note, though, that the principles of communicative rationality can be violated in the lifeworld, e.g., if individuals take personality, morality, and culture for granted or if these factors are under the sway of external forces that cannot be comprehended or controlled.
12. A discussion about "blending" communicative and instrumental attitudes may be found in Alford (1985, pp. 152-7).
13. I would of course expect no endorsement from MacIntyre himself, who favors a very different kind of alternative to the Western liberal tradition.
14. John Dewey arguably constructed a similar kind of defense around the same time as Popper (see Ricci, 1984, pp. 101-21). But several different readings of Dewey are possible here, one of which would make him a friend of communicative rationalization (Kaufman-Osborn, 1985) and not of the kind of instrumental rationality in politics favored by Popper.

Chapter 2

1. See Fay (1975, pp. 92-110) for an unusually clear account of this standard conception of critical theory.
2. Purists might reply that Whitlam's pragmatism did him no good. His government was ousted in a right-wing coup engineered through the offices of the Queen's Governor-General.
3. Some members of this tradition, notably Plato, believe that virtue is and should be equally centralized.
4. An offshoot of this program is developed by Friedrich A. von Hayek, who, unlike Popperians, argues for the market rather than liberal government. Hayek believes that the market is preferable to any kind of government on the grounds that a decentralized "catallaxy" of market actors offers the only way to aggregate dispersed, fleeting, and incomplete bits of social knowledge (see especially von Hayek, 1979, pp. 65-97).
5. For discussions of the importance and influence of Popper in this regard, see Magee (1973), James (1980), and Ricci (1984, pp. 114-32).
6. An extended response to critical theory's attack on positivism is offered by Keat (1981), who argues that positivism, however one defines it, does not back any particular kind of political practice. If one accepts the definition of positivism I have just given, then Keat's argument boils down to the simple claim that just because the theorist establishes a causal link between an action (such as a policy alternative) and a goal, this does not mean that the action must be taken, for other normative constraints might also be brought into

play. Although this argument sounds reasonable, all Keat does here is save positivism by abandoning it as a guide to practice. Keat goes on to make the more general claim that there is no connection between epistemology and political practice. Without being able to deal with all his arguments, let me suggest that the accounts of critical rationalism and critical theory developed in this chapter are immune to them.

7. Holistic experimentation of this sort should not be confused with Popper's equation of the term with centralized historicist planning (see Popper, 1972a).

8. Underlying this fear is a recognition of the self-subversion of vanguard strategies in Marxism and other radical movements.

9. But note here the recent vogue for a participatory community architecture.

10. Enthusiasts of information technology should, however, be wary of the push-button democracy of cable television, which would trivialize politics and reduce the citizen still further to an isolated spectator (Dagger, 1982).

11. On the functions of the mediator, see Young (1972, pp. 56–60), Raiffa (1982, pp. 108–9), and Wall (1981). Within these broad roles, there is considerable scope for what the mediator actually does, which can range from shuttle diplomacy to education in negotiation techniques.

12. Aside from the real-world cases described here, the number of proposals made for discursive problem-solving institutions in recent years in a variety of issue areas is striking. Discussions of industrial policy make frequent reference to the need for some kind of participatory forum. Proposals for discursive designs in an ecological context may be found in Dryzek (1987) and Young and Osherenko (1984).

13. On a personal note, I worked as a facilitator for a working group at the 1989 National Gathering of the U. S. Greens in Eugene, Oregon.

14. Critical rationalism does not, however, treat values as arbitrary, for ethical systems have a history that can be understood in terms of the contributions of (critically) rational actors. But whereas the evolution of ethical systems reflects rational processes, any problem-solving task at hand is independent of this evolution and its rationality. History leaves an irreducible plurality of values in the context of any given social problem.

15. Recent work in this tradition has called attention to the possibility of conditional cooperation among purely self-interested actors providing an adequate supply of public goods, though only in small groups (see, e.g., Taylor, 1976).

Chapter 3

1. For a lengthier disquisition on the inability of markets, pluralist political systems, and uncalculating ecological communes to handle complex problems, see Dryzek (1987, chaps. 7, 9, and 16).

Chapter 4

1. Whether or not the earth's resources and ecosystems are finite or infinite is a controversial question, which I cannot go into here. For a review of the arguments on both sides of the issue and my own justification for a "finite" conclusion, see Dryzek (1987, pp. 20–3).

2. Exceptions to these empirical generalizations are conceivable. Sandinista sympathizers might offer the Nicaraguan case as just such an exception.

3. Amy's critique pours cold water over his earlier (1983b) enthusiasm for mediation.

4. A public inquiry more closely in accordance with the precepts of communicative rationality is discussed in Chapter 6.

Chapter 5

1. An anarchy, by definition, lacks formal institutions at the system level. For a discussion of the anarchical nature of the international system, see Young (1978).

2. Ashley's language is also a bit different. What he refers to as technical rationality appears in this study as instrumental rationality; what he calls rationality proper is roughly the same as communicative rationality.

3. The International Joint Commission is an essentially advisory forum for the investigation and negotiation of U.S.–Canada transboundary water issues, though it does have a few limited decision-making powers (e.g., about the level of boundary waters). It was established in 1909 under the terms of the Boundary Waters Treaty signed by the United States and Canada.

4. Mediation of environmental disputes in the United States is a recent innovation because prior to the enactment around 1970 of pieces of legislation such as the National Environmental Policy Act, environmental groups had little power. Today, their veto power is established through access to the legal system.

5. One of the main underlying motivations in North Dakota's enthusiasm for the diversion may be a desire to secure Missouri water for future industrial and energy-related development (see Carroll, 1983, pp. 180–1). North Dakota feels, understandably, that if its own claim is not established, then upstream or downstream states may claim the water.

Chapter 6

1. However, his marginally more sympathetic critics on this point (e.g., Seidelman and Harpham, 1985, p. 136) allow that the technocratic Lasswell's elite of policy scientists for democracy would seek broad citizen approval.

2. The Wheatsheaf, Maids Moreton.

3. Indeed, MacPherson (1977, pp. 114–15) classifies participatory democracy as a type of liberal democracy.

4. Paris and Reynolds (1983, pp. 266–9) depart from liberal democracy somewhat in arguing that rational ideologies would be essentially public spirited. Most theorists of liberal democracy see politics in terms of the pursuit of private interests.

5. Barber is no friend of policy analysis and explicitly rejects the whole idea of a policy science (Barber, 1984, p. 169).

6. Mansbridge argues too that such common interests become less likely as the size of a political system increases, such that large democracies must be "adversarial," or liberal.

7. Restriction of policy deliberation to a small group of citizens selected by lot would eliminate the pedagogic aspect of participatory democracy. Yet there would be no need for participation to be confined to the minipopulus.
8. There is an interesting parallel between Kaufman-Osborn's treatment of Dewey and Torgerson's (1985) analysis of Lasswell. Both discuss thinkers normally associated with technocratic, social engineering conceptions of the relation between social science and public policy and proceed to argue that the received view about these thinkers is erroneous. Both then read into their thinker a conception of policy analysis broadly consistent with the policy science of participatory democracy presented here. Other discussions of policy analysis consistent with this goal include Forester (1983) and Dunn (1982).

Chapter 7

1. It is technically possible, if politically unlikely, for accountability to be reconciled with economies of scale. The solution here would produce public goods in centralized governmental units but provide them in decentralized units, presumably through contract between units. Divisible, quasi-public goods such as roads, social services, and even health care might conceivably be produced and provided in this fashion. Purer public goods such as environmental quality, security, and public health could not so easily respond to this treatment.
2. Haefele (1973) argues that public choice theorists should expect their appropriate-size governments to produce better results (in utilitarian terms) only if they function by representation and vote rather than bureaucracy.
3. Prime Minister Thatcher's tendency to restrict her circle of advisors to a small group of like-minded individuals and to dispense with potentially critical ministers has been widely noted.
4. This irreducibility does not mean that values are arbitrary. Popperians recognize that value systems have a history that can be understood as a succession of critical contributions. But this history is independent of any policy problem at hand, and hence it leaves us with an irreducible plurality in any given case.
5. A clear statement of the normative principles involved may be found in Beveridge (1942).

Chapter 8

1. My title for this chapter is adapted from Gould (1981), who exposes the bad science of attempts to demonstrate hereditarian and racialist theories of intelligence. Other things being equal, a gender-neutral title would have been preferable and more in the spirit of my critique. For feminists too argue that many of the widely used methods in political science, including survey research, are inappropriate from their point of view (see, e.g., Kelley, Ronan, and Cawley, 1987). I retain "man" in the title for reasons of style and continuity with both Gould and Aristotle.

2. Apparent increases in the coherence of issue attitudes may in fact be attributable to changes in the wording of survey questions (Sullivan, Piereson, and Marcus, 1978).

3. Explanations of this standing are subsumed under general laws. Any such law states that given a certain set of conditions, some phenomenon will always occur (see, e.g., Hempel, 1965), though probabilistic relaxations of this last principle are generally allowed in the social sciences.

4. That is, I will draw upon contemporary accounts of science as advanced by philosophers such as Kuhn, Lakatos, and Laudan, who for all their differences share a rejection of the positivist and objectivist precepts of an earlier era.

5. See Lakatos (1970, pp. 97–8) for another statement of this point. Kuhn (1970b) goes further than Popper in arguing that observations are always made through the lens of the paradigm that inspires the theories that the observations are designed to test.

6. Clausen (1968) notes that the very experience of being interviewed can change respondents' attitudes and behaviors. For example, they may become more interested in politics or more disposed to vote. Clausen discusses this phenomenon in terms of a threat to the validity of panel surveys.

7. It should be noted that all apply irrespective of the degree of sophistication in survey design, e.g., in the use of open-ended questions to get at complex attitudes.

8. Marxists might stress the ahistorical aspect of opinion surveying of political dispositions and capabilities and the taking of false consciousness at face value.

9. Some political science practitioners of public choice, itself inspired by microeconomics, make use of sample surveys. In contrast, mainstream microeconomics does not study individuals directly, focusing instead on preferences and other attributes revealed in behavior.

10. The word "action" has a special meaning to Arendt (1958, pp. 175–81), who defines political action in terms of creative and self-revealing public speech and so would see "action itself" and "action-oriented debate" as synonymous.

11. By no means do I wish to suggest Key was attuned to a classical conception of politics. In fact, he took the liberal constitutionalist American political system for granted and sought only to persuade political elites to attend to issues rather than images in their communications with the masses (see Seidelman and Harpham, 1985, p. 172), such that public opinion could better constrain leadership.

12. Identifying this gap is easy; bridging it is another matter. In fact, there are two gaps: one between attitudes and behaviors, another between these microlevel behaviors and their macropolitical consequences. This micro–macro discontinuity is embarrassingly ubiquitous in the social sciences, though it is bridged by general equilibrium theory in economics and contractarian political theory and addressed at length by social choice theorists (Coleman, 1986, pp. 1320–7). I shall suggest additional ways of bridging this gap in Chapter 9.

13. Not all classical republicans are sympathetic to democracy. For example, Arendt (1969, p. 233) believes true politics will always be for the few. Nevertheless, a republican strand exists within the democratic tradition.

14. Technically, it may be said that the unification of "verbal productions" into "texts" draws from and reproduces the discourse in question (see Alker and Sylvan, 1986, p. 18).

Chapter 9

1. The exact sample used turns out not to be crucial; any reasonably representative sample of statements will do (Brown, 1986, p. 73).

2. This silence arises inasmuch as the number and content of influences affecting an individual's Q sorting is indeterminate. Here, Q resembles quantum physics, in which observed phenomena result from the simultaneous occurrence of many different processes. Further parallels between Q and modern physics arise inasmuch as the "variable" in Q, the Q sort, is structured and internally complex, like the strings in superstring theory. See Stephenson (1986-8) for a discussion of the connections and parallels between Q and quantum theory.

3. The reason this element is *quasi*-causal is that the causality is only contingent, subject to change by the actions of the audience of the theory.

4. The occasional subject in fact proves unable to master the principle of transitivity and so cannot produce a meaningful Q sort.

Chapter 10

1. Aside from making us reject whole theories, successful falsification can also indicate the parts of a theory needing reformulation and point to the outstanding problems any future version of a theory must solve.

2. Perhaps taking Moon and Ball to heart, some political scientists have used Lakatos's criteria to justify their own research programs. See, e.g., Goodin and Dryzek (1980, pp. 274-5) and Bueno de Mesquita (1984).

3. As Agre (1982, p. 121) puts it, "Studying and solving problems has been widely understood in twentieth-century America to be the chief means by which science, technology, philosophy, education, and democratic society progress."

4. The idea that science is essentially a problem-solving activity is shared by Kuhn, Popper, Lakatos, Laudan, and other luminaries in postempiricist philosophy of science. Historically, pragmatists such as Dewey, Peirce, and James shared this notion. Logical positivists disagreed, stressing instead the explication of logical connections between theory and observation.

5. Any success of a theory can leave in its wake as many problems as does a failure. Think, e.g., of the galaxy of problems opened up by the initial successes of Copernican astronomy.

6. Lakatos (1970) believes a science may be judged mature to the extent of its immunity to external influences.

7. Kuhn (1970b) recognizes social forces in problem definition, but only internally, within the scientific community.

8. Farr (1982, pp. 698–9) makes a similar point with respect to the limited lifetimes or changing domains of political concepts.

9. Formally, rational reconstructions are "interpretations of the past predicated on assumptions of rationality" (Koertge, 1976, p. 360).

10. Moon (1975, pp. 202–4) and Ball (1976, p. 170) both believe the minimax regret theorem advanced by Ferejohn and Fiorina (1974) constitutes progress in this direction, but the theorem has since suffered badly at the hands of other public choice practitioners.

11. Against those who claim Marxism is more ideology than research tradition, it is clear that Marxism does indeed possess the three necessary features of a research tradition. First, it has a distinct ontology, in which social and political relationships are constituted by modes of production. Second, its methodology, though eclectic, can be subsumed under the general heading of critique (see essays by Farr, Ball, and Carver in Ball and Farr, 1984, pp. 217–79). Third, it clearly possesses an interrelated set of theories about imperialism, alienation, revolution, and so forth.

12. Pre-1940s and latter-day classicists share an ontology of instrumentally rational maximizing individuals, deductive methodology, and theories of general economic equilibrium and inflation. Unlike Keynesian macroeconomics, the classicists are consistent with microeconomic assumptions.

13. Malthus and latter-day Malthusians share an ontology of resource constraints, a whole-systems methodology, and theories of catastrophe via overpopulation.

14. Beyond this ontology, old and new institutionalisms share a methodological hostility to statistical aggregation and sympathy with interpretive approaches (March and Olsen, 1984, pp. 740–2) and theories about political order (March and Olsen, 1984, p. 743).

15. My point here echoes Farr (1982). Like MacIntyre (1966, pp. 1–4) and Toulmin (1972), Farr recognizes that all concepts have a history. Their meanings change through time. Even natural science concepts such as atom and matter undergo such mutation. But Farr goes further in noting the dependence of conceptual change in the social sciences on social change. It is for this reason that Farr regards political science as an essentially historical discipline.

16. MacIntyre (1988, pp. 389–91, 403) makes a similar point about traditions in moral philosophy.

17. Like all classics, Hobbes and his relation to different traditions can be interpreted in a variety of ways. One reading would classify Hobbes and his heirs as members of the broad microeconomic/public choice tradition. A distinction may also be drawn between Hobbes's own work and the tradition bearing his name. Hobbes himself might be placed in the natural law tradition, and diffidence and glory as well as scarcity contribute to his *bellum omnium contra omnes*. Perhaps the strongest defense of my stress on absolute material scarcity here is that contemporary avowed ecological Hobbists subscribe to a similar reading.

18. Ricci's own emphasis is slightly different. He argues that scientific findings have generally undermined the discipline's (arational) commitment to liberal democracy. At issue in his own account is subversion of, rather than disregard for, democracy.

Bibliography

Achen, Christopher H. 1983. Toward Theories of Data: The State of Political Methodology. 69–93 in Ada W. Finifter, ed., *Political Science: The State of the Discipline*. Washington, DC: American Political Science Association.

Adler, Peter S. 1987. Is ADR a Social Movement? *Negotiation Journal*, 3: 59–71.

Agre, Gene P. 1982. The Concept of Problem. *Educational Studies*, 13: 121–42.

Alexander, Christopher. 1965. A City Is Not a Tree. *Architectural Forum*, 122(1 and 2): 58–61 and 58–62.

Alford, C. Fred. 1985. *Science and the Revenge of Nature: Marcuse and Habermas*. Gainesville: University Presses of Florida.

Alker, Hayward R., Jr. and David Sylvan. 1986. Political Discourse Analysis. Paper presented at the annual meeting of the American Political Science Association, Washington, DC.

Allison, Graham T. 1969. Conceptual Models and the Cuban Missile Crisis. *American Political Science Review*, 63: 689–718.

——— 1971. *Essence of Decision: Explaining the Cuban Missile Crisis*. Boston: Little, Brown.

Alm, Alvin L. 1984. Building a Better EPA. *EPA Journal*, 10(5): 16–19.

Almond, Gabriel A. 1966. Political Theory and Political Science. *American Political Science Review*, 60: 869–79.

Almond, Gabriel A. and Sidney Verba. 1963. *The Civic Culture: Political Attitudes and Democracy in Five Nations*. Princeton: Princeton University Press.

Alonso, William and Edgar Rust. 1976. *The Evolving Pattern of Village Alaska*. Anchorage: Joint Federal–State Land Use Planning Commission.

Amy, Douglas J. 1983a. The Politics of Environmental Mediation. *Ecology Law Quarterly*, 11: 1–19.

——— 1983b. Environmental Mediation: An Alternative Approach to Policy Stalemates. *Policy Sciences*, 15: 345–65.

——— 1984. Why Policy Analysis and Ethics are Incompatible. *Journal of Policy Analysis and Management*, 3: 573–91.

——— 1986. The Political Ideology of Environmental Mediation. Paper presented to the Western Political Science Association, Eugene, OR.

Anonymous. 1985. Falklands Follow-up. *Nations and Needs.* Newsletter of the Center for International Development and Conflict Management, October, pp. 1–2.

Apel, Karl-Otto. 1972. The *A Priori* of Communication and the Foundation of the Humanities. *Man and World,* 5: 3–37.

Arendt, Hannah. 1958. *The Human Condition.* Chicago: University of Chicago Press.

1962. *On Revolution.* New York: Viking.

1969. *Crises of the Republic.* New York: Harcourt, Brace, Jovanovich.

1977. *Between Past and Future.* Harmondsworth, England: Penguin.

Arrow, Kenneth J. 1963. *Social Choice and Individual Values,* rev. ed. New York: Wiley.

Asher, Herbert. 1983. Voting Behavior Research in the 1980s: An Examination of Some Old and New Problem Areas. 339–88 in Ada W. Finifter, ed., *Political Science: The State of the Discipline.* Washington, DC: American Political Science Association.

Ashley, Richard K. 1980. *The Political Economy of War and Peace.* London: Frances Pinter.

1981. Political Realism and Human Interests. *International Studies Quarterly,* 25: 204–36.

Axelrod, Robert. 1984. *The Evolution of Cooperation.* New York: Basic Books.

Bacon, Robert and Walter Eltis. 1976. *Britain's Economic Problem.* London: Macmillan.

Bacow, Lawrence S. and Michael Wheeler. 1984. *Environmental Dispute Resolution.* New York: Plenum.

Ball, Terence. 1976. From Paradigms to Research Programs: Toward a Post-Kuhnian Political Science. *American Journal of Political Science,* 20: 151–77.

1983a. The Ontological Presuppositions and Political Consequences of a Social Science. 31–51 in Daniel R. Sabia, Jr. and Jerald T. Wallulis, eds., *Changing Social Science: Critical Theory and Other Critical Perspectives.* Albany: State University of New York Press.

1983b. Contradiction and Critique in Political Theory. 127–50 in John S. Nelson, ed., *What Should Political Theory Be Now?* Albany: State University of New York Press.

1984. Marxian Science and Positivist Politics. 235–60 in Terence Ball and James Farr, eds., *After Marx.* New York: Cambridge University Press.

1987a. Introduction. 1–10 in Terence Ball, ed., *Idioms of Inquiry: Critique and Renewal in Political Science.* Albany: State University of New York Press.

1987b. The Politics of Social Science in Post-War America. In Lary May, ed., *Promise and Peril: Explorations in Post-War American Politics and Culture.* Chicago: University of Chicago Press.

Ball, Terence and James Farr, eds. 1984. *After Marx.* New York: Cambridge University Press.

Barber, Benjamin. 1984. *Strong Democracy: Participatory Politics for a New Age.* Berkeley and Los Angeles: University of California Press.

Beck, Paul Allen. 1986. Choice, Context, and Consequence: Beaten and Unbeaten Paths toward a Science of Electoral Behavior. 241–83 in Herbert F. Weisberg, ed., *Political Science: The Science of Politics.* New York: Agathon.

Benhabib, Seyla. 1981. Modernity and the Aporias of Critical Theory. *Telos*, 49: 38–59.

1982. The Methodological Illusions of Political Theory: The Case of Rawls and Habermas. *Neue hefte fur Philosophie*, 21: 47–74.

1986. *Critique, Norm, and Utopia: A Study of the Foundations of Critical Theory.* New York: Columbia University Press.

Berelson, Bernard. 1952. Democratic Theory and Public Opinion. *Public Opinion Quarterly*, 16: 313–30.

Berelson, Bernard R., Paul F. Lazarsfeld, and William N. McPhee. 1954. *Voting.* Chicago: University of Chicago Press.

Berger, Thomas R. 1977. *Northern Frontier, Northern Homeland: Report of the MacKenzie Valley Pipeline Inquiry.* Toronto: James Lorimer.

1985. *Village Journey: The Report of the Alaska Native Review Commission.* New York: Hill and Wang.

Berns, Walter. 1962. Voting Studies. 1–62 in Herbert J. Storing, ed., *Essays on the Scientific Study of Politics.* New York: Holt, Rinehart, and Winston.

Bernstein, Richard J. 1983. *Beyond Objectivism and Relativism: Science, Hermeneutics, and Praxis.* Philadelphia: University of Pennsylvania Press.

1986. *Philosophical Profiles.* Philadelphia: University of Pennsylvania Press.

Beveridge, Sir William Henry. 1942. *Social Insurance and Allied Services.* London: HMSO, Cmd. 6404.

Bigjim, Frederick Seagayuk and James Ito-Adler. 1974. *Letters to Howard.* Anchorage: Tundra Times.

Bingham, Gail. 1986. *Resolving Environmental Disputes: A Decade of Experience.* Washington, DC: Conservation Foundation.

Bish, Robert L. 1978. Intergovernmental Relations in the United States: Some Concepts and Implications from a Public Choice Perspective. 19–36 in K. Hanf and F. W. Schapf, eds., *Intergovernmental Policy Making: Limits to Coordination and Central Control.* Beverly Hills: Sage.

Block, Fred. 1977. The Ruling Class Does Not Rule: Notes on the Marxist Theory of the State. *Socialist Revolution*, 33: 6–28.

Blondel, Jean. 1981. *The Discipline of Politics.* London: Butterworths.

Bobrow, Davis B. and John S. Dryzek. 1987. *Policy Analysis by Design.* Pittsburgh: University of Pittsburgh Press.

Bookchin, Murray. 1982. *The Ecology of Freedom: The Emergence and Dissolution of Hierarchy.* Palo Alto: Cheshire.

Brewer, Garry D. 1975a. Analysis of Complex Systems: An Experiment and Its Implications for Policy Making. 175–219 in Todd R. LaPorte, ed., *Organized Social Complexity: Challenge to Politics and Policy.* Princeton: Princeton University Press.

1975b. Dealing with Complex Social Problems: The Potential of the Decision Seminar. 439–61 in Garry D. Brewer and Ronald D. Brunner, eds., *Political Development and Change: A Policy Approach.* New York: Free Press.

1983. Some Costs and Consequences of Large Scale Social Systems Modeling. *Behavioral Science*, 28: 166–85.

1985. Methods for Synthesis: Policy Exercises. In W. C. Clark and R. W. Mann, eds., *Sustainable Development of the Biosphere.* Laxenburg, Austria: International Institute for Applied Systems Analysis.

Brown, Steven R. 1980. *Political Subjectivity: Applications of Q Methodology in Political Science.* New Haven: Yale University Press.

———. 1985. The Structure and Form of Subjectivity in Political Theory and Behavior. Paper presented at the annual meeting of the International Society of Political Psychology, Washington, DC.

———. 1986. Q Technique and Method: Principles and Procedures. 57–76 in William D. Berry and Michael S. Lewis-Beck, eds., *New Tools for Social Scientists: Advances and Applications in Research Methods.* Beverly Hills: Sage.

———. 1989. A Feeling for the Organism: Understanding and Interpreting Political Subjectivity. *Operant Subjectivity,* 12.

Brunner, Ronald D. 1977. An "Intentional" Alternative to Public Opinion Research. *American Journal of Political Science,* 21: 435–63.

Bueno de Mesquita, Bruce. 1984. A Critique of "A Critique of *The War Trap.*" *Journal of Conflict Resolution,* 28: 341–60.

Burian, Richard. 1977. More than a Marriage of Convenience: On the Inextricability of History and the Philosophy of Science. *Philosophy of Science,* 42: 1–42.

Burnheim, John. 1985. *Is Democracy Possible?* Cambridge: Polity.

Burton, John. 1979. *Deviance, Terrorism, and War: The Process of Solving Unsolved Social Problems.* New York: St. Martin's.

Butler, R. J. 1983. Control through Markets, Hierarchies, and Communes: A Transactional Approach to Organisations. 137–58 in Arthur Francis, Jeremy Turk, and Paul Willman, eds., *Power, Efficiency, and Institutions: A Critical Appraisal of the Markets and Hierarchies Paradigm.* London: Heinemann.

Butler, David and Donald Stokes. 1971. *Political Change in Britain: Forces Shaping Electoral Choice.* Harmondsworth, England: Penguin.

Campbell, Angus. 1966. Review of V. O. Key, *The Responsible Electorate. American Political Science Review,* 60: 1007–8.

Campbell, Donald T. 1969. Reforms as Experiments. *American Psychologist,* 24: 409–29.

Carroll, John E. 1983. *Environmental Diplomacy: An Examination and Prospective of Canadian–US Transboundary Environmental Relations.* Ann Arbor: University of Michigan Press.

Charlesworth, James C., ed. 1972. *Integration of the Social Sciences through Policy Analysis.* Philadelphia: American Academy of Political and Social Science.

Clausen, Aage. 1968. Response Validity: Vote Report. *Public Opinion Quarterly,* 32: 588–606.

Clocksin, Donald E., Michael I. Jeffery, and Clifton E. Curtis. 1979. Comments on the Beaufort Sea Draft Environmental Impact Statement. Prepared on Behalf of the Villages of Kaktovik, Nuiqsut, and Barrow. Anchorage, mimeo.

Cohen, Jean. 1985. Strategy or Identity: New Theoretical Paradigms and Contemporary Social Movements. *Social Research,* 52: 663–716.

Coleman, James S. 1986. Social Theory, Social Research, and a Theory of Action. *American Journal of Sociology,* 91: 1309–35.

Collier, David, ed. 1979. *The New Authoritarianism in Latin America.* Princeton: Princeton University Press.

Commoner, Barry. 1972. *The Closing Circle*. New York: Bantam.

Dagger, Richard. 1982. Computers, Cables, and Citizenship: On the Desirability of Direct Democracy. 132–45 in Arthur L. Kalleberg, J. Donald Moon, and Daniel R. Sabia, eds., *Dissent and Affirmation: Essays in Honor of Mulford Q. Sibley*. Bowling Green: Bowling Green State University Press.

Dahl, Robert A. 1956. *A Preface to Democratic Theory*. Chicago: University of Chicago Press.

  1970. *After the Revolution? Authority in a Good Society*. New Haven: Yale University Press.

  1984. *Modern Political Analysis*, 4th ed. Englewood Cliffs, NJ: Prentice-Hall.

  1985a. *Controlling Nuclear Weapons: Democracy versus Guardianship*. Syracuse: Syracuse University Press.

  1985b. *A Preface to Economic Democracy*. Berkeley: University of California Press.

Dawes, R., J. McTavish, and H. Shaklee. 1977. Behavior, Communications, and Assumptions about Other Peoples' Behavior in a Commons Dilemma Situation. *Journal of Personality and Social Psychology*, 35: 1–11.

Dempster, M. A. H. and Aaron Wildavsky. 1979. On Change: Or, There Is No Magic Size for an Increment. *Political Studies*, 27: 371–89.

d'Entreves, Maurizio Passerin. 1987–8. Aristotle or Burke? Some Comments on H. Schnaedelbach's "What Is Neo-Aristotelianism?" *Praxis International*, 7: 238–45.

Derrida, Jacques. 1976. *Of Grammatology*. Baltimore: Johns Hopkins University Press.

Diamond, Irene. 1988. Medical Science and the Transformation of Motherhood: The Promise of Reproductive Technologies. 155–67 in Ellen Bonepath and Emily Stoper, eds., *Women, Power and Policy: Toward the Year 2000*, 2nd ed. New York: Pergamon.

Diesing, Paul. 1962. *Reason in Society*. Urbana: University of Illinois Press.

  1983. Ideology and Objectivity. 1–17 in Robert S. Cohen and Marx W. Wartofsky, eds., *Boston Studies in the Philosophy of Science, 71: Epistemology, Methodology, and the Social Sciences*. Boston: Reidel.

Dror, Yehezkel. 1964. Muddling through: Science or Inertia? *Public Administration Review*, 24: 153–65.

Dryzek, John. 1982. Policy Analysis as a Hermeneutic Activity. *Policy Sciences*, 14: 309–29.

  1983a. *Conflict and Choice in Resource Management: The Case of Alaska*. Boulder, CO: Westview.

  1983b. Don't Toss Coins in Garbage Cans: A Prologue to Policy Design. *Journal of Public Policy*, 3: 345–68.

  1987. *Rational Ecology: Environment and Political Economy*. Oxford and New York: Basil Blackwell.

  1990. Green Reason: Communicative Ethics for the Biosphere. *Environmental Ethics*, 12.

Dryzek, John S., Margaret L. Clark, and Garry McKenzie. 1989. Subject and System in International Interaction. *International Organization*, 43: 475–503.

Dryzek, John S. and Stephen T. Leonard. 1988. History and Discipline in Political Science. *American Political Science Review*, 82: 1245–60.

Dunn, William N. 1981. *Public Policy Analysis: An Introduction.* Englewood Cliffs, NJ: Prentice-Hall.

1982. Reforms as Arguments. *Knowledge: Creation, Diffusion, Utilization,* 3: 293–326.

Dye, Thomas R. and L. Harmon Ziegler. 1987. *The Irony of Democracy: An Uncommon Introduction to American Politics,* 7th ed. Monterey, CA: Brooks/Cole.

Eckstein, Harry. 1966. *Division and Cohesion in Democracy.* Princeton: Princeton University Press.

Edelman, Murray. 1977. *Political Language: Words That Succeed and Policies That Fail.* New York: Academic.

Ehrenfeld, David. 1978. *The Arrogance of Humanism.* New York: Oxford University Press.

Elster, Jon. 1983. *Sour Grapes: Studies in the Subversion of Rationality.* Cambridge: Cambridge University Press.

Evans, Peter, Dieter Rueschemeyer, and Theda Skocpol, eds. 1985. *Bringing the State Back In.* Cambridge: Cambridge University Press.

Farr, James. 1982. Historical Concepts in Political Science: The Case of "Revolution." *American Journal of Political Science,* 26: 688–708.

1985. Situational Analysis: Explanation in Political Science. *Journal of Politics,* 47: 1085–107.

Fay, Brian. 1975. *Social Theory and Political Practice.* London: George Allen and Unwin.

1987. *Critical Social Science: Liberation and Its Limits.* Ithaca, NY: Cornell University Press.

Ferejohn, John A. and Morris P. Fiorina. 1974. The Paradox of Not Voting: A Decision-Theoretic Analysis. *American Political Science Review,* 68: 525–36.

Feyerabend, Paul K. 1970. Consolations for the Specialist. 197–230 in Imre Lakatos and Alan Musgrave, eds., *Criticism and the Growth of Knowledge.* Cambridge: Cambridge University Press.

1975. *Against Method.* London: New Left Books.

1978. *Science in a Free Society.* London: New Left Books.

1987. *Farewell to Reason.* London: New Left Books.

Fiorina, Morris P. 1981. *Retrospective Voting in American National Elections.* New Haven, CT: Yale University Press.

Fischer, Frank. 1980. *Politics, Values, and Public Policy: The Problem of Methodology.* Boulder, CO: Westview.

Fisher, Roger and William Ury. 1981. *Getting to Yes.* Boston: Houghton Mifflin.

Fisher, Ronald J. 1983. Third Party Consultation as a Method of Intergroup Conflict Resolution. *Journal of Conflict Resolution,* 27: 301–34.

Fiss, Owen. 1984. Against Settlement. *Yale Law Journal,* 93: 1073–90.

Forester, John. 1981. Questioning and Organizing Attention: Toward a Critical Theory of Planning and Administrative Practice. *Administration and Society,* 13: 161–205.

1983. What Analysts Do. 47–62 in William N. Dunn, ed., *Values, Ethics, and the Practice of Policy Analysis.* Lexington, MA: Lexington Books.

1985. Critical Theory and Planning Practice. 202–27 in John Forester, ed., *Critical Theory and Public Life.* Cambridge, MA: MIT Press.

Foucault, Michel. 1980. *Power/Knowledge: Selected Interviews and Other Writings, 1972–1977.* Brighton, England: Harvester.

Foxley, Alejandro. 1983. *Latin American Experiments in Neo-Conservative Economics.* Berkeley: University of California Press.

Freeman, Christopher. 1973. Malthus with a Computer. 5–13 in H. S. D. Cole, ed., *Models of Doom: A Critique of the Limits to Growth.* New York: Universe.

Friedman, Milton and Rose Friedman. 1962. *Capitalism and Freedom.* Chicago: University of Chicago Press.

1979. *Free to Choose.* New York: Harcourt, Brace, Jovanovich.

1984. *Tyranny of the Status Quo.* New York: Harcourt, Brace, Jovanovich.

Friends of the Earth. 1978. *The Whale Manual.* San Francisco: Friends of the Earth.

Fuller, Lon L. 1969. *The Morality of Law,* rev. ed. New Haven, CT: Yale University Press.

Gadamer, Hans-Georg. 1975. *Truth and Method.* New York: Seabury.

Galbraith, John Kenneth. 1967. *The New Industrial State.* New York: New American Library.

Gant, Michael M. and Dwight F. Davis. 1984. Mental Economy and Voter Rationality: The Informed Citizen Problem in Voter Research. *Journal of Politics,* 46: 132–53.

Garfinkel, Harold, Michael Lynch, and Eric Livingston. 1981. The Work of a Discovering Science Construed with Materials from the Optically Discovered Pulsar. *Philosophy of Social Science,* 11: 131–58.

Garrison Conservancy District. n.d. *Garrison Diversion Information Book.* Carrington, ND: Garrison Conservancy District.

George, Alexander L. 1972. The Case for Multiple Advocacy in Making Foreign Policy. *American Political Science Review,* 66: 751–85.

1980. *Presidential Decisionmaking in Foreign Policy: The Effective Use of Information and Advice.* Boulder, CO: Westview.

Geuss, Raymond. 1981. *The Idea of a Critical Theory: Habermas and the Frankfurt School.* Cambridge: Cambridge University Press.

Gewirth, Alan. 1954. Can Men Change the Laws of Social Science? *Philosophy of Science,* 21: 229–41.

Goldstone, Jack A., ed. 1986. *Revolutions: Theoretical, Comparative, and Historical Studies.* New York: Harcourt, Brace, Jovanovich.

Goodin, Robert E. 1979. The Development–Rights Tradeoff: Some Unwarranted Political and Economic Assumptions. *Universal Human Rights,* 1: 31–42.

1980. *Manipulatory Politics.* New Haven, CT: Yale University Press.

Goodin, Robert and John Dryzek. 1980. Rational Participation: The Politics of Relative Power. *British Journal of Political Science,* 10: 273–92.

Goodin, Robert and Ilmar Waldner. 1979. Thinking Big, Thinking Small, and Not Thinking at All. *Public Policy,* 27: 1–24.

Gould, Carol C. 1988. *Rethinking Democracy: Freedom and Social Cooperation in Politics, Economy, and Society.* Cambridge: Cambridge University Press.

Gould, Stephen Jay. 1981. *The Mismeasure of Man.* New York: Norton.

Grünbaum, Adolf. 1976. Can a Theory Answer More Questions Than One of Its Rivals? *British Journal for the Philosophy of Science,* 27: 1–23.

Gunnell, John G. 1986. *Between Philosophy and Politics: The Alienation of Political Theory.* Amherst: University of Massachusetts Press.

Gusman, Sam. 1981. Policy Dialogue. *Environmental Comment,* November: 14–16.

Haas, Ernst B. 1980. Why Collaborate? Issue Linkage and International Regimes. *World Politics,* 32: 357–405.

Habermas, Jürgen. 1962. *Strukturwandel der Offentlichkeit.* Neuwied: Luchterhand.

1970. Towards a Theory of Communicative Competence. *Inquiry,* 13: 360–75.

1971. *Knowledge and Human Interests.* Boston: Beacon.

1973. *Theory and Practice.* Boston: Beacon.

1975. *Legitimation Crisis.* Boston: Beacon.

1979. *Communication and the Evolution of Society.* Boston: Beacon.

1981. New Social Movements. *Telos,* 49: 33–7.

1982. A Reply to My Critics. 219–83 in John Thompson and David Held, eds., *Habermas: Critical Debates.* Cambridge, MA: MIT Press.

1984. *The Theory of Communicative Action I: Reason and the Rationalization of Society.* Boston: Beacon.

1987a. *The Theory of Communicative Action II: Lifeworld and System.* Boston: Beacon.

1987b. *The Philosophical Discourse of Modernity.* Boston: Beacon.

1989. Ethics, Politics and History: An Interview with Jürgen Habermas. Interview by Jean-Marc Ferry, translated by Stephen K. White. *Philosophy and Social Criticism,* 14.

Habermas, Jürgen and Niklas Luhmann. 1971. *Theorie der Gesellschaft oder Socialtechnologie – Was leistet die Systemforschung?* Frankfurt: Suhrkamp.

Haefele, Edwin T. 1973. *Representative Government and Environmental Management.* Baltimore: Johns Hopkins Press for Resources for the Future.

Hanson, Russell L. 1985. *The Democratic Imagination in America: Conversations with Our Past.* Princeton: Princeton University Press.

Hardin, Garrett. 1968. The Tragedy of the Commons. *Science,* 162: 1242–8.

Hare, R. M. 1963. *Freedom and Reason.* Oxford: Clarendon.

Harter, Philip J. 1982. Negotiating Rgeulations: A Cure for Malaise. *Georgetown Law Journal,* 71: 1–118.

Hauser, Philip M. 1967. Social Accounting. 839–75 in Paul F. Lazarsfeld, W. H. Sewell, and H. L. Wilensky, eds., *The Uses of Sociology.* New York: Basic Books.

Hawkesworth, M. E. 1988. *Theoretical Issues in Policy Analysis.* Albany: State University of New York Press.

Heck, C. B. 1975. Collective Arrangements for Managing Ocean Fisheries. *International Organization,* 29: 711–23.

Heelan, Patrick. 1983. Natural Science as a Hermeneutic of Instrumentation. *Philosophy of Science,* 50: 181–204.

Held, David. 1980. *Introduction to Critical Theory: Horkheimer to Habermas.* Berkeley: University of California Press.

1987. *Models of Democracy.* Cambridge: Polity.

Hempel, Carl. 1965. *Aspects of Scientific Explanation.* New York: Free Press.

Hirschman, Albert O. 1973. *Journeys toward Progress.* New York: W. W. Norton.

Horkheimer, Max. 1947. *Eclipse of Reason.* New York: Oxford University Press.
Horkheimer, Max and Theodore Adorno. 1972. *Dialectic of Enlightenment.* New York: Herder and Herder.
Horowitz, Irving Louis. 1981. Social Science and the Reagan Administration. *Journal of Policy Analysis and Management,* 1: 125–9.
Horwitz, Robert. 1962. Scientific Propaganda: Harold D. Lasswell. 225–304 in Herbert J. Storing, ed., *Essays on the Scientific Study of Politics.* New York: Holt, Rinehart, and Winston.
Huckfeldt, Robert and John Sprague. 1987. Networks in Context: The Social Flow of Political Information. *American Political Science Review,* 81: 1197–1216.
Hunter, Susan. 1984. An Inquiry into Policy Conflicts: The Ontological Basis of Environmental Policy Disputes. Ph.D. dissertation, Ohio State University.
Huntington, Samuel P. 1974. Postindustrial Politics: How Benign Will It Be? *Comparative Politics,* 6: 163–91.
Iggers, George G., ed. 1972. *The Doctrine of Saint-Simon: An Exposition.* New York: Shocken Books.
Inbar, Michael. 1979. *Routine Decision-Making.* Beverly Hills, CA: Sage.
James, Roger. 1980. *Return to Reason: Popper's Thought in Public Life.* Shepton Mallet, England: Open Books.
Janis, Irving L. 1972. *Victims of Groupthink: A Psychological Study of Foreign Policy Decisions and Fiascoes.* Boston: Houghton Mifflin.
Kaufman-Osborn, Timothy V. 1985. Pragmatism, Policy Science, and the State. *American Journal of Political Science,* 29: 827–49.
Keane, John. 1984. *Public Life and Late Capitalism.* Cambridge: Cambridge University Press.
Keat, Russell. 1981. *The Politics of Social Theory: Habermas, Freud, and the Critique of Positivism.* Chicago: University of Chicago Press.
Kelley, Rita Mae, Bernard Ronan, and Margaret E. Cawley. 1987. Liberal Positivistic Epistemology and Research on Women and Politics. *Women and Politics,* 7: 11–27.
Kelman, Herbert C. and Stephen P. Cohen. 1976. The Problem-solving Workshop: A Socio-Psychological Contribution to the Resolution of International Conflict. *Journal of Peace Research,* 13: 79–90.
Kelman, Steven. 1981. *What Price Incentives? Economists and the Environment.* Boston: Auburn House.
  1987. "Public Choice" and Public Spirit. *The Public Interest,* 87: 80–94.
Kemp, Ray. 1985. Planning, Public Hearings, and the Politics of Discourse. 177–201 in John Forester, ed., *Critical Theory and Public Life.* Cambridge, MA: MIT Press.
Keohane, Robert O. 1983. The Demand for International Regimes. 141–71 in Stephen D. Krasner, ed., *International Regimes.* Ithaca, NY: Cornell University Press.
  1984. *After Hegemony: Cooperation and Discord in the World Political Economy.* Princeton: Princeton University Press.
  1986. Reciprocity in International Relations. *International Organization,* 40: 1–27.
Key, V. O. 1966. *The Responsible Electorate.* Cambridge, MA: Belknap.

Keynes, John M. 1936. *The General Theory of Employment, Interest, and Money.* London: Macmillan.

Kinder, Donald R. 1983. Diversity and Complexity in American Public Opinion. 389–425 in Ada W. Finifter, ed., *Political Science: The State of the Discipline.* Washington, DC: American Political Science Association.

Kinder, Donald R. and David O. Sears. 1983. Public Opinion and Political Action. 659–741 in Gardner Lindzey and Elliot Aronson, eds., *The Handbook of Social Psychology,* 3rd ed., Vol. 2. New York: Random House.

Kitzinger, Celia. 1986. Introducing and Developing Q as a Feminist Methodology: A Study of Accounts of Lesbianism. 151–72 in Sue Wilkinson, ed., *Feminist Social Psychology: Developing Theory and Practice.* Milton Keynes, England: Open University Press.

Kitzinger, Celia and Rex Stainton Rogers. 1985. A Q-Methodological Study of Lesbian Identities. *European Journal of Social Psychology,* 15: 167–87.

Koertge, Noretta. 1976. Rational Reconstructions. 334–69 in R. S. Cohen, P. K. Feyerabend and M. W. Wartofsky, eds., *Boston Studies in the Philosophy of Science,* Vol. 34, *Essays in Memory of Imre Lakatos.* Boston: Reidel.

Krasner, Stephen D. 1983. Structural Causes and Regime Consequences: Regimes as Intervening Variables. 1–21 in Stephen D. Krasner, ed., *International Regimes.* Ithaca, NY: Cornell University Press.

1985. *Structural Conflict: The Third World Against Global Liberalism.* Berkeley: University of California Press.

Kuhn, Thomas. 1969. Comment. *Comparative Studies in Society and History,* 11: 403–12.

1970a. Reflections on My Critics. 231–78 in Imre Lakatos and Alan Musgrave, eds., *Criticism and the Growth of Knowledge.* Cambridge: Cambridge University Press.

1970b. *The Structure of Scientific Revolutions,* 2nd ed. Chicago: University of Chicago Press.

Lakatos, Imre. 1970. Falsification and the Methodology of Scientific Research Programs. 91–196 in Imre Lakatos and Alan Musgrave, eds., *Criticism and the Growth of Knowledge.* Cambridge: Cambridge University Press.

1971. History of Science and Its Rational Reconstruction. 91–136 in Roger G. Buck and Robert S. Cohen, eds., *Boston Studies in the Philosophy of Science,* Vol. 8, *In Memory of Rudolf Carnap.* Boston: Reidel.

Lane, Robert E. 1962. *Political Ideology.* New York: Free Press.

La Porte, Todd R., ed. 1975. *Organized Social Complexity: Challenge to Politics and Policy.* Princeton: Princeton University Press.

Lasswell, Harold D. 1930. *Psychopathology and Politics.* Chicago: University of Chicago Press.

1951. The Policy Orientation. 3–15 in Daniel Lerner and Harold Lasswell, eds., *The Policy Sciences: Recent Developments in Scope and Methods.* Stanford, CA: Stanford University Press.

1960. The Technique of Decision Seminars. *Midwest Journal of Political Science,* 4: 213–36.

1963. *The Future of Political Science.* New York: Atherton.

1965a. The World Revolution of Our Time: A Framework for Basic Research. 29–96 in Harold D. Lasswell and Daniel Lerner, eds., *World Revolutionary Elites*. Cambridge, MA: MIT Press.

1965b. *World Politics and Personal Insecurity*. New York: Free Press.

Laudan, Larry. 1977. *Progress and Its Problems*. Berkeley: University of California Press.

Leonard, Stephen T. 1990. *Critical Theory in Political Practice*. Princeton: Princeton University Press.

Lindblom, Charles E. 1959. The Science of Muddling Through. *Public Administration Review*, 19: 79–88.

1965. *The Intelligence of Democracy: Decision Making through Mutual Adjustment*. New York: Free Press.

1977. *Politics and Markets: The World's Political–Economic Systems*. New York: Basic Books.

1982a. Another State of Mind. *American Political Science Review*, 76: 9–21.

1982b. The Market as Prison. *Journal of Politics*, 44: 324–36.

Lindblom, Charles E. and David K. Cohen. 1979. *Usable Knowledge: Social Science and Social Problem Solving*. New Haven, CT: Yale University Press.

Lovins, Amory B. 1977. *Soft Energy Paths: Toward a Durable Peace*. New York: Harper & Row.

Lovrich, Nicholas P. and Max Neiman. 1984. *Public Choice Theory in Public Administration: An Annotated Bibliography*. New York: Garland.

Lowi, Theodore J. 1979. *The End of Liberalism*, 2nd ed. New York: Norton.

Luke, Timothy W. and Stephen K. White. 1985. Critical Theory, the Informational Revolution, and an Ecological Path to Modernity. 22–53 in John Forester, ed., *Critical Theory and Public Life*. Cambridge, MA: MIT Press.

Lyotard, Jean-Francois. 1984. *The Postmodern Condition*. Minneapolis: University of Minnesota Press.

McCarthy, Thomas. 1978. *The Critical Theory of Jürgen Habermas*. Cambridge, MA: MIT Press.

1984. Translator's Introduction. v–xliii in Jürgen Habermas, *The Theory of Communicative Action I: Reason and the Rationalization of Society*. Boston: Beacon Press.

McFarland, Andrew. 1984. An Experiment in Regulatory Negotiation: The National Coal Policy Project. Paper presented to the convention of the Western Political Science Association, Sacramento, CA.

MacIntyre, Alasdair. 1966. *A Short History of Ethics*. New York: Macmillan.

1973. Ideology, Social Science, and Revolution. *Comparative Politics*, 5: 321–42.

1977. Epistemological Crises, Dramatic Narratives, and the Philosophy of Science. *The Monist*, 60: 453–72.

1984a. *After Virtue: A Study in Moral Theory*, 2nd ed. Notre Dame: University of Notre Dame Press.

1984b. Does Applied Ethics Rest on a Mistake? *The Monist*, 67: 498–513.

1988. *Whose Justice? Which Rationality?* Notre Dame: University of Notre Dame Press.

McKeown, Bruce and Dan Thomas. 1988. *Q Methodology*. Newbury Park: Sage.

MacPherson, C. B. 1970. *The Political Theory of Possessive Individualism.* Oxford: Oxford University Press.

1977. *The Life and Times of Liberal Democracy.* Oxford: Oxford University Press.

Magee, Brian. 1973. *Popper.* London: Fontana.

Mansbridge, Jane J. 1980. *Beyond Adversary Democracy.* New York: Basic Books.

March, James G. 1978. Bounded Rationality, Ambiguity, and the Engineering of Choice. *Bell Journal of Economics,* 9: 587–608.

March, James G. and Johan P. Olsen. 1984. The New Institutionalism: Organizational Factors in Political Life. *American Political Science Review,* 78: 734–49.

Martin, Guy. 1976. *New Tribes for New Times.* Juneau: Alaska Department of Education.

Mason, Richard O. 1969. A Dialectical Approach to Strategic Planning. *Management Science,* 15: 403–14.

Meadows, Donella H., Dennis L. Meadows, Jorgen Randers, and William H. Behrens III. 1972. *The Limits to Growth.* New York: Universe Books.

Mendlovitz, Saul H., ed. 1975. *On the Creation of a Just World Order: Preferred Worlds for the 1980s.* New York: Free Press.

Mernitz, Scott. 1980. *Mediation of Environmental Disputes: A Sourcebook.* New York: Praeger.

Midgaard, Knut. 1980. On the Significance of Language and a Richer Concept of Rationality. 83–97 in Leif Lewin and Evert Vedung, eds., *Politics as Rational Action.* Dordrecht: Reidel.

Miller, Warren E. 1960. The Political Behavior of the Electorate. 41–60 in Earl Latham, ed., *American Government Annual, 1960–61.* New York: Holt, Rinehart, and Winston.

Mitroff, Ian I. and L. Vaughan Blankenship. 1973. On the Methodology of the Holistic Experiment. *Technological Forecasting and Social Change,* 4: 339–53.

Moon, J. Donald. 1975. The Logic of Political Inquiry: A Synthesis of Opposed Perspectives. 131–228 in Fred I. Greenstein and Nelson W. Polsby, eds., *Handbook of Political Science,* Vol. 1. Reading, MA: Addison Wesley.

1983. Political Ethics and Critical Theory. 171–88 in Daniel R. Sabia, Jr. and Jerald Wallulis, eds., *Changing Social Science: Critical Theory and Other Critical Perspectives.* Albany: State University of New York Press.

Mosher, Lawrence. 1983. Distrust of Gorsuch May Stymie EPA Attempt to Integrate Pollution Wars. *National Journal,* 15: 322–4.

Natchez, Peter. 1985. *Images of Voting/Visions of Democracy.* New York: Basic Books.

Nias, D. J. 1975. The Sorcerer's Apprentice: A Case Study of Complexity in Educational Institutions. 256–78 in Todd R. La Porte, ed., *Organized Social Complexity: Challenge to Politics and Policy.* Princeton: Princeton University Press.

Nie, Norman H., Sidney J. Verba, and John R. Petrocik. 1976. *The Changing American Voter.* Cambridge, MA: Harvard University Press.

1981. Reply. *American Political Science Review,* 75: 149–52.

Niemi, Richard G. 1986. The Dynamics of Public Opinion. 225–40 in Herbert F. Weisberg, ed., *Political Science: The Science of Politics*. New York: Agathon.

Niskanen, William A., Jr. 1971. *Bureaucracy and Representative Government*. Chicago: Aldine-Atherton.

Noelle-Neumann, Elisabeth. 1984. *The Spiral of Silence: Public Opinion – Our Social Skin*. Chicago: University of Chicago Press.

O'Donnell, Guillermo. 1973. *Modernization and Bureaucratic Authoritarianism: Studies in South American Politics*. Berkeley: Institute of International Studies, University of California.

Offe, Claus. 1984. *Contradictions of the Welfare State*. Cambridge: MIT Press.

1985. New Social Movements: Challenging the Boundaries of Institutional Politics. *Social Research*, 52: 817–68.

O'Hear, Anthony. 1980. *Karl Popper*. London: Routledge and Kegan Paul.

Olson, Mancur. 1965. *The Logic of Collective Action*. Cambridge, MA: Harvard University Press.

1982. *The Rise and Decline of Nations: Economic Growth, Stagflation, and Social Rigidities*. New Haven, CT: Yale University Press.

Ophuls, William. 1977. *Ecology and the Politics of Scarcity*. San Francisco: W. H. Freeman.

Orbell, John M., Peregrine Schwartz-Shea, and Randy T. Simmons. 1984. Do Cooperators Exit More Readily Than Defectors? *American Political Science Review*, 78: 147–62.

Orr, David W. 1977. Modernization and Conflict: The Second Image Implications of Scarcity. *International Studies Quarterly*, 21: 593–618.

Orr, David W. and Stuart Hill. 1978. Leviathan, the Open Society, and the Crisis of Ecology. *Western Political Quarterly*, 31: 457–69.

Ostrom, Elinor. 1971. Institutional Arrangements and the Measurement of Policy Consequences: Applications to Evaluating Police Performance. *Urban Affairs Quarterly*, 6: 447–75.

Palumbo, Dennis J. and David Nachmias. 1983. The Preconditions for Successful Evaluation: Is There an Ideal Paradigm? *Policy Sciences*, 16: 67–79.

Paris, David C. and James F. Reynolds. 1983. *The Logic of Policy Inquiry*. New York: Longman.

Parsons, Talcott. 1971. *The System of Modern Societies*. Englewood Cliffs, NJ: Prentice-Hall.

Pateman, Carol. 1970. *Participation and Democratic Theory*. Cambridge: Cambridge University Press.

1980. The Civic Culture: A Philosophic Critique. 57–102 in Gabriel A. Almond and Sidney Verba, eds., *The Civic Culture Revisited*. Boston: Little, Brown.

Patten, Bernard C. and Eugene P. Odum. 1981. The Cybernetic Nature of Ecosystems. *American Naturalist*, 118: 886–95.

Polanyi, Karl. 1944. *The Great Transformation*. Boston: Beacon Press.

Pollitt, Christopher. 1986. Democracy and Bureaucracy. 158–91 in David Held and Christopher Pollitt, eds., *New Forms of Democracy*. London: Sage.

Popper, Karl R. 1966. *The Open Society and Its Enemies*. London: Routledge and Kegan Paul.

1970. Normal Science and Its Dangers. 51–8 in Imre Lakatos and Alan Musgrave, eds., *Criticism and the Growth of Knowledge*. Cambridge: Cambridge University Press.

1972a. *The Poverty of Historicism*, rev. ed. London: Routledge and Kegan Paul.

1972b. *The Logic of Scientific Discovery*, 3rd ed. London: Hutchinson.

1972c. *Objective Knowledge: An Evolutionary Approach*. Oxford: Clarendon.

Poulantzas, Nicos. 1980. *State, Power, Socialism*. London: New Left Books.

Presser, Stanley. 1984. The Use of Survey Data in Basic Research in the Social Sciences. 93–114 in Charles F. Turner and Elizabeth Martin, eds., *Surveying Subjective Phenomena*, Vol. 2. New York: Russell Sage Foundation.

Prior, James. 1986. *A Balance of Power*. London: Hamish Hamilton.

Raiffa, Howard. 1982. *The Art and Science of Negotiation*. Cambridge, MA: Belknap.

Rawls, John. 1971. *A Theory of Justice*. Cambridge, MA: Harvard University Press.

Reich, Robert B. 1985. Toward a New Public Philosophy. *The Atlantic Monthly*, May: 68–79.

Ricci, David M. 1984. *The Tragedy of Political Science: Politics, Scholarship, and Democracy*. New Haven, CT: Yale University Press.

Riker, William H. 1982. The Two-Party System and Duverger's Law: An Essay on the History of Political Science. *American Political Science Review*, 76: 753–66.

Robinson, John Bridger. 1982. Apples and Horned Toads: On the Framework-determined Nature of the Energy Debate. *Policy Sciences*, 15: 23–45.

Rodger, John J. 1985. On the Degeneration of the Public Sphere. *Political Studies*, 33: 203–17.

Rorty, Richard. 1979. *Philosophy and the Mirror of Nature*. Princeton: Princeton University Press.

Rowbotham, Sheila. 1986. Feminism and Democracy. 78–109 in David Held and Christopher Pollitt, eds., *New Forms of Democracy*. London: Sage.

Sartori, Giovanni. 1962. *Democratic Theory*. Detroit: Wayne State University Press.

1987. *The Theory of Democracy Revisited*. Chatham, NJ: Chatham House.

Schnaedelbach, Herbert. 1987–8. What is Neo-Aristotelianism? *Praxis International*, 7: 225–37.

Schneider, Janet A., Nancy J. Stevens, and Louis G. Tornatzky. 1982. Policy Research and Analysis: An Empirical Profile. *Policy Sciences*, 15: 99–114.

Schoenbrod, David. 1983. Limits and Dangers of Environmental Mediation: A Review Essay. *New York University Law Review*, 58: 1453–76.

Schulman, Paul R. 1980. *Large-Scale Policy Making*. New York: Elsevier.

Schultze, Charles. 1968. *The Politics and Economics of Public Spending*. Washington, DC: Brookings.

Schuman, Howard. 1972. Attitudes vs. Actions *versus* Attitudes vs. Attitudes. *Public Opinion Quarterly*, 36: 347–54.

Sciulli, David. 1986. Voluntaristic Action as a Distinct Concept: Theoretical Foundations of Societal Constitutionalism. *American Sociological Review*, 51: 743–66.

Scott, Anthony. 1986. The Canadian–American Problem of Acid Rain. *Natural Resources Journal,* 26: 337–58.

Seidel, Gill. 1985. Political Discourse Analysis. 43–60 in Teun A. van Dijk, ed., *Handbook of Discourse Analysis,* Vol. 4. London: Academic.

Seidelman, Raymond with Edward J. Harpham. 1985. *Disenchanted Realists: Political Science and the American Crisis, 1884–1984.* Albany: State University of New York Press.

Simon, Herbert A. 1981. *The Sciences of the Artificial,* 2nd ed. Cambridge, MA: MIT Press.

Skinner, Quentin. 1985. Introduction. 1–20 in Quentin Skinner, ed., *The Return of Grand Theory in the Human Sciences.* Cambridge: Cambridge University Press.

Skocpol, Theda. 1979. *States and Social Revolutions.* Cambridge: Cambridge University Press.

Soroos, Marvin S. 1977. The Commons and the Lifeboat as Guides for International Environmental Policy. *International Studies Quarterly,* 21: 647–74.

Spretnak, Charlene. 1986. *The Spiritual Dimension of Green Politics.* Santa Fe, CA: Bear and Co.

Sprout, Harold and Margaret Sprout. 1965. *The Ecological Perspective on Human Affairs, with Special Reference to International Politics.* Princeton: Princeton University Press.

Stainton Rogers, Rex and Celia Kitzinger. 1986. Human Rights: Bedrock or Mosaic? *Operant Subjectivity,* 9: 123–30.

Stainton Rogers, Rex and Wendy Stainton Rogers. 1988. Deconstructing "Addiction." Paper presented at the Annual Conference of the Social Psychology Section of the British Psychological Society, Canterbury, England.

Stein, Arthur A. 1983. Coordination and Collaboration: Regimes in an Anarchic World. 115–40 in Stephen D. Krasner, ed., *International Regimes.* Ithaca, NY: Cornell University Press.

Stein, Robert E. 1982. The Uses of Mediation to Settle Canadian–U.S. Environmental Disputes. *Environmental Law,* February: 5–7.

   1984. The Use of Mediation and Other Techniques for the Settlement of Environmental and Natural Resources Disputes. *Industry and Environment,* 7(3): 45–7.

Stephenson, William. 1953. *The Study of Behavior: Q Technique and Its Methodology.* Chicago: University of Chicago Press.

   1978. Concourse Theory of Communication. *Communication,* 3: 21–40.

   1986–8. William James, Nils Bohr, and Complementarity, I–V. *Psychological Record.*

Stokey, Edith and Richard Zeckhauser. 1978. *A Primer for Policy Analysis.* New York: Norton.

Storing, Herbert J., ed. 1962. *Essays on the Scientific Study of Politics.* New York: Holt, Rinehart, and Winston.

Straus, Donald B. 1979. Managing Complexity: A New Look at Environmental Mediation. *Environmental Science and Technology,* 13: 661–5.

Strauss, Leo. 1959. *What Is Political Philosophy?* Glencoe, IL: Free Press.

Sudman, Seymour and Norman M. Bradburn. 1983. *Asking Questions: A Practical Guide to Questionnaire Design.* San Francisco: Jossey-Bass.

Sullivan, John L., James E. Piereson, and George E. Marcus. 1978. Ideological Constraint in the Mass Public: A Methodological Critique and Some New Findings. *American Journal of Political Science,* 22: 233–49.

Talbot, Allan. 1983. *Settling Things: Six Case Studies in Environmental Mediation.* Washington, DC: Conservation Foundation.

Taylor, Charles. 1969. Neutrality in Political Science. 25–57 in Peter Laslett and W. G. Runciman, eds., *Philosophy, Politics, and Society,* Third Series. Oxford: Basil Blackwell.

———. 1971. Interpretation and the Sciences of Man. *Review of Metaphysics,* 25: 3–51.

Taylor, Michael. 1976. *Anarchy and Cooperation.* New York: Wiley.

———. 1987. *The Possibility of Cooperation.* Cambridge: Cambridge University Press.

Taylor, Paul W. 1961. *Normative Discourse.* Englewood Cliffs, NJ: Prentice-Hall.

Thayer, Frederick C. 1981. *An End to Hierarchy and Competition.* New York: New Viewpoints.

Thomas, David. 1979. *Naturalism and Social Science.* Cambridge: Cambridge University Press.

Thomas, Lee M. 1985. Controlling Pollution for Permanent Protection: A Whole Systems Approach to Environmental Policy. *Renewable Resources Journal,* 3(3): 5–9.

Thurow, Lester C. 1980. *The Zero-Sum Society.* New York: Basic Books.

Torgerson, Douglas. 1985. Contextual Orientation in Policy Analysis: The Contribution of Harold D. Lasswell. *Policy Sciences,* 18: 241–61.

———. 1986a. Between Knowledge and Politics: Three Faces of Policy Analysis. *Policy Sciences,* 19: 33–59.

———. 1986b. Beyond Professional Ethics: The Normative Foundations of Policy Analysis. Paper presented at the Annual Research Conference of the Association for Public Policy Analysis and Mangement, Austin, TX.

Totten, George O. and John R. Schmidhauser. 1978. *The Whaling Issue in U.S.-Japan Relations.* Boulder, CO: Westview.

Toulmin, Stephen. 1972. *Human Understanding: The Collective Use and Evolution of Concepts.* Princeton: Princeton University Press.

———. 1981. The Tyranny of Principles. *The Hastings Center Report,* 11(6).

Touraine, A., F. Dubet, M. Wieviorka, and J. Strzelecki. 1983. *Solidarity: Poland 1980–81.* Cambridge: Cambridge University Press.

Tribe, Laurence H. 1972. Policy Science: Analysis or Ideology? *Philosophy and Public Affairs,* 2: 66–110.

———. 1973. Technology Assessment and the Fourth Discontinuity: The Limits of Instrumental Rationality. *Southern California Law Review,* 46: 617–60.

Ugalde, Antonio. 1985. Ideological Dimensions of Community Participation in Latin American Health Programs. *Social Science and Medicine,* 21: 41–53.

van Dijk, Teun A. 1984. *Prejudice in Discourse: An Analysis of Cognition and Conversation.* Amsterdam: John Benjamins.

———. ed. 1985. *Handbook of Discourse Analysis.* London: Academic.

von Hayek, Friedrich A. 1944. *The Road to Serfdom.* Chicago: University of Chicago Press.

———. 1978. *New Studies in Philosophy, Politics, and the History of Ideas.* London: Routledge and Kegan Paul.

1979. *Law, Legislation, and Liberty III: The Political Order of a Free People.* Chicago: University of Chicago Press.

Vroom, Victor H. and Philip W. Yetton. 1973. *Leadership and Decision-Making.* Pittsburgh: University of Pittsburgh Press.

Wall, James A., Jr. 1981. Mediation: An Analysis, Review, and Proposed Research. *Journal of Conflict Resolution,* 25: 157–80.

Watson, John L. and Luke J. Danielson. 1982. Environmental Mediation. *Natural Resources Lawyer,* 15: 687–723.

Weber, Max. 1968. Bureaucracy. 956–1005 in Max Weber, *Economy and Society.* Edited by Guenther Roth and Klaus Wittich. New York: Bedminster.

Weiner, Richard. 1981. *Cultural Marxism and Political Sociology.* Beverly Hills, CA: Sage.

Weisberg, Herbert F. 1986. Model Choice in Political Science: The Case of Voting Behavior Research, 1946–1975. 284–300 in Herbert F. Weisberg, ed., *Political Science: The Science of Politics.* New York: Agathon.

Weiss, Carol H. 1977. *Using Social Research in Public Policy Making.* Lexington, MA: D. C. Heath.

1980. Knowledge Creep and Decision Accretion. *Knowledge: Creation, Diffusion, Utilization,* 1: 381–404.

Wellmer, Albrecht. 1985. Reason, Utopia, and the *Dialectics of Enlightenment.* 35–66 in Richard J. Bernstein, ed., *Habermas and Modernity.* Cambridge: Polity.

Wells, David. 1982. Resurrecting the Dismal Parson: Malthus, Ecology, and Political Thought. *Political Studies,* 30: 1–15.

White, Stephen K. 1980. Reason and Authority in Habermas: A Critique of the Critics. *American Political Science Review,* 74: 1007–17.

1988. *The Recent Work of Jürgen Habermas: Reason, Justice and Modernity.* Cambridge: Cambridge University Press.

Wildavsky, Aaron. 1966. The Political Economy of Efficiency. *Public Administration Review,* 26: 292–310.

1979. *Speaking Truth to Power: The Art and Craft of Policy Analysis.* Boston: Little, Brown.

1987. Choosing Preferences by Constructing Institutions: A Cultural Theory of Preference Formation. *American Political Science Review,* 81: 3–21.

Wilensky, Harold L. 1967. *Organizational Intelligence.* New York: Basic Books.

Williams, Bernard. 1979. Conflicts of Values. 221–32 in Alan Ryan, ed., *The Idea of Freedom: Essays in Honour of Isaiah Berlin.* Oxford: Oxford University Press.

Williams, Douglas E. 1989. *Truth, Hope, and Power: The Thought of Karl Popper.* Toronto: University of Toronto Press.

Williamson, Oliver E. 1975. *Markets and Hierarchies: Analysis and Antitrust Implications.* New York: Free Press.

Wilson, Thomas P. 1984. On the Role of Mathematics in the Social Sciences. *Journal of Mathematical Sociology,* 10: 221–39.

Young, Oran R. 1967. *The Intermediaries: Third Parties in International Crises.* Princeton: Princeton University Press.

1972. Intermediaries: Additional Thoughts on Third Parties. *Journal of Conflict Resolution,* 16: 51–65.

1978. Anarchy and Social Choice: Reflections on the International Polity. *World Politics*, 30: 241–63.

1979. *Compliance and Public Authority: A Theory with International Applications*. Baltimore: Johns Hopkins University Press for Resources for the Future.

1981. *Natural Resources and the State: The Political Economy of Resource Mangement*. Berkeley: University of California Press.

1983. Regime Dynamics: The Rise and Fall of International Regimes. 93–113 in Stephen D. Krasner, ed., *International Regimes*. Ithaca, NY: Cornell University Press.

Young, Oran R. and Gail Osherenko. 1984. Arctic Resource Conflicts: Sources and Solutions. In William E. Westermeyer and Kurt M. Shusterich, eds., *United States Arctic Interests*. New York: Springer-Verlag.

Yupiktak Bista. 1975. *Does One Way of Life Have to Die So Another Can Live?* Anchorage: Yupiktak Bista.

Index

249